THE WORLD *of* SOFÍA VELASQUEZ

FOR THE MARKET WOMEN *of*
LA PAZ AND THE ALTIPLANO

CONTENTS

ILLUSTRATIONS

Maps

Photographs

PREFACE

An enterprise that spans more than a quarter of a century depends on the support of a large number of persons and institutions. We cannot hope to name them all. First, we wish to thank Sofía Velasquez for her enthusiastic and unfailing collaboration in this effort. Her vigor, intelligence, superb recall and her ability to reflect on herself, her culture and the turbulent events in the span of her life were crucial for this book. Our appreciation also goes to other members of her family and her friends who contributed to this project. Our own families also helped in a variety of ways, particularly our daughters, Simone and Stephanie; Hans's mother, the late Rosemarie Buechler; his father, the late Ernst Buechler; his sister, Rose Marie Jo Buechler, and Judith-Maria's mother, Hilde Hess, who encouraged and supported the research and the preparation of this manuscript. We owe June Nash the idea of taping extensive life histories. We are deeply grateful for her friendship, her example, and professional guidance. Special thanks go to Hans Schlumpf, who produced and filmed an hour-long video of Sofía's life in summer, 1988 (*Die Welt der Sofía Velasquez: La Paz, Bolivien* funded by Swiss National Television, an English version of which, *The World of Sofía Velasquez*, was premiered at the 89th Annual Meeting of the American Anthropological Association, New Orleans, November, 1990). Hans Schlumpf also participated in some of the interviews during the two weeks of filming.

Over the years, our research received the financial support of our respective institutions: Hobart and William Smith Colleges and Syracuse

University; McGill University and Columbia University; and various foundations, including the Research Institute for the Study of Man, the Peace Corps, the Canada Council, the Social Science Research Council and the National Science Foundation.

INTRODUCTION

> I have to get up at half past two in the morning. I say my prayers. I leave the house at three, all alone. I lock the room so Rocío is safe, take my stick and climb the Bautista on foot in the dark, with a heavy bundle on my back. The street is empty. I am afraid. And so, because I always deal with magicians, I have learned from them that it is a good thing to have a bottle of alcohol at hand. I always carry a little bottle with me. At the first street corner, I offer some alcohol to *Pachamama*, Mother Earth, and to the spirits of the cemetery so that they will accompany me. And, would you believe it, I really believe that they do. As I reach the street corner, no one is there. I am afraid. So I make an offering. I say: "Soul from purgatory who art in the cemetery accompany me. Transform yourselves (sic) into a woman or a man and a woman with a child." And they always appear: a wife, a husband, and babies. I follow them up the hill. Then street sweepers appear. When I reach the bus stop, some people are already sitting there. I wait. The bus leaves at quarter to four, and I arrive there at six. That's what I do on those mornings when they (the customers) didn't pay me [on time]. When they do pay me, I stay overnight there. During Rocío's school vacation, I take her along and we sleep at the house [in Llamacachi].

The quotation above encapsulates the complex life of Sofía, a second-generation, urban-born market vendor with ties in both her mother's rural community and the city of La Paz. This life demands, among other things, a grueling schedule and the full mobilization of her entrepreneurial skills and her better-than-average education, and the reliance on supernatural forces for help with those aspects of her life that are difficult or impossible to control.

We recorded Sofía's and her mother's life histories over a period of thirty years. Between 1964 and 1994 we updated her story every time we conducted research in Bolivia (1964–1965, 1967, 1969, 1975, 1976, 1981, 1984, 1988, and 1994).

We first met Sofía in 1964 in Llamacachi, on the shores of Lake Titicaca, where we were undertaking long-term fieldwork. She was only nineteen at the time, but she was already fully involved in community affairs. Her mother's store, which Sofía helped to run, was a center of information on all community happenings. In addition, she routinely travelled to the city of La Paz, some sixty miles away, to sell onions produced on family plots and purchased from neighbors. During our stay in the community, she became Judith-Maria's assistant and interpreter and later assisted Hans in a study of rural and urban rituals, and, in 1981, in our research on small-scale enterprises in La Paz. She also assisted Jane Benton, a British

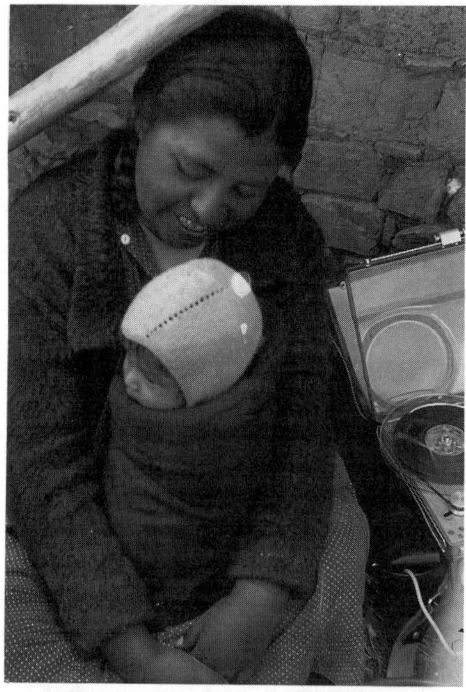

Sofía assisting Judith-Maria with fieldwork in Llamacachi (1965)

geographer, who studied marketing in Llamacachi and neighboring Chua in the early 1970s, and she worked with a team of anthropologists with CIPCA (Center for the Investigation and Promotion of the Peasantry) in La Paz. In 1988, she became the principal protagonist in a film we produced jointly with Hans Schlumpf, a Swiss filmmaker.

Sofía was born in La Paz in 1945, the daughter of Aymara rural-urban migrants. Sofía's mother, Doña Saturnina, grew up in poverty as an orphan after her father, who was from a wealthy peasant family, was killed for his land around 1905. As a teenager, she went to work in La Paz carrying sand for construction. When she was fifteen, she had an illegitimate son, Pedro, by a foreman engaging in roadwork in Llamacachi. Pedro became known as a first-rate boxer, later as a notorious militia leader, and finally, as a truck owner and factory worker. Three years after Pedro's birth, upon meeting her future husband during one of her stints in La Paz, she went to live with him and later married him. Her second son, Moises, was born after another three years. When her husband—a railroad worker—had an accident on the job and became an invalid, they took up candlemaking. Doña Saturnina's candle business enabled the family to prosper. Soon she had enough money to engage two vendors of her own, and, over the years, she was able to provide employment for a number of kin. In addition, she owned a bus. After driving his mother's bus for a while, Moises became a shoemaker. Later, he switched back to driving and ultimately landed a job as a driver for the national health service that he held until his retirement. Moises maintains two households, taking turns living with women who, for all intents and purposes, are co-wives.

During Moises's childhood, Doña Saturnina gave birth to three other children, all of whom died in infancy. By the time she gave birth to Sofía, Pedro was already married and had his first child. Thanks to her family's relative prosperity, Sofía was able to obtain a sixth grade education in a private Catholic school, a major accomplishment in those days. In the early 1960s, Sofía and her parents returned to the mother's home community on Lake Titicaca, where they opened a grocery store. Sofía helped tend the store, assisted a Catholic team of nuns and health practitioners in administering health care to the community and served as confidante and advisor to her less-travelled peers. She also continued selling produce in the La Paz markets. By 1969, our third trip to Bolivia associated with this project, Sofía had become the leader of the onion vendors from her natal community selling in La Paz and she also held a minor office in the union of her street market. Later, she switched to selling pork. She continues to purchase pork, weekly, in a rural fair near her mother's natal

A picnic during the fiesta of San Pedro (Compi 1975). Left to right: *Hans Schlumpf, a renter from La Paz, Sofía's mother, a nephew and his wife, Sofía, Stephanie Buechler, a Brazilian friend of Hans Schlumpf, Simone Buechler, Judith-Maria Buechler.*

community and to sell it on the street next to her home in La Paz. Sofía promotes her market activities and her relationships with men through magic. She regularly consults with both urban and rural magicians who stage elaborate magical ceremonies on her behalf. She claims to have lured back her erstwhile lover and father of her sixteen-year-old daughter by magic. And she has become adept at remembering and interpreting the omens in her dreams.

Anthropology and the Life History Method

The idea of recording Sofía's life history did not come to us at an early stage in fieldwork. Perhaps reflecting our more positivistic approach to anthropology, Sofía initially acted more in the role of facilitator-translator and sounding board for ideas. She frequently spoke to us, particularly to Judith-Maria, about her life, but we did not systematically tape or write down her narratives. Rather, they became an inspiration for interviews with other persons. Thus, Judith-Maria's Ph.D. dissertation on peasant and urban marketing contains but two or three lengthy examples from Sofía's life. It was only after we had become convinced of the power of first-person narratives through our reading of an early version of June Nash's book *He agotado mi vida en la mina* (1976) later translated as *I Spent My Life in the Mines* (1992) and after having initiated the taping of a book-length life history of a Spanish Galician woman in 1972 (Buechler and Buechler 1981), that we decided to record Sofía's life systematically.

Anthropology may be seen as a series of attempts at contextualizing events and sequences of events. The life history method is but one among many possible avenues of achieving such an end. The highly intensive nature of this method lends itself more to a comparison of individuals with respect to one another and in a wider context than to a process of generalizing from a single case to the society at large (as is sometimes erroneously claimed). The method then leads to a series of what one might call triangulations among individuals' lives and, at the same time to a search for explanations of these lives in terms of information gathered by more extensive means. The lives in question thereby present the reader with the possibilities and limitations within a particular society.

Our use of the life history method was, in fact, a logical progression from our increasing interest in social network analysis. Judith-Maria's dissertation was based on a network model, as was our book *The Bolivian Aymara* (1971). We saw individuals as positioned within and understandable through the social networks in which they were involved and that they helped to create. Such an approach enables generalization by abstracting network configurations, while it also emphasizes the unique position of individual actors vis-à-vis others. Network analysis and spatial and historical contextualization, and placing Sofía's experiences into the context of those of other individuals she knew was central to the purpose of recording her story. As anthropologists inspired by a variety of anthropological traditions, which in addition to network approaches ranged from culture and personality approaches of Margaret Mead and Lévi-Straussian structuralism to decision-making approaches of Richard Salisbury and Harrisian cultural materialism, our joint endeavor with Sofía was a way of anchoring our research on a variety of topics, contextualizing these topics within a more emic framework and, at the same time raising new questions to be explored with other respondents.

Initially, our approach to social networks was principally oriented toward (and, to this day, we continue to place a heavy emphasis on) discerning regularities in interpersonal behavior, irrespective of whether they are cognicized or not. Our introduction into the life history method via our interests in social networks explains the emphasis we placed on investigating with Sofía the various individuals with whom she associated throughout her life.[1]

However, the utility of network analysis is not confined to the understanding of changing social configurations. It can also serve as a framework for understanding cognitive categories. Our efforts in combining network analysis and cognitive analysis (H. Buechler 1969b, 1980) prefigure the postmodern emphasis on the discovery of multiple voices. In that effort, in which Sofía figured prominently both as an assistant and as one of his principal consultants, Hans attempted to show how individuals place themselves and others socially by their presence, assumption of traditional roles, and the innovations they contribute in rites of passage and saints' fiestas. We contend that the concern of some postmodernists for multivocality vis-à-vis other cultures and within a particular culture (see, in particular, Clifford 1988) is complementary or even congruent with the network analyst's concern for understanding the respective positions of individuals in a social network and the manner in which each individual expresses and explores those positions, employing a shared symbolic framework. One of our main concerns will be to view Sofía's life in the context of the individuals she interacts with and to explore the manner in which she constructs her identity with reference to those who surround her and how she is, in turn, situated by others.

Whose Voice is Represented in Life Histories?

At first glance, it would appear that the life history method, or, more generally, the personal narrative, should solve the problem of giving a voice to individuals from societies studied by social scientists. Lately, however, anthropologists have been concerned about whose voice is speaking even in a life history; for the life history can itself be regarded as directed (see e.g., Crapanzano 1984, Rabinow 1977). The production of a life history is shaped by the selective interests of the consultant and the ethnographer(s). Sometimes, the former takes precedent over the latter (Okely and Callaway 1992, presentation), while at other times, the interests are more mutual. For example, the choice to emphasize magic and dream interpretation was Sofía's, the systematic inquiry about marketing combined the mutual concerns of Judith-Maria and Sofía, and ritual activities were one of Hans's main theoretical concerns and one of Sofía's consuming passions. In making the reader aware of our separate and overlapping interests, we try to displace the colonial anthropological model of "speaking for" and the dialogic hope of speaking with, while maintaining the supposition that we "can give voice." At the same time, we recognize the flawed and partial nature of that endeavor (Viswesaran 1994: 100).

One way of facilitating the task of the reader to determine how a narrative is shaped by the interaction between the consultant and the investigator is to characterize the elicitor, and explain the relationship between the anthropologist and the person whose life history is being elicited or recorded.[2] Is the relationship always that of the outsider versus the "other," the "native?" The question of whether the outsider (whether the term stands for a stereotyped "westerner," "the powerful," or some narrower concept) is readily separable from the "other" (in the form of the stereotyped, "colonized" member of a "nonwestern" society, or member of a specific culture to which the researcher does not belong) has been addressed only recently (e.g., Clifford 1988: 277–346, Behar 1993). Kumar reminds us of Geertz's contention that all fieldwork is "person-specific" and all writing reflects a specific time, place, consultant's culture and class. But her memoir of Banaras also reveals the failure of the old dichotomies which are incapable of acknowledging the actual and simultaneous "otherness" and "oneness" of the anthropological field worker/writer (1992: 6). Abu-Lughod criticizes Bourdieu for assuming separability, arguing instead that "the outsider self never simply stands outside; he or she always stands in a definite relation with the 'other' of the study, not just as a Westerner or even halfie, but as a Frenchman in Algeria during the war of independence. . . . What we call the outside, or even the partial outside, is always a position *within* a larger political-historical complex" (1993: 40). Similarly, the close collaboration between Sofía and us problematizes the dualism between "insider" and "other."

We argue, then, for the dissolution of the dichotomy generally. We propose, that the best one can do to situate the anthropologist is to establish a series of approximations of the respective positions of the anthropologist and the person studied. Our relationship with Sofía is undoubtedly affected by the differential of economic means which, in part, forms the basis for the joint enterprise. This relationship took a variety of forms. At one level, Sofía saw Hans as the son of a successful La Paz businessman, a *caballero*: a man she respected and for whom she cared, but from whom she also felt separated by social class. During a period of scarcity, she persuaded a vendor to sell bread to Hans's father, but when he died, she did not dare to enter the cemetery during his funeral, remaining outside the gate to offer her condolences. Although we, Hans and Judith-Maria, were her employers, it was clear to her that we would never condone the stereotyped relationship of dominance and submission often expected between members of different social classes in La Paz. During a summer's fieldwork in La Paz, Hans and Judith-Maria took care of the house of an American diplomat. We lived rent-free in the house, but the arrangement required that we pay the salaries of a staff of a maid, a cook, and a butler. Much to the annoyance of the three of us, the butler, in spite of repeated instructions, refused to announce Sofía's arrival at the house, or to let her into the house to look for us herself. Instead, he would force her to wait in the garden until we discovered that she had come. We later savored a moment of triumph together, when it turned out that the snooty butler had engaged in acts of petty larceny that led to his dismissal by our hosts.

On the other hand, differences in social class did not enter into other strands of our relationship. Echoing the experience of most anthropologists, Judith-Maria's first contact with Sofía occurred in the context of weakness: the marginality of the newcomer in a strange community and culture, inverting the power relationship. At first, and to a degree later on as well, the relationship was that of a teacher and student, a role that, to be sure, Sofía engaged in with utmost tact. Only as Judith-Maria's own knowledge about marketing progressed, did their interaction become more of a dialogue between colleagues. It should be noted that this relationship is also consonant with the egalitarian relationship implied in the relationship of the market vendor with her *caseros/as* (preferred customers), irrespective of the social status of the *casero/a*.

The cross-cultural nature of our own identification makes the application of the "outsider"/"other" dichotomy, in its cultural sense, even more problematic. Hans's childhood was spent in La Paz too, and he spent many years visiting a rural village near Sofía's mother's natal community where he, like Sofía, was considered both a member and a partial stranger. Born to German refugees in China and educated in the United States and Canada, Judith-Maria is "at home" and a stranger in many places too. An attempt at demarcating the "self" and the "other" culturally, then, is fraught with the danger of constructing false dichotomies (and neglecting more significant ones—dichotomies that are perhaps too painful for the investigator to acknowledge).

Our identities and identification merge and separate in ways that are unexpected even to ourselves. Sofía's disrespect for officialdom is mirrored in Hans's own sentiments regarding authority, born from common enculturation. Her assertiveness as a woman, in harmony with expectations of the behavior of an established vendor, but in disharmony with traditional stereotypes of Latin American female behavior, is echoed in Judith-Maria's feminist orientation. Neither of us could probably have envisioned spending countless hours over a period of thirty years chronicling the life of a woman who closely conformed to those stereotypes. At the same time, cultural differences form, as already indicated, one of the principal pillars of our relationship, as they do, in one way or another, for all anthropologists. We were both fascinated and honored to be allowed to participate in a magical ceremony, while our visit to a Chinese restaurant in La Paz was appreciated by Sofía both as a novel culinary experience and as a window into the normally closed aspects of upper-middle class life: the restaurant doubled as a locale for the military top brass after normal dining hours, a fact that Sofía was quick to discover.

Finally, in many instances, even to speak of our relationship in terms of commonalities and differences makes little sense. For example, Hans undertook the major portion of the effort of translating Sofía's narrative during the Gulf War, permitting him to escape into a world that was simultaneously different and hearkened back to carefree childhood years spent in Bolivia.

The relationship is further complicated by the fact that Sofía became our assistant and both assimilated many of our methodologies (and indeed applied them in her work with another anthropological team and while working for a geographer) and provided direction for our own interests. In fact, it becomes difficult to say whether such methodologies as network analysis were imposed by us or whether they were so plausible to Sofía that a mutual narrative reinforcement occurred. A trope focusing on concrete ties and sequences of events as opposed to statements about ideals and norms certainly became so ingrained in our taped conversations that the more idea-oriented dialogue in which film maker Hans Schlumpf engaged Sofía, on occasion, during the filming of her life, came as a surprise to us.[3] Although, particularly in our earliest fieldwork, we had both elicited normative statements from consultants, such statements rarely served as points of departure for life history interviews. We moved from the description of events to cognition, rather than the other way around.

We are, then, aware of the fact that Sofía's story would probably have been quite different if told to a different audience. We are also aware of the fact that our views of rural and urban Aymara were molded by the interpretations, agenda, and frames of reference of our Aymara assistants, including—perhaps principally—Sofía herself (see H. Buechler 1969a).

The wider sociopolitical context also influences the range of topics we broached. Thus, the fact that the bulk of Sofía's life history and the biographies she narrated of her brothers were taped during various military dictatorships limited the detailed treatment of some political topics. Finally, we are aware of the fact that the respective contribution to this joint ethnographic endeavor (including that of the relative contribution of the two anthropologists) is not readily dissectible.

The fact that Sofía was a party in one way or another to all our research endeavors in Bolivia, also means that her voice permeates all our other publications. It would be impossible to assemble all the passages from our writings in which this is the case. Sofía's fascinating reconstructions of the rituals in which she has participated have been largely excluded from the present narrative. Her descriptions have been quoted at length in *The Masked Media* (H. Buechler 1980) and her more recent involvement in fiestas are mentioned in *Manufacturing Against the Odds* (Buechler and Buechler 1992: 232). Her description of her father's illness and cure, published in part in 1981, has also not been included here, nor has her portrayal of her brothers' lives, which was part of the original manuscript.

An issue related to the shaping of a life history is whether anthropologists by requesting consultants whose life histories they are recording are not "torturing" them by forcing to objectify their life world (Caplan 1992: 80, quoting Crapanzano 1984). Like Caplan, we would deny the applicability of this charge to our relationship with the individuals whose life histories we recorded. We feel that this fear may be overdrawn. Even when our friend Hans Schlumpf engaged in a line of inquiry which we thought was too closely patterned on European and North American concerns and thought patterns, Sofía simply reinterpreted the questions to fit her own cognitive framework. Like Caplan—and Behar (1993: 11)—we feel that consultants cast the role of the anthropologist as much as the anthropologist shapes their role. Variously anthropologists play roles as confessors/psychologists, audience, or means for the consultant's voice to be heard. Thereby both the agenda of the anthropologist and that of the consultant find their expression. In the long process of working with Sofía, we, like Visweswaran, became aware of "temporality, silence, and the multiple identities set into play by silence" (1994: 42). Sofía chose the time when she was ready to reveal "sensitive" knowledge about magical material and social power. Therefore, we have included different versions of some of her stories to stress, as Visweswaran does, how both speech and silences are strategic (1994: 59).

Sofía's Agenda

Postmodern anthropology has paid a great deal of attention to the need for reflexivity on the part of the researcher. Perhaps, it is time for the concern with self-awareness on the part of the author(s) to include the critical scrutiny of the subject of the life history as well (see Crapanzano 1980). Indeed, we posit that the reflexivity on the part of the consultant is the most salient example of reflexive thinking in modern ethnography. In Sofía's case, this reflexivity was enhanced by her enculturation into ethnographic inquiry in general, and also by her unique position in her mother's natal community and by her efforts to establish a niche for herself in La Paz society. Her agenda in telling her story was influenced by the desire to bring to the fore her hard-won acceptance as a member of her mother's rural home community, her competence as a consultant about what she considered to be her world, her competence as a vendor, her competence and compassion as a leader, her assertiveness as a woman and vis-à-vis her lover, brothers, and other kin, including affines with airs of class superiority, and in her role as an upwardly mobile member of a group, discriminated against in the city.

Unlike some of our consultants from the *clase media*,[4] she rarely portrays herself as a victim. The former cast themselves more readily in that role than those with a recent rural Aymara background (for contrasting examples see Buechler and Buechler 1992: chapter 11).[5]

In a discussion of anthropology and autobiography, Judith Okely (1992: 7) contrasts the "great white man" tradition of heroic biographies (see also Tedlock 1993) with the autobiographies of the marginalized and powerless which "have not inevitably been a celebration of uniqueness, let alone public achievement, but a record of questions and subversion." From our experience of a range of life histories situated in different contexts, this contrast is stereotypical and overdrawn. We found a range of presentations of self from heroic to victim, from self-aggrandizement to self-deprecation by different persons and by the same person (Buechler and Buechler 1992). Sofía herself combines all these modes, but she gives more emphasis to the positive. At the same time she reveals her failings with refreshing candor. Her's is not a glorification of the *chola*[6] intermediary! Sofía's portrayal of others may have been colored by a particular agenda as well.

Since the lives of the consultant and ethnographers are lived over a period of time and, in this case, the conversations occurred over thirty years, the resulting monograph is, by its very nature, historically contingent. As we shall see, Sofía's central emotional concerns change with her life stage. Thus, as the story unfolds, the welfare of her daughter takes precedence over that of her mother, while some of our own life cycle transitions, some which foreshadowed and others that coincided with hers, led to a shift in our focus over time.

Sofía's Position in the Wider Society

We did not regard Sofía as a typical member of her community. Hans, in fact, was reluctant to recommend her to Judith-Maria as an assistant and interpreter, in spite of the fact that he had been very impressed by her openness and knowledge when he interviewed her several months prior to Judith-Maria's arrival in Bolivia. The reasons for his hesitation—which turned out to be unfounded—were symptomatic of the changing social stratification system in the Bolivian highlands.[7] Thus, Hans assumed that, with her long-term urban background and relatively high education, Sofía would maintain a distanced relationship with the other members of the community and would therefore make a poor bridge to the community members.

Hans was soon proven wrong. We first hired a nineteen-year-old girl who had worked in La Paz as a market vendor whose deficient Spanish and shyness in interviews rapidly lead to an untenable situation (see H. Buechler 1969a: 13). Judith-Maria met Sofía at a fiesta. She was observing women coming to pray to the image of Saint Peter, when a young woman approached her and began to translate and explain what was going on. Delighted with this outgoing, intelligent woman, Judith-Maria decided to hire her right away. It soon became apparent that in the four years that she had lived in the community, Sofía had become well integrated into the community, and while her age-mates deferred to her because of her education and her urban experience, she had established some close friendships, particularly with her kinswomen. In her role as a store keeper, she became the center of a network of communication, and young women consulted her about boyfriends, clothing, health, and other matters. Thus, while adapting to her new life had not been easy, by the time we initiated fieldwork in Compi/Llamacachi, Sofía had made a role for herself in Llamacachi and in neighboring communities. Her collaboration in our fieldwork became indispensable.

Theoretical Frameworks to Place Sofía's Life into the Context of Rural and Urban Aymara Society

When we were writing about individuals like our assistants Sofía and Paz and others who appeared to play salient roles in the community, but who also seemed to be marginalized, we groped for a theoretical framework that would do justice to the intricacies of the positions of such individuals. Initially, we were intrigued by the concept of "cultural broker" developed by Useem (1952), Wolf (1956), Geertz (1960), and Silverman (1967), among others. However, we rapidly became disillusioned with the seeming reification implied by the concept of cultural broker. In an article criticizing the concept (Buechler and Buechler 1971–72) we argued that while a handful of individuals, like Sofía, who were prominent in introducing critical socioeconomic and political changes in community affairs, fit the definition of cultural broker in that they mediated between Llamacachi peasants and the national system, they could not be viewed as a discrete group. We argued instead that such individuals should be viewed as parts of social network segments in which each played unique roles understandable by their particular backgrounds.

The concept of "hinge group" has reemerged under a new guise in such studies as Orlove's (1977) analysis of mutual aid in Peruvian rural communities that stressed the asymmetrical nature of many instances of economic exchanges and Lagos's descriptions of the "emergence of new upwardly mobile families of rural merchants, transporters, and entrepreneurs" who exploit peasants (1993: 57–58). Unlike many of the earlier studies on cultural brokers, both of these studies downplay the role of such individuals as agents of change in their home communities, stressing instead their exploitative role. In addition, there is a new focus on the cognitive dimension of the interaction between groups: i.e., the manipulation of traditional concepts connoting egalitarian relationships among peasants for exploitative ends. Orlove shows how asymmetrical economic relations were couched in terms of supposed "mutual assistance," while Lagos stresses the self-serving nature of the entrepreneurs' continued identification with the peasantry. She writes:

> Most of the members of this mercantile class have emerged from the peasantry or the poor of rural towns, establishing production alliances with peasant households and manipulating aspects of peasant-village culture such as reciprocity, coparenthood, and "community" in order to consolidate their hold over production and exchange . . . Simultaneously, peasants have increased their participation in markets as producers of commodities and surplus labor. Thus, the fact that since the agrarian reform of 1953 these rural producers have come to be addressed as *campesinos* (peasants) rather than *indios* (Indians) reflects not a mere semantic twist in a populist discourse but structural transformations in their productive strategies—transformations that make these landowning peasants vulnerable to new forms of domination and exploitation. (1993: 57–58)

Models that view relations between upwardly mobile peasants and their less fortunate peers mainly in terms of domination or exploitation also may fail to address certain aspects of status dynamics. For example, as we shall see, Sofía enjoyed a higher status in the national class hierarchy than most of her peers in Llamacachi but was also disadvantaged by her (partial) outsider status and the small size of her family's holdings in the community: descent from community members, preferably through the male line, and the size of a family's holdings are important factors in determining a family's, and hence an individual's, standing in the community.

We prefer to stress the continuities between the "emergent class" and that of the "land-owning peasants." Sofía does, in a way, fit Lagos's category of a new "mercantile class," in that she has benefited from the new possibilities opened up by the agrarian reform. But, as we shall see presently, such a categorization fails to reveal both her similarities with less successful market vendors from her community, on the one hand, and traditional prereform urban *chola* market vendors—whose dress (wide skirts, silk or nylon tassel-fringed shawl, and bowler hat) she ultimately adopted—on the other. In addition, such a label would not do justice to the seesaw vagaries of the family's fortunes which rose and declined with personal tragedies and changing economic opportunities.[8] During this trajectory, the family occupied a variety of statuses in the community, both consecutively and simultaneously, only some of which were conducive to the exploitation of others. Sofía was not above shortchanging a peasant on the weight of the pork he had brought her or bringing down the price of a pork carcass by telling a lie, but her relations with members of *her* community were, in general, markedly egalitarian and included the establishment of lasting friendships and liaisons.

Sofía's Position Within La Paz Society

In La Paz, Sofía found herself involved in an even more complex system of social stratification (Buechler and Buechler 1992: 284–85). Her class relations and identification are not comprehensible by a single model of social stratification. Multiple stratification systems and more than one parallel cognitive framework guided her behavior. Three were foremost in our estimation. One was based on rural-urban migration, another on economic activities, and a third on the expressed values of both "traditional" and "modern" bourgeois and elites, that are also emulated by poorer persons. As we shall see, she puts a great deal of effort in continuing her contacts with her mother's place of origin, by maintaining her ownership of land and a house, participating in and sponsoring rural fiestas and by providing aid to more recent migrants. As an urban-based market trader, she participates more in urban fiestas and in trade organizations. As an educated woman, she has also worn "western" dress and is in the process of educating her daughter who also wears western dress. These three modalities intersect and change as Sofía grows older.

Her acknowledgement of class differences are most apparent in her gender-framed experiences in a convent school, her difficulties in adapting to rural life, her choice of profession (against her family's wishes), her legal battles, and her struggles against police and government abuse through her union, and other activities. She employs migrant, trader, and educated lower-middle class urban frameworks to her advantage. For example, she decided to wear *chola* dress after a protracted period of wearing modified "modern" western-style clothing when such dress facilitated her social relations in rural fairs and urban markets.

Narrative Style and Style of Presentation[9]

Commensurate with Sofía's role as an interpreter of her culture, as a network analyst in her own right as explained above, and her love of a juicy story, the narrative moves from providing information within a more traditional ethnographic mode to telling stories in an entertaining manner to the anthropologists as audience, to providing both an extended version to the anthropologists (in the interviews taped in 1975 and updated in subsequent years), as well as a capsule version of her life to a broader, or at least more readily palpable audience (in the filmed narratives), since Sofía is familiar with documentaries presented on television. There is no strict division between these modes. For example, in 1988, during the filming of her life, Sofía told us about events in her life which were of such a private nature, that she had never told them to anyone including her parents. In addition, she repeated the major events of her life for the audience she imagined her film would have. She also answered specific ethnographic questions posed by the film maker. Similarly, taping sessions geared towards obtaining specific information about peasant or urban institutions merged seamlessly with vivid, carefully constructed stories about individuals and events. Presumably the stress in our joint ethnographic endeavors on network analysis with its emphasis on concrete events and sequences of interaction facilitated the combination of these various modes of dialogue and monologue into the same recording session.

Sofía also taped some of the narratives for our benefit after we had left Bolivia. These narratives exhibit an eye for the dramatic incident, such as her friend's separation from her husband and the Fiesta de las Ñatitas, a ritual held in La Paz a week after All Saints and All Souls Day, which involves the use of skulls stolen from the cemetery (see H. Buechler 1980: 360–63). We do not believe that this narrative style was to any significant degree predicated on a felt need to report exotic customs. Rather, the same sense of drama infuses her telling of episodes in her own life and that of others. The independently taped narratives are also characterized by an attention to detail which, if anything, surpasses that of our interviews. By including samples of Sofía's own writing, our intent is to give Sofía a greater share in evolving the narrative style and in so doing, renegotiate, in some measure, the control of our "collaborative effort," allowing her to "talk back" to us and the reader (see Smith 1993: 404). She becomes, we hope, a human being who generates "new descriptions rather than someone whom [we] hope[d] to describe accurately." (Stivers 1993: 425).

We have followed the topical structure of key interviews, reorganizing these, when necessary (usually following the chronological order in which events occurred), to enhance readability, and inserting fragments of other interviews that constitute an elaboration of the topics covered.

Because of the nature of the interviews, a topical mode of presentation, rather than one based purely on the narrative structure of each interview, imposed itself on the organization of the book. The interviews were, in turn, influenced by the nature of our relationship. On the one hand, we were interested in Sofía's expertise on local matters, marketing, and economic conditions. On the other hand, we were intrigued by her relationship with ritual and the roles it played in events in her own life and in those of individuals in her immediate network. This framework became internalized by the three of us to such a degree that Sofía would maintain it, even when there had been a shift in emphasis in Judith-Maria and Hans's interests. Sometimes, Sofía introduced topics freely according to what may have been foremost in her mind. At other times, we asked specific questions, often to update conversations we had had during previous visits. The fact that we had begun our research in Bolivia with a general community study and a study on child rearing and adolescence meant that we had a continued interest in a broad range of topics beyond those we were focussing on specifically at any given time. However, we are aware that we did not cover many subjects. Thus it was Hans Schlumpf who introduced questions about sexuality, a theme that Judith-Maria had explored in her research for her Master's thesis but that we did not feel comfortable inquiring about in terms of Sofía's own life.

Most of the interviews were transcribed by Sofía herself. Within practical limits she has maintained a high degree of fidelity to the taped version.

The fact that our taped conversations took place over a period of thirty years put us into the dilemma of either strictly maintaining the topical mode just outlined and merging narratives taped in widely spaced years but dealing with similar topics in addition to employing a topical mode of presentation of narratives recorded in a given year or in adjoining years, or following a mode that highlighted the passage of time. A strict adherence to a topical mode risked confusing the reader with respect to the sequence of events,[10] while a strictly chronological account could easily have led to fragmentation and the obscuring of the threads that run through Sofía's life. We have chosen a compromise between these two extremes.

For the benefit of the Spanish reader, key phrases with nuances that are difficult to render in English, or that have ambiguous or multiple meanings in Spanish are also given in Spanish. For Aymara words, we follow the orthography proposed by Juan de Dios Yapita of the Museo Nacional de Etnografía y Folklore, using only three vowels: i, a, u. We employ ' to designate a glottal stop and x, j, and " for the three degrees of aspiration. We deviate from these conventions when an Aymara word has been adopted into Bolivian Spanish. In that case, we spell it the way it would be pronounced in Spanish.

THE WORLD *of* SOFÍA VELASQUEZ

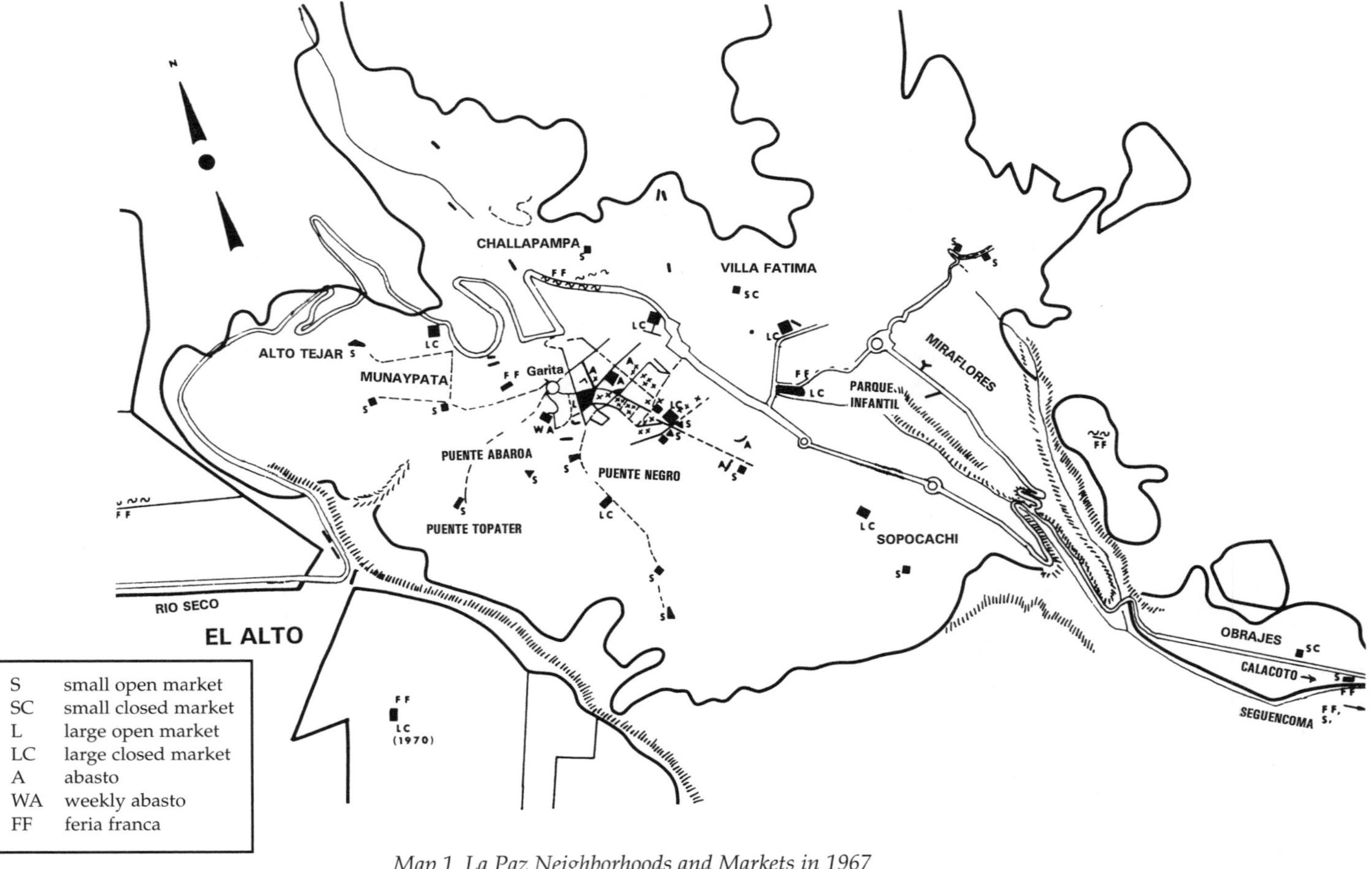

Map 1 La Paz Neighborhoods and Markets in 1967

1

CHILDHOOD *Memories*

Childhood Games

All my memories are from this house, because my mother tells me that I was born in this house in the Calle Incachaca in the room where my brother now lives. I remember when I was playing in the Garita[1] in the evening and when my mother would tell me to throw away the garbage. When I was small, I acted more like a boy than like a girl. I liked to play with the boys. I liked to play ball and play with marbles. And I liked to be the *mono mayor* (the leader in "follow the leader"). In that game, boys stand in line and if the first one climbs a wall, all the others have to climb the wall too; if he hits another boy, then all have to hit one another; if he jumps, all must jump; and if he breaks off a flower, all the others have to do so too. That's how we played.

I had a childhood friend called Yola Aguilar who is now married to a lawyer, Isidro Arismende. Her mother is from Peru. She doesn't have a father.

[The mother] lived with a friend called Agustina Quiñones. They came from Peru together. She earned a living embroidering petticoats and things like that. She had already done that in Peru. She came to La Paz because she had many brothers and sisters and her parents couldn't take care of all of them and people had told her that life was easier here in Bolivia. To this day, neither one of them is married and they are still living together. They are inseparable friends.

Yolanda came to live in our house when she was one year old and I was one year old too. She was born on October 25th and I on September 30th. I am 25 days older than she. When I meet Yola, we reminisce about our childhood and laugh about what we did. There were seven boys living in the house, all renters. We always played follow the leader, marbles, or with a ball. Yola and I always acted as goal keepers when we played soccer. Every time we played with the boys, my parents would whip me because they didn't like me to play with boys. I remember that once we went to relieve ourselves near a stream because we didn't have a bathroom in our house. There were lots of brambles along the shore and the water was so dirty it was black. Yola used to be rather timid. She didn't talk with ease, while I was never afraid to do things, even when I was very small. Well, she told me to climb up the slope first. So I did. Yola followed me, and when she was about to slip, she held on to my dress and the two of us tumbled and tumbled, right into the dirty black water. My dress was covered with black mud. I stood up and cried, "What am I going to do? My mother will beat me." Yola cried too. She took me to a public faucet and we washed ourselves and then we returned to the house. She still remembers it clearly. "What a sight we must have been tumbling down that hill," she will say. And I tell her that it was all her fault.

Also, we would always hunt for chicken feathers in the garbage dumps. They were our playthings. Once we went to look for some—Yola and I always went together—and there were some older girls there. We fought over the feathers, each saying that she had found it first. There was a battle royal. A girl knocked me on the head and I had a large bump. I cried and Yola told me, "Don't cry. Your mother will scold you." "What am I going to do to make this disappear," I answered. "Put a wet a rag on it and go to bed and you will be all right the next morning," Yola said. So my mother never found out.

Yola had dolls and so did I, and my mother would buy me small earthen ware pots and plates. I have kept my toys to this day. I had three dolls. One was of the kind that one can put to sleep and another had little braids. I only had little dolls, while Yola had large ones. One of Yola's dolls was called Pepe—a little boy. The other was Margarita. We would bury them and play funeral. For example, my Josefa would die and I would begin to cry, "My child has died." And then we would have a solemn funeral. All the children would join us. Near our house there was a pile of dirt where we would go and bury the doll, crying all the while. Then we would return and play "daddy" and "mommy." We also liked to play at performing dances. We would dance *cullawa* and *llamerada*.

Yola's mother was very kind. My mother was not like that at all. She was very strict. Yola would tell her mother that we wanted to dance the *llamerada* and she would give her an old *awayo* (carrying cloth) and she would make a *pollera* (wide skirt) out of it. I didn't have one, but I used to make the bed for my parents, and they always put some old *awayos* over the mattress. I would take one, and Yola's mother would sew it into a *pollera* for me. We would always play from six to seven in the evening. The boys who lived in our house: Lucho; my nephew José; Raúl and Eloy, the sons of my other renter—they are both married now—and Yola's little brother would bang on tin cans representing a brass band, while we would dance until we were tired. Our dolls were our children. Then we would play "wedding." Yola would always get married to Eloy, while my nephew José was always the priest. He would also baptize the dolls.

What I liked to do best, however, was to play at selling. Yola and I would pretend to be selling lard. We would "sell" mud, pretending it was flour. Really fine dirt was sugar and little stones were fish. Berries called *ñuñumaya* we found near the stream became hot peppers. Our money was pieces of paper. And I remember José, my brother Pedro's oldest son, acted as a policeman. He would come and beat us, the way policemen do. And we would pretend to cry and say that we would go and complain.

[I did not have to work] when I was a small child. My mother did that. She worked with my sister-in-law. Since I was the only, beloved daughter, I could spend the entire time playing. That's why we played at weddings, fiesta sponsorships, and baptisms. We would act out terrible quarrels. We would act as though we were drunk. Yola recently told me, "The children today are much more awake than we were. When we were children, we were not like that. We would play like brothers and sisters. It's no longer like that. There is much more malice." And it is true. We would play like siblings with the boys. We played with marbles and soccer balls and we even learned how to box. Yes, we used to box with the boys! I was always full of mischief. José would go to play near the stream and I remember that one day my brother told me to fetch him. But, instead, I played with him there. José was playing *cobohuy*: the bandit and the boy with his friends. I called him, "José, José, your father wants you to come." He answered, "Yes, just a moment, I am playing." He never called me "*tía*" even though I *am* his aunt. Ever since I was small, he always called me "*gorda*" (fat one). "Wait *gorda*, we will come soon." Then his friends said, "Why doesn't *la gorda* come and play the role of the girl?" I agreed and started to play with them. They took me prisoner, tied me up, and put me in a corner. At that point, my brother came with the whip, and José and all his friends escaped. But I couldn't escape because

I was all tied up. My brother released me, and when we got home my brother whipped José and my father whipped me. We both received a terrible whipping.[2]

After what happened with José near the stream, I no longer played with the boys. I mostly played with Yola. We sewed dresses, everything.

[I also remember accompanying my mother on her trips to barter cracklings for corn.] I remember one time, I can still picture it vividly. It happened in Ilabaya during the fiesta of Rosario in October. My father would arrive there a week before the fiesta and set up the tent. I was very small. All I did was play and play. I liked to dance. There were some nice *llamerada* dance groups. The migrants to La Paz from Ilabaya organized an Inca dance. They looked like real Incas. I followed them and started to dance along. My mother laughed. Then a *diablada* came and I danced along with them. Then I gathered some *wayruritos*, little black and red seeds. They were my treasure. I spent hours gathering them. I didn't even have time to eat. It was the eve of the fiesta. My mother's tent was not the only one there. There were two others. The other two were set up by butchers who had also come to trade. I remember it clearly. Firecrackers were set off in a large open area surrounded by straw thatched houses. I think that there were two *prestes* [who sponsored the fiesta and the firecrackers]. I went to the church to look at the Virgin. The migrants to La Paz had the custom of buying new clothes for the Virgin and changing her clothes. Ever curious as I was, I went to watch them change the clothes and saw the Virgin all naked. It seemed strange to me. They called her "Virgin," but the Virgin was made out of rags. Her body was made out of rags! I watched with my mouth open. Then I went back to the tent, sat down next to my mother and asked her, "Mamita, how can they say that it's the Virgin? The Virgin has a body made out of rags just like my doll. And they dressed her like I dress my doll." My mother answered, "Why did you go and look. You shouldn't have looked how the *prestes* dress the Virgin. She might get angry."

Later that evening the Virgin *did* get angry. Or so it appeared to me. They began to set off the firecrackers, with the two *prestes* competing [to see whose display was more magnificent]. I was watching from under the tent. Suddenly a firecracker landed on one of the straw roofs. It was the county judge's office. The roof caught fire. I began to scream. I couldn't watch any longer. I screamed, "Father, father, let's leave!" I imagined that the Virgin had become angry, that we would all burn and that end of the world had arrived. Everybody was screaming. I didn't know what to do. My mother tried to hold on to me but everybody was running all over the place and so I escaped. My father ran after me. I ran down to the river because I thought that if I jumped into the river the fire couldn't reach me. Next to our tent was the tent of a butcher who had a daughter the same age[3] as I but she was *de pollera* (a woman who wears a wide, gathered skirt) and I was *de vestido* (a woman who wears European-style[4] dress). She was hard of hearing. But she too ran down to the river. When my father finally caught up with me I refused to return to the tent and had to be carried. That night I couldn't sleep. I was totally disturbed. The next day my mother asked me why I had run away. I answered that water couldn't catch fire. Well, five or six houses had burned. It was a terrible fire that they couldn't extinguish. I had had the shock of my life. I thought that the end of the world had come because the Virgin became angry and had put a curse on me for watching her clothes being changed.

[I also remember another frightening experience]. At the time, my mother already owned a plot of land in El Alto. She had not built a house there yet. I was small and full of mischief. I loved to explore everything. I remember that there was a pile of rocks there and I started to pick up stones. I saw an enormous toad and I began to scream. I had a bad scare and escaped screaming. My father was alarmed, wondering what had happened. I thought that the toad would gobble me up. I almost died of that *susto* (fright). That evening I became very ill. I had a high temperature, perhaps because of the scare I had. Also I had caught the measles. My father tells me that I almost died then. I was delirious. My mother also tells me that I was about to die because I was no longer conscious and no longer could speak. My father was crying, "How can my daughter die?" To cure me, they washed me with a herb called *hakana*. That herb burns the skin. That's why I am dark. They say that I was supposed to be light-skinned. My mother sometimes curses my father because he washed my entire body including my face and she wanted him to wash only my body. I have not been ill since then, except for high blood pressure, but that time I almost died because of that toad.

School

Time passed. School started. They took me for the first time to the Victor Muñoz Reyes School (a public school). It's located at the corner of the Buenos Aires and the Max Paredes and is known as the Eduardo Abaroa School in the morning and Victor Muñoz Reyes in the afternoon. It was a girls' school. My father didn't like mixed schools for boys and girls. He always put me in schools for girls. I don't remember much about the

Victor Muñoz Reyes school. I think that I was there for [only] two years. I went to school there for the first time when I was seven. It must have been in 1952 or 1951 [just before the revolution]. I remember well how I cried for my brothers during the revolution on April ninth [1952]. It seemed to me that the whole city was going to burn from all the fires. My mother was crying because Moises wasn't at home and neither was Pedro nor my father. They had gone to join the revolution. We went out on the street and stopped at the street corner down from our house and I saw the sad sight of cadavers stacked in the back of trucks like beef. The prisoners too were being loaded in rows with their hands tied behind their backs. Then I saw that one of the persons leading the prisoners with a rifle slung over his shoulder was my brother Moises.

I only remember from that time that the teacher would frequently hit me. She would grab me by the hair and knock my head against my book because I couldn't learn how to read. I also remember that my brother Moises had a quarrel with my teacher. He scolded her. I am sure that she must have hit me badly.

[She hit the other children too.] She was mean. But I think that I got used to [school] during that year, and in the second year when I was in the second grade I no longer found it difficult. I had the same teacher but she no longer hit me. Rather, I had become her favorite pupil. In that school I also had a terrible quarrel with one of the other girls over a copy book. I also remember that once they had me march dressed as a nurse in the Sixth of August (Independence Day) parade. That's what I remember.

When I was small I only spoke Aymara. My cousin Juana, the oldest daughter of my aunt Fabiana, would criticize me for being a monolingual Aymara speaker (*porque era aymara cerrada*). She would say [to my mother], "Your daughter won't be able to learn Spanish, *tía*, she is an *aymarista*." Because my mother doesn't speak Spanish, I learned how to speak only Aymara too. My teacher probably hit me for the same reason: I was unable to learn, and I didn't know any Spanish at all. I only learned how to speak Spanish in school. In that class some girls spoke Aymara as well as Spanish but they spoke Spanish most of the time. With Yola I always spoke Aymara and a little Spanish because her mother spoke Spanish.

Then my brother Moises took me to Sagrados Corazones and I remember everything about that school. He took me there because he felt that the girls in Muñoz Reyes were willful and quarrelsome. I don't know why, but we often hit one another. Perhaps because I am fat, the girls didn't like me. They always pulled my hair or shoved me. They didn't want me to stand in line next to them. They would always bother me.

Sofía's experiences included an incident involving her schoolmates that was so upsetting that she didn't even tell her mother about it. Another factor that led her to change schools was the constant pressure to give gifts to the teachers:

The following year, when I was still attending the same school, I remember that there was a scarcity of sugar, bread, and cooking alcohol. So the pupils would bring these items to school to give to the teachers. I told my brother Moises what they were doing to me. I told him, "Because I don't bring presents to the teacher she makes me sit on the floor." So one day, my brother went and had a bad quarrel with the teacher. That's why Moises changed his mind about the school. My father also preferred me to be with the nuns. There I went to school both in the morning and in the afternoon, while in the Muñoz Reyes, classes were only held in the afternoon. I liked Sagrados Corazones.

[My friend Yola] went to another school because Yola's mother was a more educated person (*siempre preparativa*). She spoke Spanish. She was a bit better than my family. So they looked for a school that was better than mine: Yola attended the 16 de Julio school in the Tumusla where girls from good families went. My father didn't know about that. That's why he put me in Victor Muñoz Reyes where lower [class] girls went. Realizing that, Moises took me out of there and placed me in Sagrados Corazones. Now I was in a better school than she. She was in a public school while I was in a private one.

The nuns accepted me readily. There were no problems. The nuns never punished me. The *madre* liked me. You see, I already knew things. Mother Maria Chantal was the director. The nuns always raised girls and some of them became teachers. They continued to live there. When I entered the third grade I also had first communion. But I didn't have *madrinas* (godmothers) because my mother didn't know about things like that. They prepared me for first communion together with eighty or hundred girls. The nuns had dresses and veils for us. We celebrated it during Corpus Cristi. The nuns prepared chocolate, cookies, and bread [for all those who didn't have *madrinas de comunión*]. When I told my mother that we had celebrated our first communion all she said was, "Fine."

At Sagrados Corazones they taught me embroidery and knitting. I learned how to pray and to go to communion and confession every

Friday. They taught us cleanliness much better than in the first school. I was always very neat. I was well-behaved and no longer quarreled with the girls. We were on the right path (*yá hemos ido bien*). We learned how to read and write well. I knew everything well: religion, sacred history. Of the different subject matters we were taught, I remember anatomy, zoology, arithmetic, geography, geometry, Bolivian history, and physics. We had gym lessons only once a month because we didn't have a gym teacher. And we only wore skirts. The *madre* didn't want us to wear shorts. She didn't want us to be half-naked. She also didn't want us to go to church in short sleeves. Now Mother Chantal has changed her mind about this. Now [the pupils] are allowed to wear what they want. But at that time she didn't want to see anything. [Imagine], she would [even] get angry if she saw us playing with marbles! We only wore uniforms twice a year for the parades on July 16th (the Day of La Paz) and August 6th (the Bolivian national holiday). When I finished primary school, I entered the *segundo clásico*. That school was already called Henriette de Chevarier. There we did have gymnastics. For this we wore pants. I still have them stored away. At the time, the school was poor and free of charge. The part higher up was for poor girls. The lower part charged tuition and was for *gente buena*.

We never mixed with people from below. We were separated by some very dense pine trees. If a ball landed in our part from the other side, a nun would carry it over. Well, I do remember once I was over there. I think that it was in fifth grade. It was during a large celebration that the nuns organized during the fiesta of Corpus Cristi. They had a beautiful procession. Each floor was adorned with pine trees and beautiful ornaments that looked like flowers. The pupils walked in the procession carrying candles and we followed singing religious hymns. And the parents from below and our own parents both attended. Yes, that time we did come together, and we all seemed equal. However, our clothing did look a bit sad, because they were wearing good clothing.

We ate at home. School was out at noon and we returned at two in the afternoon. We did receive chocolate and some very good bread that the nuns had made for religious fiestas.

Then the nuns also showed movies twice in a large hall in the school and we had "civic hours" (*horas cívicas*) where we presented dances. I danced as a black. Each class presented a dance. There was a *llamerada*, a *diablada*, "Spaniards," things like that. I had to dance with a "corporal."[5] One of the girls played that role dressed as a man. I think that it was on Mother's day. People came to watch paying admission. The nuns also directed plays and charged the children and parents that came to see them. They used the money to improve the school because the classrooms were very ugly. There were only two floors. Now I think that there are three. The school was very poor.

School Friends

When I went to school [in Sagrados Corazones] I had a friend called Eva Mamani. She lived [nearby] in the Bautista farther up than the Garita de Lima. She is an only daughter, just like me. Her father worked in a hotel as a waiter and her mother was a housewife. Her right foot was crippled from birth and so her mother would often bring her to school. Because she limped, the girls [in school] didn't like her. We became friends because we sat next to each other in class and we were both hardworking pupils. Our classmates hated both of us because Mother Chantal liked us. They didn't hit me, but they hit her because she couldn't defend herself. I often had to defend her. She cried a lot and I felt pity for her because she couldn't defend herself. That's how we became friends.

Eva's mother was well aware of our friendship. When she came to school with Eva in the mornings she would ask me to watch out for her. "Sofía," she would say, "take care that nothing happens to her." And she would give me sweets and chocolate.

She was my only friend in school. We would always play marbles together. It was the only game we played during recess. Because Eva was crippled, she didn't like to jump rope or run. But she was good at playing marbles. After school, we would go out on the street and get into all sorts of mischief. We would stick our heads into a store and poke fun at the owner. One would push the other and the other would escape. We would play like that until we reached home. We were always together.

I would do my homework in the evening. Then I would play with my friend Yola. We played with dolls in her room.

We continued to go to school together until we finished grade school. After that, we took leave from each other. We didn't see one another until one day my nephew José, who by then was grown up as I was, told me that he had a fiancée whom he wanted to marry. My brother suggested that we invite her here for lunch and when José presented her to me I realized that she was my old school friend. She looked at me and cried out "Sofía!" and I cried "Eva!" and we gave each other a wild hug. The others were stunned. Finally José asked, "How come you know one another?" "She is a school friend of mine and now she will become my niece," I answered. Now Eva is a commercial secretary and works for Urdi Moto.

Catechism

On Sundays I would go to catechism because I liked religion. I wanted to become a nun. I fancied wearing their robes. So, when I was an adolescent I didn't go to the movies or to fiestas. My only pastime was to go to the Recoleta church for catechism. I would pray and sing and they taught me religion: the ten commandments, the sacraments, and all the things in the Bible. The Recoleta church is in the Calle América. The monks there wore almost the same habits as the Franciscan monks do. I believe that they were foreigners. They came from all over, even from San Pedro and Villa Victoria. But the only girls I knew were my cousins Lidia and Rita. I had a small card, that the padres gave us when we first came, and on that card there were small squares that they would stamp every time we attended. The girls that had gone every Sunday would have the card full of stamps and would receive a prize at Christmas time. I really went all the time because I wanted to get that prize. I went every Sunday at three in the afternoon and we would get out at five thirty. My cousins, the daughters of my mother's sister, first introduced me to catechism. There were four of them. They came by one day and asked me whether I wanted to come along. So I went to pray every Sunday and for Christmas I received cookies, sweets, and clothing and I liked that a lot. Upon entering the church, I would first pray in front of the Virgin of Lourdes—I think that they brought her from Lourdes. They said that she was the mother of unmarried girls and so I would ask her for favors. I was nine or ten years old when I first went and I continued going for four years.

I remember that once the *padres* who taught us catechism prepared a dance performance. All the older girls danced for the parents in a large hall in the Don Bosco school. They also showed us a nice movie about soldiers in Spain who wore skirts. By that time, I was twelve or thirteen and I must already have known a lot about religion and so they switched me to the Juventud Obrera Católica in the Church of the Holy Spirit in the Avenida Perú. A *padre* from France, *padre* José, lived there. He had a secretary called Elvira Galló who I think was from Belgium. I was transferred there together with my cousins Lidia and Rita and three other girls. We went there on Sundays and Elvira Galló taught us how to embroider, sew, knit, and bake little buns, and gave us lectures about becoming a woman. Then the *padre* would come and teach us religion.

We would also go to confession. At the end, we again performed dances. The *padre* filmed the occasion and showed us the film. The *padre* was very good. Every two weeks, they would give us ten to twelve pounds of flour and sugar. This suited my mother just fine, and so she would always urge me to go. That was one of the main reasons I went.

I remember that once the *padre* decided to celebrate San Juan with a little fiesta and a bonfire for us, something he had never done before. Twenty-five girls from all over La Paz, including Sopocachi and Tembladerani, came along. The *padre* had two vehicles, a large white station wagon and a Jeep, like the one you have. Elvira drove the Jeep and the *padre* the station wagon.

The *padre* came up with the idea of picking up some firewood in Caiconi for the bonfire and we all loaded the firewood into the two vehicles. Even the *padre* helped pick up sticks, hiking up his robe. But the *padre* grabbed some nettles by mistake and began to scream, "Ay, Ay." We were all upset and wondered what to do about it. But I was familiar with the customs in rural areas because my mother had taught me and I told the *padre* that urine was good for nettle burns. So the *padre* told us to go to one side so he could pee and wash his hands with his own urine. It worked, but we were not allowed to watch because it's supposed to be a sin to watch a *padre* . . . Well, we reached the house and he prepared a very special meal for us. I went home to change and we made a bonfire. I asked my mother to let me stay until ten o'clock. The girls loved the dance because boys had been invited too. The *padre* was the only adult man. He danced and danced until he was exhausted from dancing with all the girls. He made himself really popular with the girls. We danced until midnight and we were all afraid to go home, so the *padre* had to work hard dropping us off one by one at our homes. I don't know when he went to bed that night! My mother didn't get angry that time because it was our first late fiesta.

Another event I remember is the time we went with the *padre* to the Yungas valley for a one-day outing. I still have a little earth from the Yungas stored away from that trip. The *padre* wanted to go to Yanacachi in the Yungas where there is a school run by nuns. He told us each to prepare food to take along. So Yola and I prepared food and we asked my sister-in-law Lidia Laura, the younger sister of my brother Pedro's wife, to come along too. The *padre*, Mecha, María (the pretty one), Yola, Lidia, and I went in the station wagon and the others came in the Jeep. The poor girls whose mothers wouldn't give them the money for the quota to pay for gas stayed behind. We left at seven as happy as can be. The *padre* was happy too.

But something terrible happened to me. Nothing happened to the others, it happened to me alone. We were about to reach Unduavi. I still remember exactly where it was. It was a place where a lot of water comes down the river. I was pressed against the door as was another girl. The *padre* was talking or singing and suddenly the door flew open and Sofía went flying. I don't remember a thing that happened after that. Apparently I fell on the back of my head. They told me later that the *padre* only stopped the car quite a distance away. He hadn't noticed what had happened until Mecha screamed that Sofía had disappeared. And there was Sofía, stretched on the road! I only remember that they picked me up and cleaned the dirt off, nothing else. They told me that they had run like mad to where I was. But nothing was broken. Only the back of my neck hurt a lot. The *padre* was frightened. "Maybe something is wrong with Sofía," he said. "Let's not continue but return home." But I wanted to see what the Yungas looked like and assured him that I was all right. But in reality I was not in good shape. It hurt a lot and I couldn't eat anything. The *padre* was no longer in good spirits. He was deeply preoccupied. I was vomiting when we arrived in Yanacachi. It must have been both from the knock I had received and from the shock. The *madres* did everything they could to help me get over my headache. They were very good. Now they live in my parish, Exaltación, in La Paz. They invited us to eat with them and with the girls in their school, and after that we went to steal oranges and to buy some to take home with us. Everybody had a good time but me. I no longer enjoyed the trip. My head hurt too much.

When we got to the site where I had fallen out of the station wagon I asked the *padre* to stop and I picked up some earth and stones. I have kept them to this day. The *padre* asked me, "Why did you pick up this dirt, leave it." But I answered, "No, if something happens to me I can accuse this earth of having done it to me." Mecha tried to cheer me up by singing, "*Tio, tiorile*, the *padre* married the station wagon. *Tio, tiorile*, Sofía married the earth." The *padre* joined in too. But my headache became worse and worse until I could barely stand the pain. The *padre* wanted me to tell my mother about what had happened but Yola and my cousins told me not to tell her anything. I arrived here [in La Paz], gave my mother the oranges I had bought and only told her that I was not feeling well. When she asked what was wrong I said that it must be the change of climate. I waited two whole months before telling my mother that I had fallen out of the vehicle and had lost consciousness. My mother got very angry and wouldn't let me go anywhere anymore.

I continued to like to go to the Juventud Obrera Católica. But then we had the surprise of our lives. Mecha had swallowed some ten sleeping pills and had died. Maybe it was suicide. The *padre* was wondering about that possibility. But he thought that it couldn't have been. He was sure that it had been an accident. It was a terrible death. But they held a beautiful funeral. Mecha looked like the Virgin of Lourdes. She had a blue ribbon and they had made almost the same clothing. The *padre* had ordered a coffin of the best quality with a large glass window so that one could see the entire body. So we went to the cemetery to bury her. We cried a lot. We couldn't forget our grief. So they [transferred me to another club]. I was appointed president of the Juventud Católica Obrera in Villa Victoria. A black girl, older than I, called Mercedes Vargas who came from the Yungas was also appointed. But I was there only for a short time. I did everything I could so that the girls would come, but they didn't. So I gave up. I just continued going to school, that's all.

Learning Dressmaking

After finishing primary school,[6] I began to study dressmaking at the same school, Sagrados Corazones. It was my mother's idea for me to become a seamstress. That's why I took lessons on Sundays. My teacher at Sagrados Corazones was Doña Aida de Fuentes, who happened to be Pedro's wedding godmother. She already knew me because she and my mother were *comadres*. [She was surprised when she saw me] and she told my mother, "Oh! She is your daughter! I want her to come to my house an extra day and I will teach her more." So I went to the school on Sundays and on Wednesdays I went to the lady's house in the Calle Murillo. There she told me how to use patterns. I went every Sunday, and so one day Yola asked me about it and I told her to come too and so we studied together for two years. We were supposed to obtain a diploma, but I couldn't finish because my father became ill. My [real] desire was to become a nurse, but unfortunately my father became ill and so we went to live there (in Llamacachi).

[To be a nurse] I would have had to study everything and get a *bachiller* (high school) degree and study medicine. Yola herself wanted to become a commercial secretary. Well, she hasn't become a commercial secretary either.

Later I got to know you and then I went to school in the evening. Remember, Sr. Hans? I took evening classes and dressmaking as well as typing.[7] If Mother Chantal had continued I would have become someone, but unfortunately she left for France to ask for aid, as she told me. There were two nuns left: Madre Natividad, who was nice, and Madre

Margarita, a Peruvian, who took a dislike to me. I worked there in the laundry too. She made life impossible for us. So when vacation came, I asked for permission to leave and didn't return to school to this day.

For Bolivia, Sofía had a relatively privileged early childhood. She was the only daughter and was the apple of her father's eye. Furthermore, she was not expected to contribute to the household. Perhaps these facts contributed to her self-assuredness as an adult.

As her description of her travels with her parents show, Sofía often must have played alone, but in her recollections, she constructs her identity as a child as a heavy Aymara girl who was attuned to the supernatural. First she emulated boys until her brother and her father put a stop to it. This is not the only time that her brothers intervene (indeed, sometimes meddle) in her life, a fact that was facilitated by the considerable age difference (twenty-six years with Pedro and fifteen years with Moises) between her and her siblings. Subsequently, Sofía entered into a competitive relationship with her friend Yola. She recalls that Yola had larger dolls than she did. Later they competed in terms of the schools they attended, in selling in the market, and in buying jewelry.

Sofía's experience in her first school, her brother's choice of the second school, her relationship to her Pazeño kin, and her friendship with Yola all underscore the extreme social class and ethnic consciousness that prevails in Bolivia. Her cousin looked down on her and criticized her mother for speaking only Aymara at home. The term "aymara cerrada," that the cousin employed, connotes isolation from the mainstream. Aymara descent has racial overtones, but the imagined and real linguistic differences and cultural differences are more significant. Discrimination took the form of bullying and physical violence. Sofía eventually overcame her linguistic handicap and was well liked by her teachers in the second school she attended, but with the exception of her friend Eva, she mentions no other school friends. That relationship shows her empathy for another person discriminated against because of her membership in a despised category, in this case, a person with a physical handicap.

Sofía's relationship to Yola, whose mother considered herself as belonging to a higher social class than Sofía's mother, in spite of her lower economic standing, also had social class overtones. Sofía's mother largely played along with her sons' and daughter's status games as long as this did not entail transforming her own way of life. Thus, she took note and seemed pleased that Sofía had taken first com-

munion, a strictly urban custom, but she had obviously not attended the ceremony herself. Also, while it is customary to select godparents for the event, thereby creating ties that may have long-term importance, Sofía had no first communion godparents.

Sofía's mother's decision to move back to Llamacachi consolidated the family's rural ties but it may have limited Sofía's social mobility. She was unable to complete her studies of dressmaking and she never studied nursing.

Coming to terms with supernatural forces under traumatic circumstances also marks her identity from early childhood on. She regards childhood traumas—accidents and fires—that figure prominently in her narrative as directly related to supernatural causes, or to her fear of supernatural intervention. In at least one instance, the mitigation of supernatural forces in turn required the involvement of other supernatural forces. The close relationship with the supernatural, her later searches for diviners and her own increasing competence in dreaming and dream interpretation have their roots in childhood. Interestingly, her Catholic upbringing does not appear to have had an impact on her life commensurate with the intensity of her involvement in the Catholic church as a child and as an adolescent, except initially, when she assisted the nuns with health care in Llamacachi.

2

LEARNING *How to Sell*

Sofía began to sell during one of the most eventful periods in Bolivian history: the social revolution and agrarian reform of 1952–53 and its aftermath. During the first part of the century, peasants had few rights. When Sofía's mother left Llamacachi for La Paz, rural-urban migrants were equally despised. Hans's aunt remembered an episode that occurred in the early forties: an elite mother who, after her small son had accidentally stepped on the toes of an Aymara in a store, said to her son, "Písalo, písalo, nomás. Solo es un indio." (Go ahead and step on him, he is only an Indian). The Chaco war, during which the government depended on the peasants for the ultimately unsuccessful struggle against the encroaching Paraguayans, led to some improvement in the rights of peasants, but it was not until the 1950s that these incipient movements came to fruition. While for Sofía's mother and for Sofía herself the fifties and early sixties were a time of hardship, when the family's candle industry declined and they had to re-establish themselves in Llamacachi, at least one member of the family, Pedro, benefitted—if only temporarily—from the political enfranchisement of a new social class. Eventually Sofía and her mother also benefitted from the increased purchasing power of the peasants following the agrarian reform and from the opening of rural markets to the direct sale of produce to urban customers. Sofía also participated in the grassroots movement (cum government manipulation) towards more powerful representation of market and small-scale producer organizations in local government.

Ever since I was a small child I would always accompany my mother to sell candles and I would help her carry the candles. [My parents] made the candles and [my mother] sold them. We made candles in various sizes. There were five centavo and ten centavo candles, large candles and tiny ones that people bought to burn on Tuesdays and Fridays. They said that this was good against enemies. The sales were best whenever they wanted to get rid of a government. Then, for January 24th, my mother made even smaller Alasitas[1] candles.

I carried a small basket large enough for two *sart'as* of candles; each *sart'a* has a dozen candles. Today my mother is bitter about it. She tells me, "you are small because you had to carry all those candles. You were supposed to be tall like I am." I must have accompanied her and carried candles ever since I was five or four years old.[2] I never went to sell candles on my own, always with my mother, and when I began to go to school I no longer went along anymore. I preferred to help out at home. The only thing I continued to do was to deliver the orders of candles on Mondays at the Church of Gran Poder Viejo where my mother had three *caseras*: Doña Manuela, Doña Luisa, and Doña Antonia, with whom my mother had regular contracts. I would put twenty dozen candles into a basket and deliver them there.

When I finished primary school I studied to become a seamstress and then I wanted to have my own money. I was already fifteen years old. Yola already had her own business. She was selling peas wholesale and she was talking about the marvelous things she did with her money. She had her own money and was making clothes for herself and she told me that I was a fool to continue working for my mother. She said, "You should tell your mother to give you some capital so that you can sell on your own." So one day I decided to tell my mother that I was grown up now and wanted to handle some money of my own. My mother agreed and gave me I think it was forty pesos as capital. She told me, "You may sell, but you [also] have to study. So how can you do it? Why don't you make candles just once a week here and we will go together to sell. My mother bought an *arrobita* (sixteen pounds) of fat and so I had an *arrobita* of fat. Then she told me that I would have to buy a ball of wick twine. As for the *cabo liqui* (candle rests purchased from churches to improve the quality of the candles), I told her that she would have to give it to me, for after all I was her daughter. So every week I put up nine pounds of fat that cost 120 pesos (or US$10 per pound, with 1080 pesos equaling US$90). So I knew how much capital I had invested. When my mother figured the profit, she would figure a profit of one half (*sic*). Let's say there was a capital of ten pesos. The profit would be twenty pesos, which meant that we ended up with a capital of thirty pesos. So my mother must have earned [double] the capital. She made easy money. And so did I. We would go together to sell and when we arrived at home my mother would say, "This much is yours."

I was earning well [selling with my mother] and had some money. [But] one day[3] Yola told me, "You are foolish to go with your mother. You should get a hold of something and sell on your own. Don't go with your mother anymore. She knows how much you earn and [so] she has control over you. If you go on your own, she won't know whether you have earned money or not.

[When I sold together with my mother, she would keep the money I earned for me and I could only buy those things with it that she wanted me to buy]. I didn't use it for sweets and things like that. Half of what I earned was for me, but my mother kept the money and she bought me a lunch pail with it, a brown jacket, a red skirt, and even a small radio. That's why Yola told me, "What are you doing selling with your mother. Since you already have something [you can use as starting capital] come and sell here with me." So I told my mother one day, "I don't want to go with you anymore. I want to sell on my own. I am going to go and sell every day in the Max Paredes." I really wanted to be able to brag to Yola and tell her that I was earning more than she was. My mother answered, "O.K., go ahead, child. If you like Yola better than me go and sell with her." At that time, the Max Paredes was not lined with kiosks with people selling cloth, the way it is now. It was empty. There were no vendors except for us. Yola and I and one other girl sat near the entrance to the [Rodriguez] market.

[Now I could buy what I wanted]. I bought clothing for myself: sweaters, things like that. I no longer had to content myself with what my mother bought for me. I didn't like the things that my mother bought me. This way I could buy what I liked.

After that, I went back to studying to become a seamstress. I went together with Yola. Yola continued to sell on Saturdays and Mondays. On Sundays we studied. Every Sunday we went for lessons and during the rest of the week we sold.

But that's how I found out how lovely it is to have one's own money. Before that I didn't know anything about money matters. But thanks to Yola I found out. Thanks to Yola I handled money marvelously. I knew how to do business. She is the one who egged me on.

Yola's story is as follows. As I have already told you, her mother was from Peru. She lived with a friend, Agustina Quiñones, and they used to embroider. And it seems to me that this woman didn't earn enough with her embroideries. They lived very poorly. Sometimes they had nothing to eat. Sometimes they would have to content themselves with a little coca. It seemed to me that they were very sad. There was a woman who also lived in the house, called Juana Katunta, who was from Pakullo, near Sorata. She was married to Isidro Chique. My mother had gotten to know her travelling to Atahuallpani, in the Sorata valley, because she came to buy from her. So when Juana moved to La Paz from Sorata, she came to live in our house. I don't know why. This Juana Katunta began to sell *purexa* potatoes, a black potato [from her area of origin]. And because she knew people there she was able to buy them on credit. In the meantime, Clorinda [Yola's mother] and Agustina continued with their embroideries. Juana [saw this and] was sad that they sometimes did not have enough to eat. Sometimes she even would pay their rent for them. They were very nice women. They took care of the house as though it were their own. One could trust them and so my mother liked them and did not want to throw them out.

Well, I think that this Katunta talked to Agustina Quiñones and one day I saw that Agustina was selling potatoes too. Since Agustina spoke Spanish well she was successful. Clorinda also helped Agustina. She cooked and occasionally sold as well. The business progressed and soon Agustina was ordering potatoes from Sorata in quantity. That's how Yola began to sell. Agustina taught her. Yola sold peas and broadbeans while her mother and Agustina sold *papa purexa* and *papalisa* (*Ullucus tuberosus*). She told me that her mother had given her a capital of one hundred pesos with which she bought a bag of peas. Her first business was selling peas. That's how she earned money. Later, she had contracts to buy peas in large quantities. She went to a special market place (*agencia*) where peas arrived from Sorata. She made the contacts with the merchants from Sorata through her mother and bought large quantities. When she was twelve, she was already making a lot of money. Now they had money and ate the best food. They were wearing better clothing.

The first time I went [to sell with Yola, she] got an *arroba* (twenty-five pounds) of peas and an *arroba* of green *habas* for me, and I began to sell. I sold them for twenty centavos (US$0.20) a pound. It must have been in 1958, when I was thirteen, because I had my front teeth rimmed with gold when I was fifteen. At that time I didn't have them yet. I was only a child.

At first, I only sold in the afternoon. I went down at two. The person who sold me the peas and beans was Yola's mother: that is her second mother—her real mother is Agustina. She obtained them by the *carga* (150 pounds). I would earn one peso for the *arroba* of peas and another peso for the *arroba* of *habas*. I was happy with that. And the next day the same thing.

Then we also went down to sell in that same spot early in the morning. At the time, it was very difficult to sell in the mornings because there was a lot of control by the municipal police. It was prohibited to sell there because it was an empty place. So we went to sell in the Buenos Aires. It was also prohibited to sell in the Buenos Aires, but we sold there anyway near Cuevas's house: the two of us alone, she with her produce tied in a cloth and I with mine also in a cloth. When the policeman was not around, we would sell, and when he came, we would run away. Now one can sell there without problems. They no longer stop you. But at that time it was prohibited. But for me it was fun, because Yola and I were free to laugh and make fun of the policemen. I was no longer tied to my home. I earned good money. I bought ice cream. I bought soft drinks. If someone passed by with food, I bought some and I went to the movies. My mother didn't ask me how much I earned. She left me alone. So that's how I learned how to sell peas and *habas*.

[I never had to give my mother anything]. She bought my clothes, food, and shoes. I never showed her my earnings. She probably wanted me to learn a thing or two, so that I would know how to earn a living. That's why she gave me all this freedom. But I never let my little capital that my mother had given me die. I always kept it invested in produce.

Then, one afternoon, my brother Pedro saw me selling on the street. Pedro was no longer living in our house. He was living on the other side of the city in Vino Tinto where he had bought a house [of his own]. My mother had helped him buy it. He lived there with his first wife whom he had married in church and whom my mother had taught how to make candles. He saw me in the Max Paredes selling peas and *habas* when he was passing by with two friends. He didn't like it at all that I was selling there. After he had said goodbye to his friends, he went up to our house and confronted my mother. "How can you allow my sister go and sell there? What are my friends going to say? They will say that my sister is a street vendor! Shame on you! You can't even raise an only daughter. Can't you provide for her? You only have one daughter and you send her out to sell on the street!" My mother answered, "I am not forcing her. She wants to go and sell. That's why I am letting her do it. Is she doing anything wrong? Has she stolen anything?" They had a big argument! "From now on," Pedro said, "I will tell my sister that she is no longer my sister. It is shameful for her to be selling on the street." That's why I say God is great. Because my brother was ashamed, I didn't want to be his sister either. He said that it was unseemly for me to sit in the street and that his friends would criticize him. He saw himself as a gentleman. He must have wanted me to continue with my studies and become a society lady. But I didn't want that. When I returned home that night, my mother began to scold me telling me what my brother had told her. She didn't want me to go anymore either. So I had a big quarrel with her too. I said that I didn't want to stop. I liked to sell. Selling was pleasant. I could go and sell whenever I wanted and I was earning money. I started to cry. "I won't stop, Mother," I told her. "Let him go ahead and say that I am not his sister. It's fine with me. They (the other vendors) will help me." And so I continued to sell.

I started to sell during winter vacations. I sold every day, both in the mornings and in the afternoons. Then, [just a few months after I started to sell produce], I began to sell onions. Later, Yola went to school in the morning and sold in the afternoon, while I went to school both in the morning and in the afternoon, like I did before. But on Saturdays and Sundays when there were no classes, I continued to sell.

But I was ashamed myself. I was afraid that my schoolmates would see me. I would watch out for people I knew. Fortunately no one ever did see me. I was very careful about that. I didn't want them to wonder why I was a vendor and at the same time studying in the best school.

The first time I dealt in onions was when Elena's father, Andrés Quispe—Moises's father-in-law—brought some from Llamacachi. I still remember it. They were really large. When he saw that I was selling *habas* and peas he told me, "Why don't you sell these onions? I have brought three hundred of them, retail them." Andrés brought them to the house and I bought them from him. Three hundred is a lot of onions. I was only a little girl. I carried a bundle of one hundred of them down to the sales site. It was a very large bundle. My mother helped me load it on my back and cautioned me to be careful not to fall. But when I reached the corner of our street, I had a terrible fall. I had to gather up all the onions and ask someone to load the bundle on my back again. I went down and sold the onions, but some were missing. That evening I became ill. My mother said that it was *qaxa*, an illness brought about by the *achachilas* (mountain spirits). You see, I had never fallen on our street. *Qaxa* is from the earth, from *Pachamama* (Mother Earth). Because I fell at that place it got a hold of me. I became ill. I was limping and couldn't walk. I didn't have any appetite. I had to vomit and had a headache. I was sick in bed for a week. My mother blamed the whole thing on Andrés Quispe, "This old man brings onions here and now my daughter is sick." She didn't know why I was sick. So she called a *brujo* (spiritist, diviner, and healer) who said that it was a *qaxa* from the Callejón Incachaca and that we would have to *milluchar*. *Millu* is black and earth-like. It's supposed to be bad to eat *millu* because it makes one's teeth fall out. My mother took some rotten urine—people in rural areas always wash their hair in rotten urine—and heated it in a basin. The *brujo* put the urine on my feet for almost an hour while I was sleeping. Then he rubbed my entire body with it, calling out [for the illness] to leave. He said something like, "Why did you give her *qaxa*, why did you make this child sick at that spot?" And he rubbed my head, my body, and my bad foot. He put [the rag with which he had rubbed me] into the hot urine and covered the pot with my sweater. After a long while he uncovered it and the urine had foamed like beaten egg. He said, "Look, here is the Callejón. This is where she fell." Apparently, there was a path in the foam that looked just like the Callejón. Then they took the urine out in a new earthenware pot, and they threw it down at the spot where I had fallen. I had to remain in the house for three days and not walk on that spot. They warned me that if I stepped on it again, the same thing would happen to me. That's how I became well. I will always remember that fall.

[The *brujo*] was Qolla Achila (literally, Old Man Medicine) from here, from Munaypata. My mother always dealt with him. He was a close friend of Pedro's first wife. He was ancient. He was a hundred years old and really mean. He must have died by now. He used to come and hit us with a stick when we had sinned.[4] He also prepared magical offerings for my mother to improve her business luck. I only remember that he would read her fortune in the coca leaves. I think that he used to prepare and make the offering during the entire night. He would come at nine o'clock with his stick and that's when he would hit us all asking how we were behaving. He even pulled *Pedro* by the ear and asked him if *he* had behaved well. My mother would give him food and coffee. I would watch with curiosity. I would sit in front of my mother and watch him read the coca and he would read the fortune of every one of us. Then I would go to sleep. I don't know how long the old manwould continue but he would only leave the next morning and I would wake up with some yarn tied to me here and there. He went around curing people: he was a *brujo de Dios*, a believer in the Catholic faith and did not have contact with the devil. I think that he was a follower of the apostle Saint James.

That's how I began to sell onions. And I studied at the same time. I continued selling in the Buenos Aires and the Max Paredes. I didn't have a fixed site but the policemen didn't fine me because I was a little girl and they were not allowed to detain me. I had some earnings and I had a little bag that my mother gave me as a present to keep my money. But I lost it. I think that I had some one hundred pesos (US$8.33) in the bag. I had good money and I had my *habas*, peas, and onions.

I would go to the Rodriguez and buy [the onions] wholesale by the hundred. I didn't know who was from Llamacachi. But then, my sister-in-law Elena took me to the Rodriguez market and told me to buy *tocuro*. *Tocuros* are the onions that are already flowering. She told me that I was stupid [to buy from strangers] and [introduced me to people from Llamacachi] saying, "This is your aunt." This way I earned almost double and was happy with my profit.[5]

I finally stopped selling when Yola became angry with me. I think that she was jealous. She said that I was selling better than she and I answered back. I told my mother about it and she advised me to stop selling, "Teach her a lesson. Tell her that you are quitting. Some day she will tell you that you became someone just because of her. No, my child. Don't sell any longer. People will say that the daughter of a landlady has gone to sell on the street." So I no longer went out to sell. However, my capital had grown by now. So I bought fat wholesale. My mother told me to make candles again. This must have been in 1961 (when Sofía was fifteen). At that time I also finished primary school. She had changed her mind about my future. She told me, "You can earn something by making candles for me. Remember how you became ill carrying onions. Your brother was right to get angry. You are my only daughter. Make candles and I will go sell them for you. At the same time you will go to study tailoring and you will become a seamstress."

On Tuesdays and Saturdays my mother made candles for me: no longer just out of ten pounds [of tallow] as before, but from an entire *arroba*. I think that I had a capital of 150 (US$12.50). I was buying fat by the hundredweight and I had my own ball of wick twine. I prepared the twine myself. My mother would go and buy the fat and I would accompany her. She taught me how to buy. I believe that an honest person can't make a profit nowadays. My mother had two large scales, one was accurate and the other stole some extra (*robaba más*)—two hundredweights weighed only something over one hundredweight on that scale. That is how my mother was able to benefit and how she was able to buy a house. Some meat vendors [from whom my mother bought the fat] didn't know about scales. She also taught me [some other tricks]. She would climb some steps and have me push the fat upwards with a hidden stick so that it would weigh less. And my mother was happy about our success in tricking people. So my mother went to sell and my father made the candles while I made the twine for the wicks and helped my father. I also did the cooking. Finally, my mother taught me how to make candles myself.

One day, I made some with my lard and they came out very thick. My mother scolded me and told me that I would lose money. "How can I sell candles like that," she said, "They are a disgrace. Go sell them yourself." So I put them in a basket and took them to her own *casera*, telling her that my mother had sent me. That's how I learned how to make candles. I also continued to help my father.

At this point, my mother told me to take my candles to her *caseras* near Gran Poder Viejo on Tuesdays. So I would go there in the afternoon and deliver my candles personally, and on Thursdays I went to collect the money. Soon I had at least 350 pesos (US$29.17).

Then, my mother told me that she would like me to have my front teeth trimmed with gold. I was already fifteen years old and liked the idea too. I told my mother, "Yes, I would like that. Yola will not be the only one with gold-trimmed teeth." For Yola had just had them trimmed herself. It was strange. Whenever Yola got something, I had to have it too. We were in constant competition. So my mother said, "Yola has one trimmed tooth. You must have two of yours trimmed." Yola had her left front tooth trimmed. "Don't tell anyone about it though," she continued, "not even your father or your brothers." So one day we went down to sell candles. Because I carried candles around all the time my feet were hurting, and they told me that there was something wrong with them. Well, we passed a sign on the Perez Velasco: Doctora Victoria Jordan Velasquez. I had always heard on the radio that she was the best dentist. I told my mother, "She is a doctor. Why don't we go in. Maybe she can cure me." So we entered quite by chance. The señora quickly took me and said, "Let's do it right away," and my mother agreed. She ground the teeth and measured them. That time she charged me 80 pesos (US$6.67) per tooth. We paid 160 (US$13.33) or 190 (US$15.83). I had 100 pesos (US$8.33). It was two days before my birthday, so [my mother] said: "All right, but let's not tell your father. Let's make it a surprise for your sixteenth birthday." No one said anything about it. Yola looked at me and I looked at her, [but she didn't say anything either]. Now I had one up on her. She only had one and I had two. I did it with the money I earned making and selling candles. And my mother helped me too. Then one day we went for a walk with my mother and met Moises on the street near San Pedro. I didn't want him to see me but he did anyway and he looked at me and scolded me and told me that I was crazy. But I had my wish. My father didn't say anything, he was happy about it.

Then [some five months later] Yola got herself a pair of golden earrings.[6] I wanted a pair too. I told my mother, "Mother, I want earrings. Yola has some already." My mother answered, "Yes, child, just wait a little. I will buy you some if you don't have [enough] money." I barely had 100 pesos stashed away, so she added some of her own and she bought a pair of earrings, a ring and a little chain—an entire set. I think that she paid some 150 pesos (US$12.50). I have put them away. They have large square stones and large golden leaves. When Yola saw them, she [again] didn't say a thing. That's how we competed. My earrings were nicer than hers. Hers were small with blue stones, while mine were long with red ones. Also I had earrings, a ring, and a chain, and Yola only had earrings. We have been competing with one another ever since we had that quarrel at our sale site.

Some two years after I stopped selling on the street, when I had already gone to sewing school for a year, Yola found out about it and asked me to take her along. "I don't want to sell any longer," she said. "I want to become a seamstress." So the following year we both took classes—Yola wearing braids and I with my hair loose. Then Yola copied me and also wore her hair open. Then, when my mother bought me a tight skirt, she bought one just like it. Our competition continued. We went to school together for a year and then Yola married. At that point,

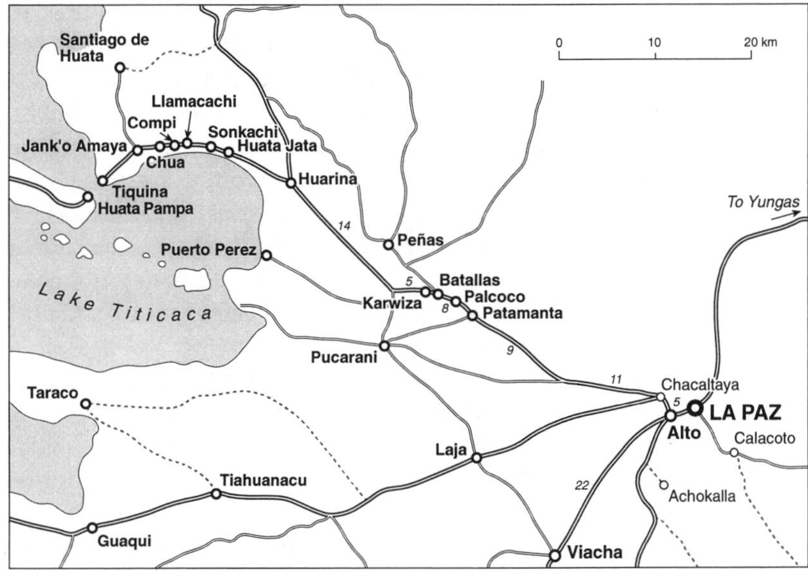

Map 2 La Paz and Lake Titicaca area

Yola changed her business to selling clothing and cloth. I myself left [for Llamacachi in 1962].

My father became ill making candles. In addition, my mother had changed her mind about making candles because sales were low. So she said, "Lets go there." With no sales for weeks on end, we could no longer make a living. It seems to me that that contributed to my father's illness and his becoming deranged. We stayed at Manuel Parra's house. He lived near the lake in a straw thatched hut and we rented a small room that he used as a store room.

We always used to stay there. We used to go and exchange cracklings for produce. He was the only relative with whom we stayed during fiestas, vacations or on any other occasion. He is a cousin of my mother's, a good friend. They also stayed at our house in La Paz. We trusted one another and that's why my mother preferred to stay with him rather than with her brother [with whom she was less close].

The Move to Llamacachi

After we arrived in Llamacachi, I remember that my mother went to visit my great-uncle Pedro Moya, my mother's uncle, and asked for the plot of land and he told her that they could give her her inheritance from her grandmother. In addition, my great uncle owed a bull to my mother. That time I think we stayed for only a week and returned to La Paz where we stayed for another year. I think that my father and mother both worked in order to be able to build a house, but my father always travelled back and forth. My father had some money. He had a house in Vino Tinto and he sold that. He also had a large lot in the neighborhood of 16 de Julio in El Alto. He sold that plot only recently (i.e., in the early 1970s).

[During that year,] my father and my mother continued to make candles. My father was already a bit deranged. He would go to contract mud bricks but, according to what people told us later, he would actually go to other places near Achacachi.[7]

[Before that, my mother had always wanted to build a house in Llamacachi, but only as] a place to stay when she was there, not to live permanently. It was always difficult to stay at someone else's place. Manuel Parra couldn't be trusted [entirely] either. Some fruit or bread always got lost.

So then when my father became ill, we went to live in Chua Visalaya with Isidro Choke where we stayed for almost a month. At the same time we were still having my father treated, but he was already much better.

We had to move because Isidro became irritated. He got tired of us. So we moved from Chua to Llamacachi and stayed with Manuel Parra until my mother had finished the house. We lived in Manuel Parra's house for only two months [because Teodoro, Moises's son, who was living with us got into a fight with Manuel's son]. So we had to move again, crying to the straw house. It wasn't even finished yet. Not even the door had been installed.

So we started to live in the new house in Llamacachi. [For a living] we sold or bartered the cracklings we had accumulated for produce and helped people in the fields in return for some *ocas* (*Oxalis tuberosa*, a tuber) and potatoes. They would pay us an *arroba* or an *arroba* and a half of produce—depending on the harvest—for a day's work. We would start at seven in the morning and work until the field was harvested. We would go to the persons who had large fields. [It didn't matter if we were related or not]. Our life was sad. We didn't own any land except for a little plot we had from my great-grandmother on my mother's side where we built a house. It had remained abandoned until my grand-aunt came to visit us and gave us the land. The house served as sleeping quarters and as a kitchen at the same time. In one corner was the "bedroom," in the other the "kitchen." We stayed there until the store was finished. I frankly got sick and tired of it. Then my father [who was well again by that time] had the store built farther down towards the road. That cost a lot of money because the rocks had to be dynamited away.

Opening a Store and Selling Beer at Fairs

After my mother opened the store, we would go from fiesta to fiesta to sell beer. We went to Sonkachi and Chua. In Compi, we went to the fiestas of San Pedro and Carmen. And we went to the fiestas of Rosario in Chua, San Sebastián, San Miguel in Lakachi, and Cristo Asunción in Sonkachi. We also sold bread and fruit. For the bread, my mother had a contract with a woman who lives in Villa Victoria in La Paz. She has a large oven there and is very well known. She is called Mercedes Cuaquira. She originally came from Peru. She was a friend of my brother Pedro, so my brother went to see her and convinced her to sell bread to my mother on credit. That's how we obtained baskets full of bread on credit. We did well because ours was the only store around. And we went to sell beer. I sold beer and my mother bread, fruit, and sugar. We brought the beer in trucks. On each case of beer we earned fifteen pesos (US$1.25) which in those days was a lot of money. Now I think that they earn 40 pesos (US$2) per case. I would go to La Paz and buy the beer from a *casera* at the corner of the Calle Bustamante and the Santa Cruz. Facing the Chijini police station, there was a beer depot [with beer from Oruro] owned by a very nice man from Oruro from whom my father had already bought beer earlier. Now, that man no longer sells beer. [At that time,] I had to pay cash, but could bring the empty bottles back later if I left some item as security. My mother had an old merino *awayo* that she had bought from an old woman. It was pretty and finely woven and had the words "Viva Bolivia" and "Abajo Paraguay"[8] and the date of the Chaco War woven into it. It still looks like new and I still wear it. I would bring him that *awayo* and he would let me have the beer bottles without paying a deposit. I went again and again and he knew me so well that I finally just sent the truck drivers with a note to pick some beer up for me. He has a large dry goods store. At the fiestas, everyone knew us after a while. We sold at fiestas for almost three years.

Switching to Eggs

When I was in Llamacachi I didn't sell [in La Paz] any longer. It would have been difficult to come to La Paz and since I am the only daughter, I was supposed to stay with my mother. She was afraid to let me go on my own. But then one day I started to buy eggs during the fiesta of [the] Ascension of the Virgin. My mother no longer wanted to sell beer because she said that there were too many drunk people and suggested that I buy eggs instead. "It seems that people are buying a lot of eggs [to resell]," she said. The first time I went was in Sonkachi, just before the government fell in 1964. That afternoon, I got almost five hundred eggs together, spending all the money I had. So I sent my mother a message and the next day she brought more money. When I saw that one could make a good profit, I never wanted to stop dealing with eggs. I wanted to stay with it all my life. One earns more than with beer because if one sells beer one has to attend to customers, spend the night [in the tent], and one gets into arguments with drunkards. Some of the drunks want to fool around with you or they tell you that they have already paid you, things like that. I could earn as much from buying and selling one hundred eggs as the entire profit I made from selling beer. At that time, eggs cost me thirty centavos (US$.025) or three hundred bolivianos[9] in the countryside while here in La Paz they sold for fifty centavos (US$.04). So one earned twenty centavos (US$.017), almost half. That meant that from five hundred eggs one earned ten pesos (US$.83) or ten thousand bolivianos, which was a lot of money.

I liked that, so I told my mother that I wanted to switch to eggs. Since I had come to Sonkachi to sell beer, people already knew me. I sat down [at the market site] and started to buy and no one scolded me. I always bought the eggs for cash. I never bartered for other things. However, I did bring cheap sweets (confites) and oregano to give as a *yapa* (a little extra) when someone brought a lot of eggs. We took those [five hundred] eggs to La Paz and I asked my mother, "What am I going to do with all these eggs?" But my mother remembered a client to whom we used to sell candles wholesale—a very nice woman called Doña Paulita, who has a store in San Pedro. My mother said, "She buys five hundred or six hundred eggs or whatever people bring her. I know that she will buy the eggs from us." So we went there and my mother talked to her and I told her my story, and she paid us for the eggs right away. So my mother told her that I would be bringing her eggs [regularly from then on]. Doña Paulita even asked her if she would bring her candles again. My mother answered that she was not living in the city any more and didn't make candles any longer but that she would bring her eggs every time she had gotten some together. Doña Paulita said, "Fine." From then on I brought her eggs every time I went to a fiesta. I didn't go to weekly fairs yet, only to fiestas.

Then [when my father was better again] he began to rent land. First he rented parcels of land in the hills. When the harvest came, we had our own produce. My father said that luck was following him. We harvested more than other people. My father used cow's and sheep's dung he bought in Cawaya from Feliciano Yujra and Lucas Mamani who kept animals in the hills and we produced the best harvest around. We continue to buy from the same persons every year. We used the same amount of dung as everyone else in the community but we either had better luck, or my father prepared the fields better; whatever it was, we produced beautiful potatoes and everyone admired them.

Then my father began to rent land farther down where it can be irrigated. He rented from Pedro Copana in Compi. We still rent from him. We have been renting from him for eleven or twelve years now. There, my father planted onions for the first time.[10] [When they were ready to be harvested], my mother and I took them in bundles to the Rodriguez street market. When I went there for the first time, there was no one selling in the upper part of the street yet, only in the lower section. I started to sell and asked [the other vendors] how much I should charge. They told me how much, and I still remember that Lino Condori's wife and Crisostomo Condori's wife taught me how to sell onions. Perhaps I was foolish, because the onions disappeared just like that. People were all over me trying to buy onions and soon there weren't any left. [The other vendors] warned me, "Be careful, you are asking too little." I think that what happened was that I sold small and large ones at the same price, so everyone wanted to buy from me. I began to travel together with [my friend] Raimunda with our own onions. Raimunda would leave her son withher mother [in Llamacachi] and we would travel together. She would stay over in my room here in La Paz. My mother had full confidence in her and often sent onions with her. When I went around with her, I came to know all the onion vendors in the Rodriguez and the Camacho. Since I came every Friday, I got to know all of them.

That's how I began to sell in the Rodriguez. I arrived there every Friday. I sold only our own onions. When they were all gone I stopped selling. Seeing that one could earn well with onions, my father rented some additional land from Remigio Paucara. When I was working for you [in 1965] my mother would go and sell the onions. At that time—it was during the presidency of Barrientos—the government decreed that there would be free fairs[11] (*ferias francas*). Policemen were posted on the Alto and in Rio Abajo to redirect the vendors to the fair in the Avenida Montes. So, when my mother arrived in La Paz, she was taken straight to the Avenida Montes where she had to scramble for a sales site. She got one on the far side of everyone else. I am still selling there because I didn't want to get into a quarrel with the other girls nor with men like Bonifacio Laura and Tiburcio Laura who were squabbling [for the better sites] as though they were dying of hunger. My mother told me, "All the other vendors [from the community] have better sites. I have the one way at the end." "It's better like that," I answered. "Let them fight." It turned out that my mother had arrived for the first time on the Saturday after the fair had opened. I began selling there too under the control of the police and am still selling there today.[12] At first my mother and I went together. That time we sold 350 pesos (US$29.17) worth of onions and she gave me fifty as a present. But the next time she told me to go alone because if both of us sold we would merely double our costs. So the third time I went alone. I made at least ten trips with our own onions and the *feria franca* continued. I told my father that I hadgotten used to selling, so what was I going to do now. Since I had come to Llamacachi I had spent my capital. I was a crazy girl and liked to be *madrina* (godmother or sponsor) of a soccer ball and things like that. A boy called Willi asked me to act as *madrina* and I bought shoes and everything [for the team]. I liked to amuse myself a bit. I received formal letters with requests of all sorts, and soon I didn't have any money any longer. I spent everything buying soccer balls, uniforms, and things like that. My mother pardoned me, sold my father's donkey, and gave me the proceeds. We had a really mean donkey that didn't let anyone near him. He was called Mariano and would kick. He had not been neutered like our present donkey, also called Mariano. My father sold the donkey for 450 pesos (US$37.50) and he gave me the entire sum. With that money I went to buy onions from Benito Mamani of Compi, known as Jach'a Benito [because he was very tall] who had a field right next to his house. That time alone I earned one hundred pesos (US$8.33). And I continued coming and going.

Then, one day, my mother and I went to the fair of Jank'o Amaya to make purchases and I met a friend, Graciela, whom I had gotten to know selling on the street in La Paz a long time ago. Graciela had been buying eggs in the market of Jank'o Amaya. We chatted and I saw that she had bought three or four hundred eggs in a single day. My mother saw it too, and that evening she asked me, "Why don't you go and buy eggs there too? [Even] strangers are coming to buy eggs. You are from the area and have every right to buy eggs."[13] So the following Thursday I approached Graciela at the fair and told her, "I came to buy some eggs, because my brother asked me to buy twenty-five eggs for him. That's why I have come today." I was being careful because I was afraid that she might get angry. People always get upset when someone comes and competes with them. So I was being wily and told her a lie. She is a good person and so she invited me to sit and I bought sixty eggs. The next Thursday I no longer said that I was buying eggs for my brother. I just greeted her and told her that I had come again and I sat down and bought ninety eggs. The next time I bought 100, then 120, and finally 300 to 500. Graciela wasn't angry. She was happy [that we sold together] because we were both *de vestido* and got along well together. She told me that Andrea, a *cholita* that sat next to her at the time, was very mean. She was envious and insulted her. She said that she was happy that I had come to buy and that she would pass on her site to me because she was about to get married and her future husband, a sign painter, didn't want her to continue selling there. She said, "My husband paints Pepsi Cola signs and things like that all over the Alto and so I am no longer going to come and you can buy instead." So I stayed.

Launching a Market Career

MARKETING AND SOCIAL STATUS

As in the choice of a school for Sofía, class consciousness affected her brother Pedro's reaction to her selling. The fact that his sister was selling as a market vendor, and in a street market (rather than in a covered market where long-term migrants and urban-born vendors sell (J.-M. Buechler

1972)), did not befit the image of a man who was becoming a political figure in the Movimiento Nacionalista Revolucionario (M.N.R.) party. He held this attitude irrespective of the fact that socially more suitable activities, such as embroidery, were not necessarily more lucrative, as Yola's mother and her friend Agustina had discovered. Sofía's mother supported Pedro and ultimately convinced Sofía to return to the less public activity of producing and selling candles and to take sewing lessons. Sofía had her revenge, when her brother's fortune changed and his wife was forced to join Sofía as a trader in the same market.

Unlike her brother, who saw marketing as contrary to the family's social standing, Sofía did not see entering the world of marketing as a step to downward mobility. Nevertheless, she was at first ambivalent about selling. She hid her marketing activities from her school friends, but at the same time regarded selling as a means of engaging in her own status games. Striving for success took the form of a competitive game with Yola. Gold-trimmed front teeth are among the symbols of wealth of a chola. *Although Sofía was wearing European dress at the time, she appears to have emulated* chola *prestige symbols to some extent. For one, her friend Yola was wearing her hair in braids in the* chola *style. We shall see later that Sofía's ambiguous position with respect to the* chola *and* de vestido *social stratification systems made it easy for her to switch to* chola *clothing when she felt that it was to her advantage to do so. Learning how to become a seamstress and make European-style clothing moved her—and later Yola—in the opposite "Latin" direction, symbolized in Yola's copying Sofía's loose hair style.*

Another aspect of the competition with Yola is the tug of family and friendship allegiances. Sofía's mother cleverly exploits the quarrel between her daughter and her friend to lure her back into the family enterprise. She frames the issue in terms of Sofía's independence. She argues that Yola might say that Sofía's success as a market vendor was all her (namely Yola's) doing. Making it on one's own and making it within the confines of a family enterprise are equated and contrasted with dependency on outside assistance.

CARVING A MARKET NICHE

Establishing herself in society entailed more than dealing with her brother's disapproval. It also meant facing competition and the city bureaucracy's heavy-handed attempts to regulate markets and limit selling on the streets. Young vendors with only small quantities to sell were in a better position to play cat-and-mouse with the police than were older ones with more goods to sell. Market vendors frequently remember setting up a sales site at a new location as a disagreeable experience. It often entailed crossing swords with the police, who, depending on the politics of the moment, tried to impede the formation of new street markets with more or less vigor. Founders of new markets are often treated with particular respect by those who follow later, and may even enjoy special privileges, such as not being forced to sponsor the market fiesta.

After the social revolution of 1952–53, new markets were established with increasing frequency. Indeed, the government officially opened two new markets for producer/vendors in an attempt to reduce food costs for urban consumers and in response to peasants who, freed from serfdom, had more time to sell their produce personally and who had gained in political influence under the M.N.R. regime. An alternative way for a young vendor to gain access to a sales site is through inheritance from a mother, aunt, or other close kinswoman, or by paying a fee to join a market union of a street market that is in the process of becoming officially recognized.

Throughout her enculturation into the art and business of marketing, Sofía used her mother's network connections in intricate ways. Agustina, her mother's tenant in the Velasquez compound and Yola's mother's friend, helped Sofía obtain produce. Agustina, in turn, had been assisted in establishing herself in business by Sofía's mother's regular client from Atahuallpani, who bought her cracklings.

It was Sofía's sister-in-law's father who persuaded her to buy onions from him and retail them instead of peas and beans. Interestingly, this switch did not, at the time, lead to a complete reliance on members of her mother's natal community as a source of onions. Sofía undertook that move only later, when her family was living in Llamacachi.

The roles Sofía and her mother played in the regional marketing network after the family's move to Llamacachi continued to be anchored in La Paz. The sale of beer at rural fiestas and of urban baked bread depended upon pre-existing ties in the city. At the time, and to a degree, even in recent years, such activities were generally undertaken by paceños *and persons from towns. Similarly, egg buyers were often* paceños, *with or without kin connections in the area where a fair was located. Sofía's entry into the egg business was facilitated because of her connection with another egg vendor whom she had met in La Paz earlier and who, like she, was* de vestido. *At the same time, Sofía's mother took advantage of a connection with a former candle customer in La Paz to gain an outlet for the eggs. However, in the interim, after Sofía's father began harvesting onions on land he had rented, Sofía and her mother imitated the local producer/vendors and sold local produce in La Paz. Later, Sofía began selling onions again alone. The source of produce, site of sales and clients reflect intricate rural-urban social networks that one inherits and weaves for oneself.*

Trauma and Magic

From Sofía and her mother's description of Sofía's fall and the resulting illness and from Sofía's stories about her fall from a vehicle in the Yungas and her encounter with a toad in El Alto a pattern of diagnosing and treating illness begins to emerge. This pattern is consistent with the literature on Andean disease etiologies and curing practices. It is also echoed by certain disease etiologies elsewhere in Latin America.[14] *Soul loss, or* susto (*Aymara* q'atxa)[15] *is regarded as a frequent cause of illness. According to at least one Aymara cosmology,*[16] *a person has three spirits: the* ánimo, *that is likened to the Spanish soul; the* coraje, *that gives people initiative and courage and the* ajayu.[17] *"According to Oblitas (1971: 199) and Tschopik (1951: 212–13) the* ajayu *detaches itself from the body during sleep to take a tour of the outside world. Its impressions are recorded in the sleeper's dreams. When a person suffers from* q'atxa, *the* ajayu *becomes similarly detached (if perhaps only partially) when the patient is awake, and may be captured by the spirit of the place where the untoward event occurred, e.g., by the* Pachamama *or by a more specific place spirit (see La Barre 1948: 220–21, Tschopik 1951: 212–13, and Paredes 1963: 257). In the case of* q'atxa, *the soul is the victim of an accidentally angered spirit, but, as Tschopik points out (1951: 213), an evil spirit may also capture a victim's soul at the behest of a sorcerer. In both cases, the patient suffers a loss which must be recovered" (H. Buechler 1981: 46).*[18] *The measures that Sofía takes in situations of soul loss or potential soul loss are both preventative and curative. First, Sofía remembers that when she woke up in the morning after the family magician had come for his annual visit to ensure the family's well-being, she would find pieces of yarn tied to her body. Carter and Mamani (1982: 311) mention that, among other things, the magician who was called to cure a patient from* susto *tied a piece of yarn to the patient's hand. The patient was admonished not to remove the piece of yarn for three days. In both cases this act may have signified tying the soul to the patient: in Sofía's case prophylactically, in order to prevent the soul's departure, and in Carter and Mamani's example, in order to secure the recently called back—and therefore still vulnerable—soul to the body. When Sofía fell out of the station wagon on a trip to the Yungas, she made the priest stop at the site where the accident had occurred and gathered some earth and stones, which she has kept to this day. Presumably, they would have come in handy if Sofía had fallen ill after her ordeal and a curing ritual would have become necessary. When she explained to the priest that she was gathering the earth because in case she became ill, she could accuse the earth of harming her, she was echoing Oblitas Pobletes's consultants who told him that "if the earth has caused the suffering, it is only just if the same earth takes charge of the cure." (1963: 40) According to the same author (1963: 34) the proper thing to do under those circumstances would have been to eat a small amount of earth from the site where the* susto *had occurred, or to spit or urinate there, so that the spirits would be content with a substitute for the soul.*[19]

When Sofía fell in the Callejón Incachaca, her mother and the magician rubbed her with millu *(aluminum oxide) and urine and threw the container down at the spot where she had fallen. The same medium, urine, served both divinatory and curative purposes. Its foam produced by* millu *both signaled and embodied the culpable site. In an otherwise almost identical description of the same ritual Oblitas Poblete (1963: 37–38) adds that the Callawaya magician cuts the shape of the cross through the foam, presumably to neutralize the force it represents. At the same time, as a preventative measure (presumably because the soul was not yet well anchored in its usual abode), Sofía was not supposed to leave the house at all, and later she was admonished to avoid walking near the spot where she had fallen.*

Aymara feel that they have to maintain a balanced relationship among humans, various aspects of the natural world, and the supernatural (see Buechler and Buechler 1972: 90–103). This balance is maintained through divination, offerings, and sacrifices. The spirits are fed and otherwise placated by providing them with appropriate "foods" and "stimulants." As in ritual systems elsewhere, less expensive ingredients may be substituted for more costly ones. For example, llama fat represents sacrifices of entire animals. Sofía's mother's version of the story, the ingredients of the concoction with which Sofía was washed seem to have served as an offering to placate Pachamama as well as a means of removing the illness.[20]

A common thread in the episodes Sofía recounts surrounding illness associated with susto *is the fact that the spirits appear to have acted on their own. All they needed was an opening, which was provided by the soul's vulnerable state when she was frightened. In later chapters, we will examine examples where spirits act on the behalf of human beings to inflict harm.*

3

ADAPTING *to Life in Llamacachi*

I had great difficulty getting used to life in Llamacachi. It seemed to me that people there were very different from La Paz. It seemed to me that nobody wanted to talk to me. I looked at them and they looked at me [and that was all]. The place appeared like an empty desert to me and so I would cry and cry. I also found the food strange. I had eaten good meat here in La Paz. I had eaten good things. But there they didn't exist. My mother made *chuño* soups and other things including fish. But I wanted fresh meat and I became bitter about it.

During an early interview, in January 1966 in Llamacachi, when Sofía's initial discomfort was even fresher in her mind, she expressed the difficulties she had establishing friendships with young men in Llamacachi.

I wanted to do things like I was accustomed to doing them in La Paz. But here [in Llamacachi] they didn't do them that way. For example, if a young man meets a young women, they immediately talk about love. In La Paz it's not like that. There they treat each other and get to know each other with respect. Here the boy quickly steals something from the girl as a souvenir. I would watch how my nieces and nephews carried on near the rivers. Here there is little [in the way of entertainment]. There are no movie theaters and there are no *paseos* (Sunday promenades). Instead of *paseos* young people go on *kachuas*.[1] People don't have fun. The youth here have no joy. When one makes a joke, they already think that it means something more. I have seen young women here who met young men for

Sofía in 1965

the first time and they began to talk, play, and laugh and soon afterwards they were already married. In La Paz it's different, they have more respect. If a girl gets to know a young man he becomes a friend, but he treats her well. It's not like here where they elope right away and then marry. That's ugly. People here are not well educated. They are rather ignorant. If they see someone from La Paz, like you, they laugh and make fun of them; they refuse to talk and they escape. In La Paz it would be different. So, I felt very out of place here.

Later Sofía began to find ways around these difficulties by only soliciting the attention of men with an urban background. In 1975, Sofía described her encounters with men.

Once I even confronted my mother and told her that I hadn't been born in Llamacachi, so why had she brought me there. If she had wanted me to live my life there why hadn't she given birth to me in Llamacachi rather than in La Paz? I suffered for at least two years. But when we had the store, I slowly changed. Everybody came to buy, and so I became friends with all the girls. But before that, it was difficult to talk to them and they didn't want to talk either. I had no friends at all. They seemed hostile. They saw me as a stranger. Now people are more civilized. But it wasn't like that back then.

[At work] I didn't talk either. I only talked to my mother. I was always very timid. When we finished harvesting, [the families we worked for] would invite us to eat and I would sit behind my mother while the others sat around in a circle. They would tell me to eat and I would refuse to serve myself. My mother would pass me the food. I also found it very difficult to work in the fields. I wasn't able to finish harvesting the furrow that I had been assigned. My mother would complete harvesting hers as fast as possible and then she would help me with mine. When the field was not even half finished my hands would already be full of burst blisters because I didn't know how to harvest. Then, the next day everything would hurt me and my mother would rub me with urine, her favorite medicine, to make me feel better. [They paid us] an *arroba* each. But they always gave my mother a little more than that and they gave her large potatoes while they gave me small ones. I would ask my mother why

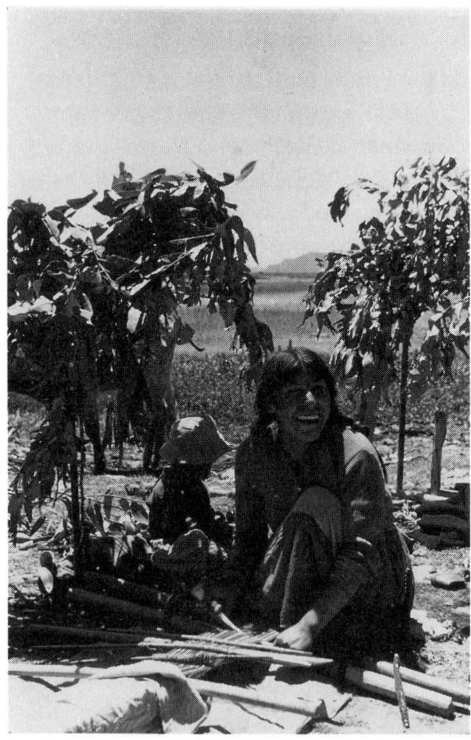

Sofía's friend Raimunda and her illegitimate son weaving in Llamacachi (1965)

Doing the wash in the river (Compi 1965)

they were paying me so little and she would say that it was because I was small and was barely doing anything. So she told me, "Don't be upset. They just are that way." But I was happy that we were getting some *ocas*, potatoes, *papaliza* (another tuber), and things like that.

Friendships

My first friend [in Llamacachi] was Raimunda, whom you know. She was my only friend then. We would chat and laugh together and meet at the river where we would go to wash clothing. Later I got to know Marujita Quispe. She is married now. Then Margarita, who also married recently, became my friend. These are the three intimate friends I had there. The others used to greet me and talk to me and laugh and play with me, but the ones I have a relationship of deep confidence continue to be Raimunda, Maruja, and Margarita.

[Also], when we began selling in our store I came to know the girls from Chua better. Since we lived near the border with Chua, they came to buy. Raimunda was my friend because her father is my mother's *compadre*. My brother Pedro baptized his son and so [Raimunda and her brother] called my mother "godmother." Raimunda was poor and continues to be poor. She would go around helping other people in the fields. She would take me along and we would work together. That's why we became friends. Even before she had her child, she was my only friend then. [Now] they all live in La Paz.

[As I told you earlier, Raimunda and I travelled together to sell onions in La Paz]. [In Llamacachi, Raimunda] directed me. She would tell me, "Let's go to such and such a place to work in the fields. The potato harvest is good there." Or she would say, "On such and such a day I am going to wash clothes. Take your clothes there too." I would agree. It was as though she was courting me. She would whistle and I would come out and we would go and wash together. She is older than I am so she would talk about her boyfriends and we would almost die of laughter.

We would also go to fiestas together. She would say, "There is going to be a fiesta in such and such a place. I will come and pick you up." Mostly we went to Chua, but we also went to Huatajata where they celebrate the national holiday in August.[2] Once we also went to Jank'o Amaya. We would always go and watch together. I knew that she had boyfriends. But I didn't know anything more than that. But we would always encounter some young men and we would laugh and they would invite us to soft drinks. She would tell her parents that she was going with me and so they would let her go because they trusted me. But she was lively and full of mischief. I didn't know what was going on. Once she told me to come to the river and that she would go there too. Earlier, she had told her mother that she was going to wash clothing with Sofía and her mother had told her, "Go ahead. Since you are going with the daughter of my *comadre* it's alright." But Raimunda had arranged to meet a boy there. She had more friendships with boys from Huatajata than from her own community. That day she must have told one of them to meet her at the river. We were washing and laughing, telling one another all sorts of wonderful stories. I was joking with her wondering whom she was going to marry, when a young man appeared riding a bicycle. He stopped and I looked at him. I had never seen him before. He talked to her and he lay down on the ground while she washed. He even took photos of us washing.

She [knew the boys from Huatajata because she] was a Protestant from childhood on. And they always had field outings and Baptist meetings there. Raimunda even asked her whether she could take me along, but my mother told her that I was her only daughter and she wouldn't allow it. But Raimunda went herself and she must have gotten to know the

Flirting (Llamacachi 1965)

boys from Huatajata in this manner. They came to visit her by bicycle. She also got to know a [man with the surname] Chura from Compi. He is the father of the little boy, who is my godchild.

When the fairs were opened there, Raimunda continued to come to La Paz with me, and I think that she had a sales site in the Rodriguez and was selling there on a daily basis. She was working here and living in La Paz, in Vino Tinto, where the boy's father lives and so they got to know one another and they eloped. They were supposed to get married. He even went to her parents to ask for her hand in marriage. I think that they gave him three months to get married and in that time the child was born. She said that the man was very mean. He beat her every time he got drunk and so she separated. She didn't want to marry him any longer. She said that they were, after all, not married and so she didn't have to be with him. She had him sign a document that he would pay child support. He was also very close to his family and did what they told him and they were hostile towards her. After she got separated, she returned to Llamacachi and so when you came she was living with her parents. Then, when she got to know her present husband, she came back to La Paz. Her life [in Llamacachi] had been difficult too because her older brother made life impossible for her. He would say, "Why did you have a child? What sort of child is he?" They would quarrel every day about it until Raimunda got sick and tired of it and came back to La Paz. Then one day she came and told me, "*Comadre* (I had baptized her son), I think that I am going to get married. I am telling you this because you are my close friend." I couldn't believe it. But she said, "Yes, *comadre*, it's true. He is younger than I am but I will marry him anyway." And she even married in white. He is from Jank'o Amaya and I think that he works for the Figliozzi bread and noodle factory. She married here [in La Paz] in the church of Saint Sebastian at nine in the morning and at eleven they went to Jank'o Amaya. They had a beautiful wedding.

I think that she got to know Apolinar, her husband, through Chabela, a woman who sells here in the Rodriguez. It seems to me that this Chabela and the young man were both renters in the same house. That's how Raimunda got to know him. Now they are married and they live happily. She says that he likes her little boy a lot. It's as though he were his own son. She says that she is very happy because she loves him and he loves her son. She married some five years ago and she already has two children from this man, a daughter and another son. The daughter is already quite big and the baby son must be seven months old. They live here in Munaypata. She stopped selling onions when she married. She is at home and she says that there are fairs on Saturday around there where she sells noodles. Her husband can obtain them at a cheaper price because he works for the factory. She also has her small son whom she sends to school. I think that he is in second or third grade.

Boyfriends

I got to know [my boyfriend] in Llamacachi. I knew him in 1971, for one year. I had always been living here and going there. I would be here for three days and stay there two. My mother would ask me why I had stayed in La Paz that long and I would say that my clients hadn't paid me. But it wasn't true at all. I was just having fun.

In the meantime, this young man had been there. I didn't know him yet. Remember that there were lots of trees in Chua? Well now there aren't any left. The Matilde Mine bought them and cut them up for tunnel supports. They came with two large trucks. A man called Juan Escobar came to work as a supervisor. Well, he had a driver called Hugo Santiago driving a Volvo diesel truck of the kind they use in Riberalta to transport logs. It was a large red and white truck. I didn't know him, or at least only superficially, but he said that he knew me.

[I do remember the first time I noticed him]. It was at the fiesta of Rosario in October. I went to buy some bananas and I was walking back up with [my nephew], Leán, when a group of musicians from La Paz came along and bothered me, calling my name. I looked at them angrily and wondered why they knew my name when I had never seen them before. My parents were standing a little farther away, while on the other side there was a young man who was smiling and looking at me. I wondered who he was. He was thin and dark. I thought that he was bothering me just for the fun of it. I told him, "Llokalla,[3] don't bother me!" and didn't pay him any attention. But I was curious and asked other people who he was. That's how I first met him, because he bothered me. Soon, I forgot entirely about the whole episode. But then, one Friday, I was travelling to La Paz as usual. I was sitting in the back of the truck with my head covered with a black manta. Well, when I travel I always like to joke with all the passengers, so I was joking and laughing when I looked to one side and saw that the same young man was sitting right next to me. He looked at me and I looked at him and he smiled and wanted to talk to me. But I looked away covering myself with the manta. He is from Laja, but he had been working there in Chua since the fiesta of Rosario. He would follow me around and bother me. In Huarina he disappeared. Apparently he went to the Matilde Mine from there. I wanted to know who this guy was.

Time passed. Then one day I was resting in Llamacachi. My mother and I were sitting in the sun between the store and the road. A truck passed and later returned and the driver came out, greeted my mother and me and entered the store. There he greeted my father by name and my father returned the greeting as though he knew him. It turned out that they were friends already. I didn't know anything about it. He ordered some "papaya (a yellow soft drink) with foam" as he called beer. When I asked my mother who this man was, she said that he was my father's friend. "He comes by all the time and buys from me." He stared and stared at me, but I didn't pay any attention. Then, on another occasion, he came to buy cigarettes. I again didn't talk to him.

Some time later I went around in search of guinea pigs.[4] I heard a rumor that Lidia, the daughter of Andrés Quispe, who was married to Edmundo Gutierrez, was having an affair with the pastor of the Jehovah's Witnesses and everybody in Llamacachi was commenting and criticizing them. I ran all the way home bursting to tell my parents the big news. When I entered the store my parents were drinking beer. I entered gloating to tell my story, when I saw that he was there. He greeted me, "Señorita Sofía." But I ignored him angrily. I said to my mother, "What is happening in this community?" At that point he interjected, "Excuse me for talking to you by name, but how wrong of that woman to do a thing like that." So we discussed the whole thing. That's how we started talking to each other. I left the store while he continued drinking. After a while he was quite drunk and he came out and talked to me. He told me that he had fallen in love with me from the moment that he had first seen me, and wanted me to be his girlfriend. I told him that was impossible. I didn't know who he was and that he must be crazy to say such things. But he pleaded and pleaded until I said, "OK, let's be friends." That's how I got to know this Hugo Santiago Alejo Quino.

[Before that, I had another boyfriend]. Remember, I used to make el Señor Hans angry when I didn't come to work and he had to go and look for me at home? We were working in the Hermanos Manchego together with Pascual. Well, that time I was friendly with a young man whom I don't see any longer. His name was Jaime Cabrera. He was from my neighborhood in La Paz. He lived across the street from our house. But he was not very nice. He drank a lot and my mother didn't like that. He knew very well that I was working and he wanted me to stay away from my work. My brothers didn't like that at all. I got angry at him myself and that's why I no longer talk to him. Our friendship lasted only three or four months.

After that I took more care. Hugo suspected that I had already had a boyfriend, but I told him that I didn't. He would always visit me at nine o'clock in the evening, hoping that I would come out. But I didn't. My mother didn't let me. The poor fellow would come with the pretext of buying Colorado cigarettes but I wouldn't open the door. Then one day—let me tell you all about it, señora—it was the first of May and he had the day off, he came to the house already quite drunk and continued to drink in the store where almost all the members of the Chua cooperative were gathered because it was Labor Day. He and others started to play music. He was well liked by everybody. He made friends with everybody and everybody said that he was a good person, that he was quick to invite people for drinks. He liked to spend money on friends and people there always have a good opinion of people like that. I myself didn't mind it either. I was happy that my sales were good. We earned a lot that day. They left late that night and he stayed on until we finally urged him to go home. He left and we all retired but then he came back and knocked at the door. The young man's plan was to take me with him. So he knocked at the door and I asked, "Who is it?" And he answered, "Sell me some alcohol." "Who are you?" I insisted. "I am from Chua," was the response. He no longer wanted any alcohol but wanted to take me with him. I told him, "How are you going to take me with you? You don't know me well. We have become friends only recently. Go home. You can't take me to La Paz. It's the middle of the night." "No," he answered, "We are going to my boss's place. He knows all about it. We'll go to the chalet [in Chua] and sleep there and we will go to La Paz tomorrow." It was difficult to get rid of the man. I was afraid that my mother would come out and scold me. So I told him, "Look Hugo, I am going to come right away. Take this *manta*." When he took it, I told him, "Look, my mother hasn't eaten yet. I have to cook for her. When I am done I am going to come out. Don't knock at the door, but promise to wait." "Yes," he said, "I will wait for you." He made me swear that I would come out again and I promised him that he could do whatever he wanted with me. Then I went up. We had, in fact already eaten. I was scared. I didn't have my *manta* but my mother didn't notice that I had gone out with a manta on and had returned without it. She just asked me what had happened and I told her that I had made a sale and had left the money in the store. In reality, I hadn't sold anything. I made sure that the door was locked, took my blankets, and told my mother that I wanted to go to sleep and that I didn't want her to answer if someone knocked at the door because some drunkards might come. I was sure that someone would knock at the door and ask for beer. And he did. He knocked and knocked shouting, "Sell me some beer." I didn't react. But the stupid ass must have thought that I would [eventually] come out. He sat down next to the door to the store and must have fallen asleep waiting for me. What finally woke him up was my dog Sandro. The dog licked his face and he woke up freezing at three o'clock in the morning. Imagine! He fell asleep at the door thinking that Sofía was going to come out. So he finally left without saying a word, still clutching my manta.

A week later he brought the manta back. I had told him to bring it back. But he told me, "Why did you deceive me? You should have come out and gone with me." I answered, "I am no one's toy. I am not an easy lay. You were stupid to stay and fall asleep. Who is going to come out because of you?" I did a lot of mean things to the poor fellow. I don't deny it. I made him suffer a lot. When he came to buy cheese I got angry. I didn't want to talk to him. I told him that I didn't know who he was; that there were men who came to amuse themselves passing themselves off as bachelors when they in fact had wives.

He knew that I was angry, but he didn't know how to win me back. He came on the pretext of buying cheese or eggs and I would sell him cheese worth seven pesos for twenty and he would have to plead with me to give it to him even at that price. I didn't come down with the price easily. He would tell my father, "Don Velasquez, tell your daughter to sell me some." And my father would tell me, "Sell him some, he is a stranger here. Poor man, sell him some." I didn't want to sell him anything. So I put the price up so that he would stop bothering me. I made him suffer for an entire year. I started talking to him again only when my father died. He even said that I should become his sweetheart. I agreed. He won me over when my mother became seriously ill after my father died. My mother couldn't walk and so he took her to the Matilde Mine to have her cured. He had her see a doctor there who gave her some injections and since then her feet no longer hurt. At that point, I said to myself that this man must love me.

His father is a tailor and before that he worked as a doorman at the Volcán factory until they retired him. Since then he has been sewing. His mother used to travel to fairs with eggs and cheese like I do. He tells me that he was the youngest son. I don't know whether I will continue with him. My destiny will tell me the answer, but I am planning to marry whoever comes along next year (i.e., 1976), as long as he is someone responsible.

Becoming Integrated into Life in a Rural Community

As we have seen in earlier chapters, the Velasquez family were far from being strangers in Llamacachi. A constant stream of visitors came to stay for varying lengths of time in their La Paz house and Sofía's mother often went to the country to exchange cracklings for produce. In the aftermath of the agrarian reform and with the improvement of the road to La Paz, rural-urban contacts accelerated. The integration of Llamacachi into the regional cash economy was further stimulated by the fact that neighboring Compeños, with whom Llamacacheños have traditionally intermarried, shared rituals and, more recently, a school, were freed from their labor obligations and thus also had more opportunity and time to travel to the city with produce. Onions, grown year round on the valley's irrigable land, became an increasingly important cash crop, involving frequent trips to the city, where both Llamacacheños and Compeños sold and continue to sell them. Nevertheless, the fact that the Velasquez family had access to only a small amount of land made them in some ways marginal, for land ownership is the basis of full community membership. Also, although Sofía's parents eventually acted as the chief sponsors of the community's major fiesta and thereby validated their claim to full recognition as senior members, her father was not from the community and always appeared to us as somewhat of a loner.

Sofía herself relied on her role as Llamacachi's and Chua Visalaya's only storekeeper to expand her social network. As we have seen in the introduction, this role eventually placed her in a central position in a network of communication in Llamacachi and beyond. Her closest ties, however, were associated with multigenerational links between related families. One of her best friends, Raimunda, was a distant relative whose family was linked to the Velasquez family through fictive kinship ties. Having gained the complete trust of Sofía's mother while selling onions, she also became Sofía's friend and travel companion on her trips to the city with onions. Raimunda's parents reciprocated this confidence by entrusting Sofía with the role of chaperoning their daughter. The fact that the two young women's friendship left room for (and even acted as a cover for) Raimunda's trysts and her eventually becoming pregnant, would not have been seen as a matter of the same gravity as in clase media *and elite society. Among Aymara peasants, trial marriage—albeit usually preceded by a more formalized ritual elopement—is a common practice. The fact that Raimunda refused to marry her child's father because of his abusive manner provides testimony of the considerable independence enjoyed by Aymara women. Nonetheless, her brother's criticism contributed to her decision to migrate to La Paz. As in the case of many other rural-urban migrants, Raimunda's move to the city expanded her social network and she eventually married a man from another community. But, again typically, the man was from a neighboring community. His family would therefore have been known by Llamacacheños.*

In contrast to Raimunda, Sofía's boyfriends had more varied backgrounds. One was from her neighborhood in La Paz, another was from Laja, some eighty miles from Llamacachi. However, she was not to marry any of these men, whose networks were unknown. The man with whom she was living in 1988 and by whom she bore a child came from neighboring Chua, a community where she knows as many people as in her own community.

In Llamacachi, then, Sofía formed an identity in terms of kinship allegiances, customer circles, and common urban background rather than in terms of membership in a closed corporate peasant community.

The identity she constructed was unlike that of peasants with little migratory experience and that of the traditional vecino, *or rural town residents who would never have treated a peasant as an equal. Even she ultimately began to differentiate herself increasingly from rural dwellers without urban experience and sometimes sided with urban market vendors against "the peasants."*

4

LIFE *as a Market Vendor*

In chapters 2 and 3 Sofía told how she learned how to sell, made various changes in the kinds of goods she sold, and, after the family moved to her mother's natal community, Llamacachi, progressed from selling onions to selling eggs purchased in the fair in neighboring Jank'o Amaya. In this chapter we take up her description of her activities as a trader in the late sixties and early seventies, including her brief experiment engaging in contraband.

When General Hugo Banzer came into power in 1971 after a bloody coup, he initiated one of the most repressive regimes in Bolivia's history (see Dunkerley 1984, Ramos 1980). For seven years, civil liberties were curtailed and a series of economic measures were adopted that succeeded in drastically changing income distribution to the detriment of the poorer segments of the population. In addition, in spite of favorable terms of trade for its minerals, the nation increased its foreign debt to alarming levels, laying the foundation for the debt crisis of the early 1980s. The economic policies that had the most negative impact on Sofía's economic activities and her standard of living were a major currency devaluation in 1972, followed by the removal of subsidies for staples in 1974 while prices for produce remained frozen. Nevertheless, Sofía also sometimes benefitted from these same policies, by engaging in shrewd and sometimes illegal deals.

I already had my *caseras* [in the Jank'o Amaya fair] and began to expand. There is plenty of space. I was just afraid that [Graciela, the woman who had originally allowed me to buy eggs at the fair] would be angry at me. Now, I too become angry when [unknown buyers] come. I haven't gone to the fair during the past three weeks and I am sure that people are taking advantage of that and are happily buying eggs. There are only five of us who buy eggs there [regularly]. People always tell me, "Sofía, someone is buying eggs. Let's go and scold them." We don't like unknown women to come. We think that they are paying more for the eggs than we are and then we are left without eggs ourselves.

Some [women] came from Huatajata[1] but we stopped them from coming. There is only one new person, but she is from the community and she replaced Andrea. In addition, her father holds some official position in the fair. We are five in all, including a woman from Huarina. She had always come to the fair because she used to own a truck and would come to sell things. But it is not our custom [to go to each other's fair]. The five of us don't go to Huatajata [either]. What [those outsiders] do is that they go and sit at some distance. But we find out about it from our *caseras* who sell us eggs. They will tell us that someone is buying eggs for so and so much—they always pay ten or twenty centavos more—and so two or three of us go over and scold them. If they don't pay any attention to us, we go over to the police headquarters and fetch a man from there who forces them to take all the eggs to the police. The police help us because we always contribute money for the bullfight during the fiesta of the Holy Spirit. We take turns doing that. For example, in 1971, I had to pay for the *enjalme* to be placed on the back of the bull. I had to buy a piece of cloth and I embroidered my name on it and six five peso bills on it. In all it cost me sixty pesos (US$5). So we don't even allow the women from Huatajata to watch the bullfight.

[I have never gone to Huatajata to buy eggs]. There is a woman there, an old skinny one, who would kill us. She always comes here and I have to confront her. I tell her, "If you come here we will go there too." And she answers, "You better not come." And I tell her that I never go there. Last Thursday, when you went to Tiquina with your father, I went to buy eggs [in Jank'o Amaya] and I saw her there. I scolded her, "You always come when eggs are scarce, and when there are plenty of eggs you never come." I would like to do [that woman] some harm. In other fairs they say that they break the eggs of someone who persists in coming to buy more than once [and] she doesn't pay the weekly fee of a peso that we have to pay either. Once I had the police fine her five pesos. Eggs are seasonal: in August and September when there is a lot of barley there is an abundance of eggs while during the rainy season there are few eggs. I think that the chickens don't like to eat the grass that grows then. That's when those women come to compete with us. When there are a lot of eggs we have to suffer. We sometimes have to borrow money from the truck drivers to buy all the eggs the people bring in order not to lose *caseras*. And we don't earn anything. While when eggs are scarce we earn a lot. One sells them quickly and one can charge a little more.

Caseras

So every Thursday I would come here to La Paz with my eggs. I changed *caseras*. There is a woman who sells eggs, cheese, and *chuño* on the sidewalk in the Calle Rodriguez where they [mainly] sell onions who always asked me whether I had any eggs, so I brought her eggs. She would sell the eggs quickly and pay me, and I didn't have to do anything. When I brought eggs to the woman in San Pedro I had to find a stevedore and walk three long blocks. This way I arrived right there. So I sold and sold and one day I was sitting next to my cousin Manuela in the Mercado Uruguay and a woman came by asking for eggs and I asked her how much she was paying. She said that she was paying as much as fifty pesos (US$4.17) per hundred. I told her that I brought eggs every Friday. She didn't believe me. I said, "Yes I bring eggs every week." "How many do you bring?" she asked. "I bring three hundred or four hundred or five hundred," I answered. She still didn't believe me, but finally I convinced her. I said, "Let's make a contract. I will give you the eggs and you pay me for half and the rest you can pay the following week." It turned out that she lived near the Garita de Lima above a kiosk and served egg, cheese, and meat sandwiches, coffee, and soft drinks from nine in the evening to three in the morning. Her clients were all the people who walk around there at night: the truck drivers, policemen. So I brought her four hundred eggs and ten cheeses. It was the first time that she had bought that many eggs, but the following week she had used them all and she told me that she had had a lot of luck. She told me to bring eggs regularly and that she wanted to sign a contract. Together with her husband, we went to the police to have it stamped. Noncompliance would mean a fine of five hundred pesos (US$41.67). From then on, I brought her five hundred or three hundred or sometimes—when eggs were scarce—only one hundred eggs as well as cheese. Then, on Monday, she would give me the money and I would return to Llamacachi.

This has been going on for five years now (i.e., since 1970). For Christmas, her husband would ask for *aguinaldo* (a Christmas bonus) arguing that the baker gave them an *aguinaldo* too for selling his bread. I agreed and gave him an extra twenty or twenty-five eggs. But then I had a quarrel with the woman. The culprit was a friend of mine, Cristina, the one where we went to that birthday party. That Friday, I arrived very tired from the trip and went to bed early. I told my friend Cristina that I had brought eggs but would deliver them to Martin only the next morning. Later, my friend went and told Martin that I had arrived. When my *casera* heard about it she was angry. And she was right to be angry. "I need the eggs," she shouted. "Where is this woman? Why is she deceiving me? Now I don't have any eggs. She should have told me that she wouldn't be able to come till Saturday and then I would have been able to buy fifty eggs [from someone else] to serve my clients."

[Cristina tattled about it] out of envy. She did it on purpose so that I would quarrel with my *casera*. Later, I encountered Cristina and told her, "What you did to me hurts me a lot. It is as if you had taken a dish of food away from me. I earned money from this woman and you did this to me. You are not worthy of being my friend. That's the end of our friendship." Since then, I don't talk to her any more.

The next day, I went to sell in the Avenida Montes and then I went to deliver the eggs in the evening. The woman was angry. "How could you fail me? You should have come immediately after you arrived. There was a reason that we made a contract." I told her, "You are right, but who told you about it?" "Cristina told me," she answered. So I became angry too, "Well then let Cristina bring you eggs," I said and I left with my eggs. She still owed me three hundred pesos from before. But I didn't go to see her for two weeks. Then I went and asked for [the money]. Her husband, who is very proud, gave it to me. I noted it down in my copy book and left. He didn't say a word about bringing more eggs. So I returned to my *casera* in San Pedro and now she is my *casera* again.

Cristina has done everything possible to make amends. Even Doña Aida, who is her fiance's mother, tried to mediate twice. One day I went to the Garita and saw her. She called me and I saw that she had *empanadas* (cheese turnovers) in her hand and wanted to invite me. I escaped telling her, "Señora, do me a favor. Don't to force me to talk to this woman." I am hurt that Cristina did this to me. This Martin used to pay a little more. And then this Cristina came along and ruined it all.

I think that my old *casero* Martin is having second thoughts. His wife is trying to talk to me. She greets me when she sees me on the street. But I just give her an angry look, greet her and go my way. I don't want to [patch up with her]. I was a very good *casera*. If some of the eggs that I had brought were broken I gave them to her as a *yapa*. What other egg vendor does that? Out of five hundred eggs, ten to fifteen are usually broken. I would give those to her. Or if she complained that some of the eggs already had chicks in them, I exchanged them for good ones. I am sure that she must have difficulties now. Well, let her find out for herself! Let her friend Cristina sell her eggs!

I am sure I could [talk to her husband once more], but let him come to me first. I am sure that one of these days we will talk to one another again. . . . The wife made some really good sandwiches—some are cheese sandwiches that cost five pesos—and sometimes I would like to go and eat some, but my pride stops me from going. I would rather send someone else to buy the sandwiches. I was good to them too. [I would tell them what they should charge for their sandwiches]. I figured [his costs] out for him and told him that he was not charging enough to make a decent profit. That's why he held me in high regard. He would tell me that I had taught him a lot. You see, he doesn't know how to read and write, so I gave him advice. He was a good person. When I celebrated the *cabo de año*[2] for my father, they came with two cases of beer. It was my friend who was bad.

Cristina lives in the neighborhood. Everybody lives in the area. Even Clara (the *casera*) is Cristina's friend. See, these are all friends, and friends notice when one is angry with another friend. So we try to mediate. But with me they were not successful.

Trade with the Peruvians

In addition to eggs, I buy cheese and skinned guinea pig [in Jank'o Amaya]. Sometimes I buy thirty or forty guinea pigs and at other times only eight or ten. Then, two or three weeks before Christmas, I also buy [live] chickens. At that time, I also surreptitiously go to Huatajata to buy chickens. [The traders who buy there regularly] don't see me because I buy from people on the way to the fair. I stick [the chickens] into a burlap bag and load them on a truck, and it all looks as though I had just come to shop. There I am known as a buyer of potatoes. Eight of us went to buy potatoes by the hundredweight. Those potatoes came from Peru. We would have contracts to buy potatoes every Wednesday. Then I would bring them here [to La Paz] and deliver them to restaurants. I am going to start doing this again in September, October, and November. It is seasonal. The potatoes are very cheap: the *arroba* costs twenty pesos (US$1) or so while here they are scarce, so they sell well. Right now everybody has potatoes, so I don't get involved. When potatoes get scarce, near All Saints (November 1) I even go as far as Kasani (on the other side of the border with Peru) and I change my Bolivian money into Peruvian money and I buy by the pound in Peruvian currency. That way, I get them very reasonably and I earn well. I always bring back seven or eight *cargas* from Peru. I have a contract with a man whom I got to know in Huatajata from whom I buy every year. He and his friend brought potatoes from Peru by the boat load. They would bring twenty bags at a time. They must have seen that I buy larger quantities and so we made a contract.

Last year (1974), potatoes were very scarce in La Paz and when they found out that the Peruvians were bringing potatoes they charged import duties. So they brought them in as contraband. Those Peruvians keep their promise. That's why they don't like to sell to other persons. They wait until we come—that is, I; Margarita Quispe from Capilaya and her brother Hugo; the wife of Cisco Nacho, that fat man from Llamacachi; and Gregoria Nacho from Compi. So those persons who come from here (La Paz) return empty handed. I am kind, not to the people from here but to the girls from there. When my *casero* brings me twenty bags of potatoes and their *caseros* don't come, they ask me, "Sofía, please let me buy some too." Then I have to pass some to them. I tell them, "You take this bag and you take that bag." Each one gets the same amount.

[Nonetheless] we often [do] quarrel with those from Huatajata. The people from Huatajata buy smaller quantities: an *arroba* or so at a time to eat at home because they don't have enough land to produce for the entire year. When they come, we don't allow them to buy. We tell them that all the potatoes are reserved for us. They answer, "Are you going to swallow all these potatoes all by yourself? We eat potatoes too. This is our fair." We respond that they should be thankful that we come to do business there and make the fair known elsewhere. They often fetch policemen who force us to sell some to the women whether we want to or not.

[In a way they are right]. The poor women are often left without potatoes to use in their own households because we have bought them all up. Since we didn't want to give them any, we arranged for the [Peruvians] to bring the potatoes by boat directly to the harbor in Chua.

We also had great difficulty bringing the potatoes here [to La Paz]. It was a major struggle. If the agents from the town hall in La Paz or those of any one of the markets caught us, they would force us to sell them immediately. A long line would form and we would have to sell each person a quarter of an *arroba* at the price fixed by the mayor. This didn't suit us at all, so we would unload our potatoes in Chacaltaya, before reaching the point where the road descends to the city. Then we would load the potatoes on a city bus.

[All this happened] last year (1974). First sugar and then potatoes became scarce and so we handled the potatoes as though we were thieves. We had contracts with restaurants. They didn't mind paying more because they preferred that to not having any at all. So we would go from restaurant to restaurant offering potatoes at a certain price and later we would deliver them either by truck or by bus. We would arrange for the driver to unload the first bag or two near the cemetery where there is a restaurant called Bar Bolivar—an old client of mine—another four at the Garita, two for Sra. Betsa's restaurant, and another two for an old man nearby. Then, I unloaded another two or three in the Rodriguez. There, I would take a taxi and deliver [additional bags] at the train station. I couldn't have done all this alone. So, Margarita would get off at the cemetery and deliver the potatoes there while I would get off at the Garita. Then she would take a taxi and go to Chijini. We worked together like that. We would know how many *arrobas* each one of our bags contained. Let's say we brought ten *cargas* of which five were hers and five were mine. We would collect the money jointly and then divide it later. We would help one another. Its impossible to engage in business all alone. It was a beautiful arrangement.

The other market women who bought potatoes in Huatajata wanted to know where we were taking the potatoes. They complained a lot that they couldn't earn selling potatoes. They would unload at the Camacho market and the agents would force them to sell [at the officially established price]. They were surprised that I never haggled with the Peruvians but paid what they asked. They would ask me, "Why do you buy without trying to bargain with them? You don't say a word. Are you making a profit anyway? Where are you selling? There is a lot of control in the markets. How do you manage?" I would just laugh without telling them anything. So they tried to catch me when I was delivering the potatoes. Finally, I made a contract with my brother Pedro. He would come to the Garita with the pickup truck of the Manhattan factory and fetch five *cargas* for the factory cafeteria. See, I had a lovely business. I think that I am specially lucky with the police. If my luck should ever fail, poor Sofía! But [until now] they have never caught me. Would you believe it? When a newspaper publishes or the radio announces that prices are rising or that [some item] is scarce, I am happy. For me, it means good fortune. It means that I will earn money. And I do. I am always sure that I will.

When sugar was scarce, I earned more than you do. I knew where I could get sugar. I got it in a store where there was a very nice woman at the corner of the Granier and the Ochoa who sells staples. I would always buy a hundredweight can of alcohol from her for my mother's store and this woman took a liking to me. I think that that's why she did me this favor. When goods became scarce, this woman still had sugar because the store was in a hidden location. In order to win her over, I brought her chickens as a gift. I gave her a live cock and a hen. When she asked me why I had brought her these gifts, I told her about my plan. We would be good *caseras* and would tell no one about it. I alone knew when she would get a load of sugar. I would order sugar and she would tell me when it would arrive. I had her telephone number and everything and I would call to find out exactly when the sugar would arrive, or I would go there in person. When it came, the people would notice and come. But then we would do something interesting. We would tell the people that we would sell the sugar right away and so they would form a line. So the *señora* would tell them that she could only sell two pounds to each person and I would help her while two police agents watched. The *señora* would accept the money and her daughter and I would weigh the sugar. But whenever the policeman looked away we would ferret away a hundredweight bag of sugar in the back room and then we would continue selling as though nothing had happened. Then, when we had finished selling the contents of one bag and were in the process of opening another one, we would let another bag disappear and we would end up hiding some seven bags of sugar under the bed or under the closet or covered with something. The señora was sly. She would keep seven empty bags from earlier sales hidden away somewhere and so she would add those on the pile of newly emptied bags. The police would count all the bags that were unloaded. And we would tell everyone, "There isn't any left. We are going to keep the last one for ourselves, mister police agent." So when there was nothing left the policeman would send everybody away and count the empty bags. Then he would tell the señora that she had to give him one *arroba* of sugar from the remaining bag. The *señora* would give it to him and we would get rid of him. The people would think that there was no more sugar, but in reality we had salted away five or seven bags inside, which I would take away at night.

I also already knew where I would resell [the sugar]. I already had a contract. At eleven or two o'clock at night I leave with the sugar hidden in some dirty old bags like a thief and I would take it out to the altiplano. No one ever caught me at it. I would always say that I had distributed it here in La Paz. At that time, it was prohibited to take sugar out to rural areas. But I was doing it anyway and I was earning one hundred pesos (US$5) for every bag. Each time I would take five or six hundredweights. I earned a lot. That's why I had a broach and a pair of earrings made. Whenever I look at them I say to myself, "Those are my earnings from the sugar." My mother was very proud of me. I think that people would come and plead for some sugar. They would tell her that they had heard that I had sugar. They even brought her gifts so that they would receive some. They came as far away as Sonkachi where there are some bakers' ovens. Since they couldn't get any in La Paz, as they weren't allowed to take it out of the city,[3] they came and paid 450 pesos (US$22.50) per hundredweight without saying a word. When the price of sugar was only three-hundred-something pesos, I would say that it cost four-hundred-something and they would buy at that price. Pedro Condori would invite me to a drink so that I would sell him sugar and even my brother Pedro would ask me to get him sugar for the factory cafeteria. Pedro was surprised that I not only managed to obtain sugar, but even had a contract with someone. When he asked me about it, I told him that, thank God, I was smart.

Engaging in Contraband

In addition to her other marketing activities, Sofía smuggled goods across the border from Peru for a brief period in the early sixties.

When my brother still had his truck we engaged in contraband. At first I only brought ACE (detergent powder) and sweets from Llamacachi to La Paz.[4] The sweets were for my mother and the ACE was for myself. After a while, I had a contract with someone in the Isaac Tamayo. I would bring the sweets by the boxful. I would fill a basket half with sweets and half with eggs, and perhaps put some dead guinea pigs on top and no one knew that I was transporting contraband goods. Later, I got the idea of bringing Moba brand underwear, the finest underwear for men. And I earned a lot.

I already had quite a lot of money and so one day I told Ruth, "Let's go. One can make a lot of money that way." We would go to Jank'o Amaya by truck. From there we would take a sailboat to Huatapampa where we would stay overnight and the next morning, at five, we would walk up the steep hill to Parquipujio. Its really far to walk. In Parquipujio we would buy clothing. Then we would have to lug everything back again. Going there wasn't too bad. I just had my *awayo* to carry. But coming back, we would be carrying heavy bundles of clothing. Sometimes we would slip and the bundle would roll down the hill. Or we would be late and the boat would already be far out on the lake and we would have to make signs to make it come back.

It was really difficult to engage in contraband. Also, the first time we went, we both became seasick. You better believe it, our adventures engaging in contraband were a sad tale. Well, Ruth soon realized that this was good business and so we hired Raimunda's brother, Martin, to help us carry. He is my brother Pedro's baptismal godchild. We got to know all the people from Jank'o Amaya. Many young persons went too, so we would play on the way. It was quite an adventure. We would see who could run fastest. My problem was that I was too fat to run fast, and so was Ruth. It was very difficult, because it was too steep to run with our bundles. I already had made friends with the Peruvian customs officials. They were very nice. I even promised to bring them dark beer. Once, Ruth, the Peruvians, and I got drunk together. We must have had a premonition, because we celebrated a goodbye party. And we did in fact never go again. Our *caseros* were very nice. We would eat fricassee together and they would come and say, "Oh here are my *caseras*. These *paceña* women are very open, not like our Peruvian women. These women reciprocate right away when you invite them to drink." And it was true. When they invited us both, we would both reciprocate with four bottles of beer each. So we would get very drunk. We would make sure that Pedro wouldn't find out what we were doing, because if he did, poor us! We would sleep our hangover off in the boat and we would arrive at home as though nothing had happened. The boat would go directly to Jank'o Amaya, and from there a truck would pick us up.

Everything went all right until somebody denounced us to the authorities. The wife of a man who owns a truck denounced us here in El Alto. You see, he would have half his truck full of contraband and the customs officials discovered that and so these wicked people decided to tell on us too. They had decommissioned everything they had, and so when our truck stopped [at the same checkpoint], they told us to open the truck's toolbox, where we had our contraband. The underwear exploded like a treasure onto the ground. Ruth and I cried like crazy. We had lost all our capital! That time Ruth lost five million (US$417) and I two million (US$167). That was a lot of money then. So we called Pedro. He said some very strong words. "How were you earning money?" he asked. "Contrabandists are prostitutes and you must not have wanted to humor [the border guards] any longer and that's why they must have taken everything away from you."

We did get a part of [our goods] back. Pedro was smart. All the contraband that they took away from us at the entrance to the city was deposited at the central customs building. As a member of the M.N.R. party, Pedro was able to find out about it. He told us to hire a lawyer and we told him that we had lost much more than we had actually brought in. Ruth said that she had brought twenty rather than only ten dozen shirts and I also said I had lost double of what I had actually lost. We claimed some of the goods that had, in fact, been taken away from that other truck. We handed in a written petition and we were able to get [the goods] out. We had to pay the lawyer a good part of what the merchandise was worth. Still, after all the trouble and all the tears it had cost us, we actually came out ahead! We laughed about it; but we swore never to engage in contraband again. My father [also] told me never to do it again. [Well, we really only did it for three months].

Theft and the Lawsuit Trap

A recurring theme in the lives of Sofía and her kin is theft and other forms of loss. Lawsuits to recover stolen property often only contribute to further loss, as becomes apparent from the following story that Sofía told when she explained to us why a young girl whom her mother had "adopted" as a companion (see chapter 11) became a persona non grata.

I had some money hidden away and the day my mother and I had a quarrel she had thrown it at me. I had taken that money—it wasn't much, thirty-five hundred pesos (US$175)—along with me to La Paz. And, since we had made up, I told my mother: "Mother, I am going to buy a gas kitchen range." But she told me not to do that. "One should not let one's money go just like that if one has any. A dog might bite you or something else might happen to you. Just take it along with you." So Elena, [who was my mother's companion and helper][5], my mother, and I climbed on the truck and I gave Elena my bag. . . . And now I have taken the case to court. [This is what happened:] I had a red bag tied with a cord and I had the title of the house in the bag and I had brought it with me. I carried it all the time and never let it out of my sight. Then I bought a radio and some special buns. I told the stupid Elena to take care because there was money in the bag. At first, there was no truck but then one came and the three of us and two other persons climbed on the truck. Then my mother told me to pick up some beer bottles in a store and I climbed down without telling my mother that there was money in the bag. Only the girl knew about it. When I picked up the bottles, neither my mother nor Elena must have paid much attention. A woman from Jank'o Amaya was sitting in one corner of the truck and both my mother and the girl saw her handling the bag. Instead of saying something to my mother about it,

Elena didn't say a word. We departed with seven other persons all of whom were known to us. There were no other passengers. But when we arrived in Llamacachi that evening and I looked in the bag, the money—all thirty-five hundred pesos—was gone. When I wondered who could have stolen the money, my mother said that that woman was the only one who had handled the bag. Elena agreed. "You knew that there was money in the bag," I cried. "Why didn't you tell us about it." I made a big fuss. My mother cried too and went off in search of a diviner. He confirmed that it was that woman. I didn't know her name.

The next day was a Thursday, and we went to Jank'o Amaya to find out. We found out that she was in fact from there. Her name was Remigia Cordero de Calle. Her husband was Mateo Calle. Then we met with the judge, and he had her arrested. She half wanted and half didn't want to talk. But then she promised to return the money. It was quite a row. Even her husband and her son-in-law promised [that the money would be given back]. She was supposed to bring it that very day to the central police station [in La Paz] and I wanted to have her imprisoned but her husband and her son-in-law said, "No, we are Baptists and we know you well. So how could we do something to you? It's as though we were relatives. Give us seven days and we will make her own up to the theft and return the money to you directly without going in front of the authorities." I agreed. Even you would have agreed under the circumstances. My mother agreed too. I told my mother that she would come on Thursday. She came, but all she did was scold me. She said that I had the habit of making false accusations; that she didn't know anything about the money and that it was all a lie. She called me an exploiter and a thief and other things like that. Overcome with anger, I ran to the judge. The judge scolded me, "I told you to take her to the central office. Now seven days have gone by. What have you done?" I said that I would take her to the central police station and teach her not to be slippery. I was angry that she had insulted me. I had to drag the woman to the main police station like a policeman. In front of the police station I pleaded with her once more, "Please return the money. Don't be mean. I will give you a gift of five hundred, eight hundred, or one thousand pesos. You left me without capital. It's the only money I had. But she refused. She said, "I prefer to got to hell. I am tired of my life. My husband has made me suffer." She said all sorts of silly things like that. In spite of my pleas she insisted stubbornly that she hadn't stolen the money. [I tried once more], "Please give it to me before we go in. We will both spend money. We will both suffer. If we resolve this matter, nothing further will happen. Otherwise, I will go in front of the Ministerio Público." "I will go wherever I have to, even to jail," she answered. So I said, "All right then," and pushed her into the central police station, where they deal with crimes and robberies. I wanted to accuse her directly as a thief. But I didn't know what to do. I had never been in the central police station. I had never dealt with matters of this kind before. I acted like a stupid ass. I felt very much alone. So, since I had made peace with Pedro, I asked him to help me. He knows how to do those things. I told him what had happened, but I pretended that the money was my mother's. I didn't want him to know that it was mine and gloat about it. He said that he would come right away, but he never did. I didn't know what to do. I had the woman detained all by myself, accompanied by the renter. When I finished presenting my case, they asked me how I could prove that the woman had done it. I answered that at first I had only suspected her but then, when she had asked for seven days to give it back, I knew that she must have the money. "Now I want my money back," I said. "There were very few passengers on the truck, that's why I am accusing her. During the entire trip she didn't move her arm. I thought that it was broken, but it was because she had the bundle underneath. When her hat fell, she didn't move to pick it up and when a bundle fell on her she remained where she was and didn't say a word. That's why I suspected her and that's why I have accused her."

After they had heard my story, they put the woman in a cell and told her, "Give her the money you stole from her." "What money am I going to give her, what am I going to give her," she replied. "Well, then you will have to go to jail," he told her. But all the insolent woman said was "What do I care?" So they locked her up and told me to come back only the following Monday to resolve the matter. I was distressed. I didn't know how to follow through with those things and in those matters you really have to know how things are done. I don't know whether it was my fate or whether the devil tempted me to go to court.

Then I happened to meet one of my cousins, Angelica Mendoza, from Chua. She is *de vestido* and has a pale complexion. We never used to speak to each other. We would look at one another but we never acknowledged one another. But that day she talked to me just like that, "Hello Sofía, what has happened to you? What's your problem?" It turned out that she was accustomed to helping people in legal matters. She earned money in this manner. She was in contact with all the policemen. They were all friends of hers. She asked me what had happened. "They have robbed me," I answered sadly. "What am I going to do, sister?" Then she asked me which detective was handling the case and [when I couldn't tell her] she quickly asked a young man who told her that it was Silva, an elderly man. So she told the man, "Look, Felipe"—she addressed him by his first name—"she is my sister. She lives in the countryside and doesn't know anything. I entrust her to you. See to it that justice is done." "Sure, sure," he answered. Then she asked him when he was going to be off and he answered, "at 3:30." "Well, we are going to wait for you and invite you to some 'milk.' " It turned out that the "milk" was really beer, but I didn't know that. [It was all very secretive]. We didn't want him to say anything. [So when he came out] I asked him what I should do. He asked me [again] what had happened and I told him that the woman had stolen the money and how I had given her seven days to pay it back and how she had turned against me and had called me a thief. "She has all these relatives [to support her] and I am all alone." The thief had her son-in-law, her husband, her niece, and her aunt—almost eight (*sic*) persons—with her. You should have seen how they insulted me! They said, "You do these kinds of things all the time (*acostumbrada eres*). You probably don't even have any money. My aunt (the accused) is crazy. The woman is sick, she is insane." They really gave me a hard time! So I told [Felipe], "All these people have insulted me." Angelica was outraged, "How can they say things like that! Who is provoking you and who is behaving decently?" It turned out that it was the niece of the thief. She is *de pollera*. She spoke fearlessly. She didn't care whom she was addressing. She was very much in charge. Felipe told me to wait a moment, he would teach her a lesson. And he went into one of the offices—they were all numbered: number one, number two and so on—he entered office number two. I don't know what happened in there, but he came out with another man and, *trán6*! he had the woman detained. I remained silent, wondering what that crazy woman would do next, but he told me, "Come in, Sofía." He entered the office and asked the woman: "What's going on here? What right do you have to provoke this woman?" Angelica nudged me and so I chimed in: "Yes, this woman is insulting me." Angelica added, "My sister is all alone, she is an only child. They are probably going to beat her. Why are they butting in? It's not their problem. This matter concerns only the defendant. Let this woman sign a writ not to interfere under sanction of one million pesos (*que me lo de una garantía de un million*)." So they detained her and forced her to sign such a guarantee.

I was beginning to catch on. The next day I astutely pointed out another person to Angelica and told her that he or she too was provoking me. Angelica said: "Well, let's have him arrested too." And that person was arrested too. It went on like this until we had almost all of the seven persons involved sign guarantees. She taught me that that was necessary so that none of them could insult me or become involved. I hadn't known about any of this. She had to teach me. [And it worked].

My cousin took a *cholita* along the next time and [the two of them] began to insult the accused, and [her kinsmen] didn't say a word.

The problem was, though, that I didn't have much money with me that day, and Angelica had told Felipe that we would invite him. So when he came out from work, the policeman, Felipe, asked her, "Angelica, how about the 'milk'?" So she asked me, "Sofía, do you have twenty pesos?" I gave it to her and she handed it over to him, "Here, this is for your 'milk.' " Of course it was for beer. I didn't know that. He gave me an appointment for Monday at nine. And at nine that day, innocent as I was, I walked about not knowing what to do. I looked around for Felipe, but they told me that he had gone out. I had been warned not to forget about the defendant and so I went to information to find out if she was still detained. They told me that she was, but I didn't know what to do next. I lost the whole day. Then, that afternoon I returned and Angelica was there. "How are things going?" she asked. "Have you presented a request for a summons (*escrito de requerimiento*)?" I had no idea what that was. How could I have known? "Of course you don't know," she said. "Don't you have a doctor or a lawyer?" I answered that I didn't have a doctor. "You *are* stupid. Well, you are just a peasant," she said [condescendingly]. "Yes, it's the first time I am going to the central police station, I don't know what to do," I said. She called a man and told him, "This cousin of mine doesn't know anything, she is an innocent peasant." So they recommended a lawyer called Emilio Vargas who turned out to be very nice. He spoke Aymara and Quechua. He was well known: a man who always wins his cases. He was specialized in divorce cases and they say he always wins such cases. They call him 'el Perro Vargas' (The Dog Vargas), a nickname he earned because when he goes out on the street there are always a bunch of women following him. They said, "Angelica let her go to el Perro Vargas. Do you know him, Sofía?" "Who is this Perro Vargas? I don't know him," I replied. "Oh this one really doesn't know anybody, does she? Angelica said [disparagingly]. I know who he is. Its Emilio Vargas Machicado. Now do you know who he is?" I didn't. I asked them for his address. "His office faces the court house." [But I didn't want to go alone]. "No, no. Please come along Angelica and introduce me to him," I pleaded. So she came along and vouched for me. He invited me to enter. He asked me what I wanted and I told him and he prepared a writ for me so that they wouldn't release the woman until the matter was cleared up. He charged me forty pesos. Then he told me to present the writ to the court across the street.

However, in the meantime the infamous woman who had stolen from me had also taken a lawyer and presented a writ. And while I was bumbling about, they had asked for her to be released saying that it was all a calumny. When Angelica saw that, she was furious. "How can they do that to us," she cried. "As sure as I am called Angelica, we are going to get a hold of her. If you don't want to lose the case, do exactly as I tell you." I agreed to do whatever was necessary. She turned out to be really clever. She knew all the policemen. So I presented my writ and talked with Felipe who said that I had to present witnesses to testify. I didn't know what to do. Only my mother and the girl could act as witnesses. So I had to bring the girl [Elena] to testify. Luckily there was also a man, Tiburcio Chambi, who had testified in [Jank'o Amaya] that she had taken the money. That she had been handling the bag. I said that I had only those two witnesses. But Felipe wanted some five. I couldn't muster that many witnesses. I asked Angelica, "What am I going to do now? Where am I going to get the witnesses from? We were ten passengers and I don't know where they were from. Also, where am I going to get the money to go there?" "You silly woman," she answered, "Truth doesn't win. Lies win justice in these times. Hurry up." And she brought in three *cholas* and made them testify. She had me pay each twenty pesos. In addition she made me invite her for a meal, so it cost me almost two hundred pesos (US$10) that day. They all testified that they had seen the woman take the money out of the bag. Angelica presented those testimonies and told me to go upstairs to present my declaration, while she went downstairs to the detained woman. "We have to make her speak. Those people are clever. They may pay someone off and she will say something meaningless. The woman was already sitting there and with her was the *chola* who had given the guarantee. She was explaining what the detained woman should do. Angelica almost got into a fight with her. "What are *you* doing here? You gave a guarantee so you are not allowed to get mixed up in this." Then she addressed the detained woman, "You are the one who knows about this matter. You are the thief!" There was a big ruckus. Well, Angelica won and the detained woman did give her declaration. So now there were written declarations from both sides. Then Mr. Felipe said to me, "Well that's how things stand now. What we do now depends on you. Shall we take the case to the Ministry of Public Affairs or do you want me to plead with her?" I told him to plead with her.

By now it was late in the afternoon and so Angelica told me, "Look, Sofía, now that we have made all the declarations and everything, let's invite Felipe out for tea." I agreed, "I am grateful for what Don Felipe has done for me and I am grateful to you too, Angelica. I want to invite you too." "O.K., let's go, let's go," she answered. "Tea" turned out to be beer. Near the Sucre market there was a secret place where the policemen went to drink. When I entered I saw a bar full of drunk men and I exclaimed, "But Angelica, you had said that we were going to have some tea!" "We call beer 'tea,' stupid," she replied. Even before we had invited Felipe she had thanked everyone and proclaimed loudly for everyone to hear that we were going to go out for "tea." She said, "If you want to come along, I am inviting you." The two of us entered alone, but Angelica ordered four bottles of beer right away. Soon one policeman arrived and then another until four of them had gathered. She told me that I had to buy more beer and so I had to spend money on "tea." The policemen all made promises. They would see to it that justice was done. One of them said that this evening he would make "that Indian" talk if I paid for another four bottles of beer. Another one said that he would make her own up tomorrow. He too made me buy beer. And so it went until the entire table was covered with beer bottles. I spent almost three hundred pesos (US$15) in beer alone. By that time my total expenses to get my money back amounted to one thousand pesos (US$50) and I had nothing to show for it. I left while the others continued drinking.

When I arrived at the police station the next morning I was in for a big surprise. The woman's lawyer came up to me and scolded me. He accused me of making a lot of false accusations, that a poor peasant woman couldn't possibly have had money or even known about money. And he chided me for putting money in a bundle. I became angry, "Excuse me, doctor," I said, "I didn't put the money into the bundle, I had it in my bag." "Well, it's all a calumny," he continued. Then Angelica began to scold him as well. "You will see, we will have the satisfaction of having her incarcerated." "Well, we will see about that," the lawyer retorted. She took Felipe inside and they discussed something, since he is my cousin's friend. After a while, Felipe returned and said, "Look Sofía, the woman is offering two thousand pesos (US$100) if I let her out. What do you think. Shall we leave it at that or shall I put her back into jail?" Angelica told him, "Felipe, how can you do that to a friend? What is two thousand pesos? Why don't you want to imprison her? Felipe said that he would think about it and disappeared. The lawyer must have waited for him with money! So, that same afternoon, they took her down to the Ministry of Public Affairs where the court is. Instead of sending her to jail, they placed her in a holding cell. They told me to bring a brief and my friend Angelica told me that she would help me. So we presented a writ to prevent her from being released. This took me three days, but in the meantime the woman had been released with the judge vouching for her. Apparently, a judge is not allowed to do this, not even if the accused is a brother, a relative, or a *compadre*. However, this judge received money, so he did it anyway.

So I had to go to the lawyer they had told me to consult—Perro Vargas. He told me that he would have to run around and talk for one thousand pesos (US$50). He said that that was not much money and we would have the satisfaction of seeing the woman back in jail. I agreed and he asked me for three hundred pesos (US$15). He is a good lawyer. He goes and attends to each matter personally. He was angry at the judge and requested an audience with him. But the judge hid for eight days. He couldn't be found anywhere. We had a big problem on our hands. My mother cried a lot, "Why did you start all this?" she asked. "They pushed me to do it," I answered. The first time, my cousin Angelica told me that she would help me promising me all sorts of wonderful things. Now she has disappeared. Well, I am grateful that she helped me obtain justice in the central police station and forced the woman's relatives to guarantee that they would no longer insult me. I didn't know anything and she guided me. If she had been stupid, I am sure that the woman would have gotten away with paying [only] two thousand pesos (US$100). So now the woman is free, but we are continuing the lawsuit in the courts. They have asked for witnesses and I have presented them and now they are requesting an *hincatorio*, which means declarations. I wonder what will happen next. This week the court will adjourn for a week long vacation so I am waiting around in vain.

I must have spent thirteen hundred (US$65) just for the papers, bribes, and beer, the meals for those who testified and for the policemen who brought the woman here from [Jank'o Amaya]. And then I had her taken to the central police station and from there to the holding cell of the prison. I spent on all those things. The doctor tells me that the woman will have to pay for all those expenses too. My mother cries a lot about it.

But the day that woman returned to Jank'o Amaya, her bull died. She must be guilty. God sees everything [and must have punished her]. I think it was her largest bull and must have been worth three or four thousand pesos (US$150 or 200).

That's what has happened to me and that's why I am in court, and that's why I have gotten rid of that girl, Elena. Her father arrived and I had a quarrel with him. I told him all about the lawsuit. "I don't know, but sometimes I feel like blaming your daughter," I added. "Maybe she took the money out of the bundle. And now see what straights she has put me in! No, take her away, take her away!" And he took her with him. That's why the girl who was supposed to live with me has left.

In the meantime something else has happened. As I have told you already, I had told Pedro that I had lost my mother's money. Well, he investigated whether that was really the case. He had gone to the Uruguay market where [my sister-in-law] Elena sells and had told her, "I have heard that my mother has lost money. Was this really her money, because if it was I will do some legwork (*corretear*) to get it back. If it's Sofía's money I won't help." I would be glad. He was happy that this misfortune had befallen me. However, just eight days after he gloated, he himself lost forty-five hundred, in pesos and dollars (US$225). No one knows who stole it. It happened because he got drunk. Pedro began to cry. So I told him, "Brother, this is God's punishment. He has punished me and He has punished you. Leave things alone, but rub [those who might have done it] with a *lluta medio*, an ancient penny." I believe in this. One has to rub the penny in the hands of persons who steal and one spits. Then one puts this into some black ink and then the face of the robber turns black on its own. You must have seen men whose faces have large black splotches. Those are thieves. So he had everybody rub the coin on their hands and the only ones who refused were the son-in-law and the first wife. This means that they must have done it. They must have taken the money. "Well, how about it," I told Pedro. Because he gloated about my misfortune God has punished him. Isn't it strange? I lost money and then he did too.

So that's how things are. It's a big problem, and I am very worried about it and even my mother cries a lot. She tells me to leave the matter alone, but if I do, then they may accuse *me* of contempt of court and they may put *me* in jail. If I leave it alone, they may present a writ, in turn, accusing me of calumny, of provoking her without cause, and of dishonoring her. So they tell me to continue. So I am continuing with my declarations. The judge has asked me to.[7]

The Switch to Mutton

Between our visit to Bolivia in 1975 and Hans's visit in 1976, Sofía had made another switch in the kind of goods she sold, a switch that may have resulted from the money she had lost and the high legal expenses she incurred, which left her little choice but to assume new risks and seek a more lucrative trade.

Since I lost the money, I switched [from selling eggs] into another kind of commerce. I was in a bad situation and needed a lot of money for the "doctor" (i.e. the lawyer) and for all the paperwork. In addition, I didn't have any working capital. My mother gave me four hundred pesos (US$20) and I spent that and then a man lent me one thousand (US$50) pesos. I don't know why he did it. Maybe it was out of kindness. He did it without asking for any form of guarantee. His name is Isidro Choque and he is from Visalaya. He is a distant relative of my mother's. He is a Baptist. One day, he went to my mother's store to buy something, and my mother cried and told him about my situation, that I had entered into a lawsuit and that now I didn't have any money to engage in business. So that's how this man brought me one thousand pesos (US$50) as an interest-free loan. He told me that he could lend it to me for three months, at which time I should have been able to make some business deals and could pay it back. I went [to Jank'o Amaya] one Thursday—I always go on Thursdays to buy eggs—but that day I didn't buy a lot of eggs. I only bought one hundred (eggs) and five cheeses.

That was in January. Remember that [I lost the money on January 15th]. So it must have been around the 24th. Well, I didn't succeed in obtaining more eggs. My mother cried. I don't know how it struck me, but I suddenly thought about mutton. I told my mother, "Why don't I buy lambs? I will try with two." She answered, "Take a chance. Let's see if they will let you buy. They may scold you." There are almost five persons who engage in selling mutton. Now I have befriended them, but at that time I didn't even know who they were. Well, I took a chance, and thank God they didn't scold me. I bought two lambs saying that it was for my personal use. I greeted them politely and with a bit of humor and they didn't say anything. To this day they haven't said anything.

At the time, mutton was expensive and those were fat lambs. That time, I had no idea to whom to sell the mutton. I went around everywhere trying to sell it. After I had gone to four restaurants without success, I was beginning to despair. Then I remembered a particular woman. She is my brother's *comadre* and is called Betsa viuda de Aruquipa.

She has a large restaurant and serves fricassee, *t"impu*, and cracklings. I went in and said Doña Betsa, I have come to visit you. She invited me in, since she knew that I was Pedro's sister, and I told her that I had brought mutton and was wondering whether she would be interested in buying it. It turned out that she needed some. She asked me what I wanted for it, and I probably charged a low price and that's why she bought from me. She told me to give it to her on credit and I left. The following Monday, I returned for the money and we started talking. She told me to bring mutton regularly, whether there was a glut or whether meat was scarce. She said, "I hope you are not just bringing meat this one time. Don't get lost." So I told her, "Doña Betsa, let's make a contract." "O.K., let's make one, but don't ever let me down. Bring meat every Friday." I told her that I would bring her at least one lamb even when it was scarce, and so we made a [verbal] contract. We did it in front of her husband who is the police chief of the precinct. It suits me because I get off [the truck] in the Bautista, where you leave me off. I usually come in Tiburcio's truck, the "Gabrielito," and [the driver] leaves me off right at the corner to prevent the meat from being stepped on. Otherwise the liquid, the fat, comes out and I have a loss of three or four kilos. That's why they load it with a lot of care and they hang the lamb from the pole that runs along the middle of the truck. They already know where I get off. There I hire a stevedore, whom I know well too, and he carries it down for me. I have it weighed immediately, because if I wait another day or two, there is more weight loss. We note down the weight and [the señora] knows that I travel again on Tuesday, in the afternoon, and she pays me the entire sum—four thousand or five thousand or three thousand (US$200, 250, or 150), it depends on how much I brought.

After a while, I bought four lambs at a time, at which point Doña Betsa asked me, "Why don't you bring some pork. Bring me pork and I will buy it from you by weight."[8] She asked me how much pork bellies cost, and I said twelve hundred to eighteen hundred (US$60 to 90) but that I didn't have the capital for that. I had increased my capital from the initial one thousand to fifteen hundred (US$50 to 75) but didn't have more than that. I thought to myself, "What am I going to do? I will have to continue as before." Then, one day, I saw a large pig and Doña Modesta wanted to buy it. She offered one thousand (US$50) and the man wanted fifteen hundred (US$75). It was a purebred pig weighing fifty-four kilos—a large animal. Well, one thousand is not fifteen hundred. I fell in love with the animal but I didn't have any money. I only had seven hundred (US$35) left. So I told my mother: "Look mother, I have bought some lambs and now I would like to try out with pork." "Well how much does he want?" "They are offering him one thousand (US$50) and don't want to offer more. I could buy it for twelve hundred (US$60). You could earn a lot. Lend me some money." So she counted it out and gave it to me and told me to go and see what I could do. I surreptitiously asked the Indian how much he would accept from the woman. He said fourteen hundred (US$70). So I told him, "Don't be mean. How can it be fourteen hundred if Doña Modesta only is offering you one thousand (US$50)? I will pay you twelve hundred (US$60)." He answered that he wanted to go over and talk to her once more. So I told him that I would go to one side and that he should tell me in a way that they wouldn't notice because otherwise they would scold me. In the meantime, I was buying eggs [but I was watching them out of the corner of an eye]. It seems that they were having an argument. Modesta gave him the money and he wouldn't accept it. Then she stuffed it into his pocket and he followed her. I was praying to God because I was afraid that she might just carry the pig off and I would be without my pig. But then the Indian came. He said that he would give it to me for twelve hundred (US$60). Since that day he has been my *casero* for both pork and mutton.

[Soon] I had a lot of *caseros*: Don Manuel, Don Nicacio, Don José, Segundino—almost everybody knows me. And they come and offer me the pork directly. Now I don't deal with mutton that much. I have only brought five or six lambs. Instead, I buy three pigs or so at one thousand or eight hundred (US$50 or 40) each. I have changed my line of business. I even was able to pay off my debt. Thanks to that loan from that man, I was able to regain my footing. I am very grateful to him. Now I will never stop selling pork or meat. I will continue to be a butcher. There is a reason why those women earn so much. When I first started selling pork I would look at their bags: they would be full of red [100 peso] (US$5) bills. They must come with at least twelve thousand pesos (US$600) or so to buy meat. I would watch them shell out the money. They would do so without hesitating. So I told my mother, "Mamita, I want to be a butcher." The women don't scold me. They tell me, "Fat one, where do you sell your pork? You pay a high price for it." And it's true. I pay a bit more: some one hundred pesos more than others. So they ask me, "You are paying a lot. Where do you take it?" I tell them that I have a contract with someone in Miraflores, when, in reality, I sell it in the Garita. "Well, you are stupid. With transportation to La Paz, the kilo comes to twenty pesos (US$1). Why don't you just buy it from the people who come to the Calle Tumusla from Batallas. You wouldn't have to go through all that trouble." But I prefer the pork from Jank'o Amaya. I also have a contract with a man from Visalaya, Benancio Mamani, I have done business with him for a long time. He buys cows or bulls and sells them, he buys sheep to butcher and sell, and he brings me pigs. When I buy from him, I earn more. My mother has given me that scale that I told you she always used because it indicates more (*sic*, she means "less") than the actual weight. So I tell Benancio, "Sell me the meat at twenty pesos per kilo." And he says, "Fine." But a pig weighs maybe forty-two or fifty-two kilos [according to my scale] and I sell sixty-two kilos in La Paz. So I cheat and make a better profit. But the man doesn't notice.

I don't really know [since when there is so much pork in Jank'o Amaya]. I didn't keep track. But since last January, when I have started to buy, they have brought a lot. I think that Doña Modesta buys sixteen or twenty pigs and the other woman also buys a lot. The pigs are very large. At the same time, the meat is very good. It's very tender. It cooks rapidly. That's probably why the señora likes that pork. There are a number of persons who [raise thoroughbred pigs] in Compi and in Chua too. I don't think that there were pigs like that before.

Ever since I began to sell pork, I preferred to sell the whole carcass. As you saw, I sell to intermediaries, that is to the third hand. The first hand kills the pigs. I am the second hand, who brings them here. And the third hand cuts the pigs up into pieces. I don't like to cut up the meat (and retail it myself). I prefer to sell the pigs whole even if it means taking a loss. I have noticed that the persons who cut up the pigs and sell the meat retail always end up with a leg or a loin. This means that they lose. Or else, they let the meat rot and they have to sell the meat at half price or on credit. I wouldn't like doing that.

[I never have had meat left over that I couldn't sell. Sometimes I have to wait until the next day to be able to sell. If I don't sell on Friday, I have to sell it on Saturday in whatever way I can, even if it means selling it on credit in order not to be stuck with meat. It's bad to do what some do, letting it spoil. That way they lose. I sell a pig, even if I lose twenty or thirty pesos. In that case, I don't mind [selling on credit], even if they pay me only in a month.

[During the time I sold cheese and eggs and at the beginning when I was selling meat] I continued with the onions because my father would go around in the countryside to investigate where he could buy onions by the field. [After a while, however], I no longer sold onions in the Montes because I saw that it was much easier to sell mutton [and pork] than to sit in the fair all day selling onions. Selling onions meant selling all day from eight in the morning till seven at night. And money came in dribs and drabs of one peso or two pesos. In contrast, I receive all the money at once when I sell lamb—thirty-five or let's say twenty-five at a time. It's the same thing with pork—seventy thousand at one time.[9] So I told my mother that I didn't want to sell onions any more.

Unlike most rural vendors in Compi-Llamacachi who begin their careers as teenagers and travel to La Paz temporarily for a weekend to sell the produce of their families or neighbors (see J.-M. Buechler 1972, 1978), Sofía began her career in the city and after the family's move back to her mother's home community, continued to sell in the region with her mother in the fiesta circuit, adding eggs and meat, which required more substantial working capital and a more complex set of social rela-

tionships to reliably obtain and sell the produce. Kin, friends, fellow community members, and her own maneuvers helped her obtain and maintain sales locations in the store in Llamacachi and in La Paz. She was also lucky in having lodgings in the city and countryside. Her urban roots are also important for the development of casera *(client) ties. These are reciprocal relationships whereby Sofía maintains a regular clientele by providing a set service: quality produce at an acceptable price for fair exchange and/or credit.*

As an urban-born market vendor, Sofía also has certain other advantages not shared by first-generation vendors: she understands some of the more Latin traditions of the restaurant owners, policemen, and border guards, and has the ties that enable her to establish a clientele and, on occasion, extricate her from disagreeable situations.

Although kin ties are important for both rural born and urban born vendors, ties employed in marketing by the latter tend to be more varied (J.-M. Buechler 1972:215). Sofía employed kin ties extensively while relying on a variety of ties she and her mother had established over a lifetime in La Paz. Such ties were particularly important when there was no access to formalized sources of credit. Sofía was able to get back on her feet after her capital was stolen, thanks to the generous interest-free loans from her mother and a distant relative.

Prospering in the market in a country like Bolivia with its changing government regimes and periodic monetary crises, and weathering misfortunes such as theft, expensive lawsuits—or, as we shall see later, illness—requires a high degree of flexibility. Sofía takes advantage of international price differentials and her contacts to obtain staples in periods of scarcity. She made major changes in the kinds of produce she sold as a result of the need to counteract some misfortune.[10] *The desperation with which she pursues the thief is indicative of the importance of maintaining working capital. She thereby becomes even more vulnerable to the corruption of the legal system in which she is not only a victim but also a perpetrator.*

It is clear that establishing an identity as a market vendor must be seen as an interactive process involving many actors. In the rural fairs, Sofía's local ties played an important role. She had lived in one of the communities surrounding the fair of Jank'o Amaya, but did not belong to a community in the immediate area of influence of the nearby rival fair of Huatajata. In fact, it is not surprising that a relative stranger from more distant Huarina, was allowed to come to buy eggs, while the Huatajateñas were not: other vendors from Huarina were less likely to follow suit and thereby increase competitive pressures.

However, the mere fact of community membership would not have sufficed to gain acceptance. Sofía had to establish ties of short- and long-term reciprocity with specific more established vendors, to convince them that they had more to gain than to lose by accepting her in their clique. While she would always constitute a threat when meat was scarce, her assistance in protecting the established vendors from more massive competition from the Huatajateñas could be more valuable in the long run. She also had to show her willingness to participate in and contribute to the annual town fiesta. This showed a long-term commitment to the fair and validated her claim to buy there. The town fiesta involves not only all the vendors selling at the market, but the town authorities (and through them the wider community) as well. By the same token, requiring participation in the fiesta was an effective means of limiting competition (H. Buechler 1980: 288).

But buying in Jank'o Amaya constitutes just one part of the wholesalers' activities. The other activities limit the degree of clique solidarity. In fact, membership in a marketing clique does not entail much more than a tacit agreement to protect joint turf against outside encroachment and the recognition of the right to buy. Rivalries among clique members abound. For example, Sofía hides the identity of her regular clients in La Paz from the other vendors, especially when her operations must be kept secret from the authorities.

Through her distinctive client network in the city, each vendor gains an identity of her own. A threat to these casera *relationships may be enough to destroy long-term friendships, as was the case when Sofía's friend tattled on her to her* casera.

Rural-urban marketing (or indeed even marketing in the rural arena alone) entails asserting oneself and being categorized by others in urban bureaucratic settings as well as vis-à-vis individuals directly involved in marketing. The lawsuit places Sofía in a strange situation. In spite of her largely urban upbringing, she is categorized as a rural marketer by the urban authorities, the urban kin of the defendant, and even by her kinswoman, Angelica. She is sensitive to her ignorance of "the system" and, at first, seems to accept the ethnic putdowns and slurs by Angelica and the police officers, yet she defends her honor when the defendants employ similar tactics. She accepts Angelica's claim to superior class status, only thinly veiled by Angelica's reference to her as a sister, but considers herself equal to the members of the clan of the defendants. The lawsuit also shows that lower-class Bolivians often feel uncertain in front of urban bureaucracies and seek out the assistance of bourgeois intermediaries who often treat them with condescension and exploit their ignorance. Earlier, we encountered similar feelings vis-à-vis the school and church groups. Nevertheless, Sofía does not persist in accepting Angelica's definition of her as a powerless country bumpkin. She learns from her cousin, assists her in trying to neutralize the defendant's supporters, and accepts Angelica's strategy of hiring false witnesses. At the end of the story she sees herself as caught in the lawsuit trap, but, at the same time, as capable of assisting other victims of theft. She instructs her brother about how he can find out who robbed him, and he thereby discovers a likely suspect. Interestingly, her advice is not based on her recent experiences with the formal legal establishment, but on traditional practices. And her revenge against the defendant (and against her brother who is stingy with his assistance) is of a divine, rather than legal nature.

During the sixties and seventies, Sofía also established an identity as a marketer in the wider region. First, she sold beer in fiestas in a wide area. Then, she purchased potatoes in Huatajata. This entailed establishing casero/a *relationships with Peruvians who brought the potatoes from their country. Because she was a potato wholesaler, a role that Huatajateños had not adopted, she and the fellow buyers were not only allowed to buy at the fair but also were able to limit buying by local consumers.*

Contraband, in which Sofía engaged for but a short period in the 1960s, gave Sofía yet another persona. Like potato buying, contraband entailed working in a wider arena, but, because of the illegal nature of the activity, she risked becoming involved in situations that could have compromised her sexual morality. Therefore her brother, after saving her and his wife from a financial debacle, put an end to these activities.

5

LIVING *and Marketing in the Eighties and Nineties*

This chapter covers the period of Sofía's marketing activities between 1976 and 1994. During that time, either Hans or Judith-Maria (or both of us) interviewed her in 1980, 1981, 1984, 1988, and 1994. Sofía brought us up to date about events that occurred during a period of extreme political turmoil, when the military under President Hugo Banzer first decided to hold national elections and then took power again. The elections resulted in a split vote in which neither of the top candidates gained sufficient votes to form a government and the senate appointed a caretaker president for a year before new elections could be held. This president lasted for only a few months before he was ousted by a coterie of military officers headed by General Natusch Busch in one of the bloodiest coups in recent Bolivian history. The public uproar following the coup led Natusch Busch to resign and Lidia Gueiler, an M.N.R. politician and the first woman president in the country's history was put in office. However, she was in turn ousted by General Luís García Meza in a coup to preempt the seating of Hernán Siles Suazo, who had been elected in new elections held in 1980 (Klein 1992: 266–7). The two years García Meza was in office (during the second of which we lived in La Paz), were characterized by repression and political murders. During much of that period, a strict curfew was in force, which often meant a headlong dash for home before 11 p.m. Those unlucky enough to be caught after the magic hour were taken to the stadium and/or forced to sweep the streets. Those few who were drunk enough to protest were subjected to beatings that, according to Sofía, resulted in death in at least one instance with which she was familiar. We marveled at the courage that the Bolivians showed in the face of the constant personal danger they experienced. While Hans and Judith-Maria maintained a low profile during the period, avoiding questions of a political nature in order not to compromise their consultants, Sofía would often loudly criticize the military, sometimes within earshot of the ubiquitous soldiers. And every time there was an attempted coup against the government—at least a dozen during the eight months we were in Bolivia in 1981 and often within the military ranks themselves—resulting in a temporary relaxation of control over the media, the newspapers would immediately openly publish stories critical of the government. By the time we left Bolivia, a triumvirate of generals took over and curbed the excesses of their predecessor, and it became clear that military rule was nearing its end. In 1982, Siles Suazo was finally seated by the reconstituted congress and political activism emerged from its state of hibernation, including a veritable renaissance of grassroots political movements that bloomed as though the ten year military period had never occurred. Since then, Bolivia has undergone three successful elections and three full-term presidencies.

While political normalization was accomplished, the same did not hold for the economy until the early 1990s. Beginning in 1981 and accelerating in subsequent years, Bolivia underwent one of the most serious economic recessions in the country's history, accompanied by inflation whose severity was matched in world history only by that during the Weimar Republic in Germany. The effect of this long-lasting economic crisis, especially on poorer Bolivians, has been devastating. Describing our research in Bolivia between 1981 and 1988 we wrote:

Hyperinflation, combined with wage controls, forced women, who generally are entrusted with the family purse—chola women literally hold the purse strings under their shawls or skirts, and lower and lower-middle-class women, in general, distribute their families' pooled resources according to the joint and individual needs of the members of the household—to cut out or cut back on food, shelter, clothing, utilities, and services and to provide by their own labor goods and services they once purchased. Their goal was to provide bare sustenance during the week and, if at all possible, one "good" meal on Sunday. To that end, they went to extraordinary lengths. The number of meals per day was reduced and their content drastically altered. For breakfast, it was not uncommon to make do with coffee (brewed from the dried pulp and skin of the coffee berry). When bread vanished from the stores, oatmeal, distributed by CARITAS, a Catholic relief agency, for a nominal fee, was substituted, or the women began to bake bread themselves if they owned an electric stove and if they had legal or illegal access to both imported flour and yeast. Often, when one of the ingredients became available again, the other was not.

For the one other meal of the day, bananas, yams, yucca, and oca (a tuber) often took the place of the favored potatoes, rice or noodles, and a few eggs, some fish or cheese were often substituted for meat—now considered a luxury. Family members were up at dawn, taking turns on long lines for rations, which the poor were often forced to sell for cash. When buying food, women calculate into their decisions the subsidized meals and additional rations given to of working members of the family. A once-proud baker was relieved that her older son could eat at the factory, and she reluctantly accepted domestic service at "starvation" wages because she and her school-age son were given lunch and tea (when he helped around the house too). She had accepted this job in part because her older son feared that her baking and selling in a kiosk might endanger his salaried position. He preferred that she engage in "hidden" work.

Everyone tried to activate or reactivate the kin and community ties to inherited furrows of land or to obtain produce from the countryside. Even charitable donations of staples distributed in the countryside were carried back to and sold in the city. There, relations with officials and storekeepers were assiduously cultivated. In stores, the shelves that were conspicuously empty of dry goods during the day filled up miraculously after 8:00 p.m., when the police left. Hoarding on all levels was commonplace. Peasants held back, selling only to selected intermediaries who paid well. They, in turn, favored select clients who had sufficient cash at the right time and enough space to accumulate sizable reserves.

[Rich and poor alike engaged in barter and other unorthodox transactions. Hans brought a five-pound bag of flour from the United States in case his mother's supply ran out. A distant acquaintance of his mother telephoned her that she had an ample supply of yeast which had suddenly become scarce and his father (who ironically was involved in the distribution of sugar before his retirement) obtained a hundredweight bag of sugar from their maid's brother. Finally, on his frequent visits, the plumber (who during his adolescence had lived and worked in the household of a close friend of Hans's family) brought bread which, for a time, was more abundant in the poorer neighborhoods than in the middle-class suburbs of La Paz.]

With regard to shelter, extended families crowded together. Young married persons often did not live with their spouses but instead lived with their families of origin. Every conceivable space was rented out. For instance, a former dressmaker and her two daughters hauled stones and molded mud bricks to construct extra rooms to accommodate bohemian tourists. Clothing was altered, mended, and handed down and around. Utilities were paid at the end of the month with inflated money. To resist the price hikes in transportation, workers walked, hitched rides, and resorted to violence, road blocks, and strikes.

Perhaps the most detrimental consequences of the crisis were the deterioration in education and health care. Students had to interrupt their education due to school closures and/or costs. Even in normal times, mothers complained about the expense of school fees, supplies, and "donations"; the cost now seemed preposterous. . . .

Medical care was postponed or neglected. Western medicines, many of which are imported, were either unavailable or commanded exorbitant prices. In the recent past, health care consisted of a judicious mix of modern Western and traditional Aymara treatment. Now, there seemed to be more reliance on self-help.

Buechler and Buechler 1992: 25–26

Although, as we have seen earlier, Sofía sometimes benefited from political and economic turmoil, and she was, perhaps, more successful than most in limiting the effects of devaluation and inflation, her standard of living declined markedly during that period, and by 1988, she was forced to pawn her jewelry, following the example of countless others. When Sofía concluded in 1988 that "business is like a soapy washboard; one eventually loses one's footing and falls," she was describing not just the downturn in her own business, but the plight of the Bolivian economy in general.

Politics and Life in 1980

All the middlewomen say that one can't earn. They don't know what to do. They must have earned too much [in the past]. Now let's see what happens when another president comes to power. We don't know whether Siles or Paz is going to come to power. But people here are very angry with Paz. They don't want to have anything to do with him. That's why my brother is no longer involved in politics. He has declared in public that he no longer belongs to the M.N.R. We had told him to quit the party because people say bad things.[1] They say that "El Mono"[2] is a thief, that "La Vieja" ("The Old Hag," President Lidia Gueiler) is his mistress and other things like that. They even say that "El Mono" incited Natusch [to stage a coup]. Remember that he killed everybody . . . I was in Llamacachi. My brothers say they couldn't leave the house [here in La Paz] because my whole neighborhood was full of soldiers. There was a tank in the middle of the plaza. If there was a little boy walking on the street, they suspected that he was carrying a bomb and they would shoot him. Lots of people died. This Natusch hid it all. He had the dead thrown in the lake.

A year later (1981), Sofía elaborated on the Natusch Busch coup:

He killed the most people. They persecuted the *señoritas* of the U.D.P (Popular Democratic Union party) of Paz Zamora. They say that they threw the dead in the lake and in the river in Yungas. University students disappeared then. I told my mother that Sr. Hans had told me to go down to [where he lives in Obrajes] because in this neighborhood one can't even go out of the house. They threw gas bombs, they tried to smash the door of the Mutual with rocks but were unsuccessful. I have a *casera* who lives in Villa Fátima and she asked me over the phone whether I had any meat. I told her that I did, but that the streets were blocked. I told her not to come here because I was afraid that people would do something to her car. This neighborhood is terrible; they call it the zone of the delinquents. Whenever anything happens, those thugs come to the Garita. I was already very pregnant and a gas canister hit me on the back of my head. I don't remember what happened but I must have fainted. They made me drink some water. The gas is harmful. It causes diarrhea.

The meat vendors continued to come. They live in the Alto Tejar. I will tell you what those women did. At the time, meat was scarce. A pig's head cost four hundred pesos (US$16). They brought the meat on foot from beyond Río Seco and butchered it right in the middle of all the shooting. Then they would enter our courtyard screaming, falling down the steps head first because they were trying to escape the gas. My brother scolded them because there were so many of them, but he helped them anyway.

The reestablishment of democracy in 1979 did not erase the legacy of heavy borrowing during the Banzer regime and larceny on a grand scale during the Natusch Busch interlude. As Sofía explained in 1980:

[Natusch] took all the money. Now I think that the present president has to borrow money from all the countries. Bolivia doesn't have any money at all. People are saying that we all owe money and that even this woman (President Lidia Gueiler) will have to pay the debt. The people are very angry with the army. They don't want to even hear about them. Now we don't know who will enter as president. I am sad about it and afraid. What are we going to do?

[The power of the peasants has increased]. It was sad. With the road blocks there weren't even any fish to be had here. I was [in Llamacachi] and it was fine there. But here [in La Paz] it was sad. Perhaps your father didn't get to feel it, but we did. I would go around in the Mercado Uruguay and there was nothing to buy for three days. The peasants wanted an increase in the price of their products because they had increased the cost of transportation. The peasants protested that they were working only for other people. They blocked the roads totally. They didn't let anything come in from [the country]. So people ate up all there was here in the city and soon there was nothing to buy. We didn't know where to get meat. But some of the women I know made a lot of money. They went to Villa San Antonio. . . . A pig the size of my daughter cost millions. A leg alone cost eight hundred (US$32); a pig's head six hundred (US$24). And the people bought at those prices. When I looked around the street at five in the morning there were people in their cars waiting. I felt sorry for them. There wasn't any meat to be had.

I arrived on Thursday and had sold all my meat. I was really sorry about that. I who deal in it suffered for lack of meat! I had to eat sardines those days. It was making me sick. A head of lettuce alone cost ten pesos (US$.50).

The peasants said that they were not allowed to make direct sales any longer, [the way they were able to in the past.] They would bring a few potatoes, a lamb, or some cheese and the middlewomen would scold them, hit them, and take their produce away from them and sell it at the price that they were accustomed. So the peasants wanted a fair where they could sell freely. Those fairs [where they could sell directly] have died. They have slowly become markets where only the resellers are selling.

I think that the mayor has promised them a market, but who knows when that will happen? The peasants were giving the government a deadline or whatever that is called. So, as a result of that, they promised them something. I would like you to listen to the radio; they protest a lot. They say that the government has forgotten about them. Now they say, "Let's unite again brothers and fight."

Although, as some of the above comments show, Sofía had ambiguous feelings about the Gueiler government that reinstated democracy after Natusch Busch's bloody coup, she was enthusiastic about the populist measures the mayor of La Paz took during the brief democratic period. Hans had just had an audience with the mayor with a group of colleagues and talked to Sofía afterwards:

[Raúl Salmón is a good person.] When he comes to the Calle Incachaca... Uf! It's his favorite neighborhood. When they made the fiesta on the 14th of September, he was at the head of the procession next to the figure of Christ. He is the director of Radio América. He was also the director of the municipal theater. I am happy with that mayor. When Natusch came to power I cried a lot. He put in another mayor, but then when Lidia came in, she called Raúl Salmón back. Before Natusch Busch, the mayor would visit the neighborhood and would see whether there were public faucets. We would ask for all sorts of things including garbage collection; and now the garbage trucks come. They pick up garbage twice a week. Then we asked him to put in a gas station nearby and a public toilet. They were going to give it to us. But then everything stopped with Natusch. He is a very good person, this Raúl Salmón. He is very concerned with the whole upper part of the city. That's why the people like him a lot. He also made us obey him. He forced our entire neighborhood to paint our houses. And we painted them. The entire city did. Then he revived the fiesta of Carnival. It was beautiful. I went to watch. I stayed downtown until nine o'clock at night. The parade started at eight and ended at twelve. Lots of children participated. It was the same in the afternoon. It was quite something to see how he could persuade all the neighborhoods to be represented by their own dance groups. He himself danced in a clown's costume. Even the *señoritas* of the town hall danced as *pepinos* (clowns). The same thing happened with the market vendors. They were forcing them to dance too. It was obligatory. That's why a group from the Incachaca participated. He revived [Carnival] after I don't know how many years. Everybody is happy, admiring what the mayor has done. But it was beautiful: there were *chutas, incas, caporales*. From each neighborhood the young people were dancing as mummies, gypsies, everything. The workers of the Said factory where my niece works also had to participate. They all dressed in the same *pepino* uniform. The fair of the 24th of

Sofía selling pork on the street in front of her house (1988)

January was also beautiful. All the stalls had the same roof color—the plastic sheeting was all in matching colors. The women who sell pastries had red flowered plastic tablecloths. Those who sold plants had stalls with green roofs and green covers for their display cases. He obliged everybody to be very clean. We now have to sell wearing white aprons and everybody has to have low wooden tables to place their wares on, otherwise they fine us.

Selling Pork in 1980

Before, I used to sell to Señora Betsa, but now I am no longer selling to her. One has to give a lot of credit and it's very difficult to collect the debts. I would have to wait a lot. I almost failed with the business. One day, I decided to leave. I am friendly with the women who sell around there, so now that there is a market next to my house. I put a stand there. I have a sales site right next to the door of the movie theater. I only sell there on Fridays and sometimes, when I want to, on Mondays too. I sell there from five to nine in the morning. Recently I [also] made a contract with a woman who makes *chicharrón* (cracklings) near the zoo. I call her by telephone and she comes with her car. It's a good arrangement for me. I no longer bring large fat pigs, the way I used to for Betsa, rather, I bring skinny ones, but with a lot of meat on them for *chicharrón*. She doesn't want to see fat ones. She said that they don't serve her purpose. She claims that her clients are 'better people' and they don't like *chicharrón* with a lot of fat. She makes them with a lot of spice and everything well prepared. So she wants thin pigs with a lot of meat. In addition, I bring lamb and sell it at the door of the movie theater. I also bring pork hocks and intestines. I think they make *escabeche* (a vinegar pickle) with it.

[Now, there is a scarcity of pigs around the lake.] It's not the way it used to be. For a time there was a disease going around that killed them off. Now they are coming from Santiago de Huata. They bring the pork on donkeyback. They tell us that they go as far as Peru to look for pork: to Yunguyo, Juliaca. Then they bring it by truck. Now, the pork from [our] area is bought up by the people from Batallas, while we buy it from Peru.

Sales are fine. But one has to work with a lot of capital. It's not like it used to be when, as I told you, large carcasses cost eight hundred or nine hundred (US$40 or $45). Now it's twenty-five hundred, two thousand, eighteen hundred (US$100, $80, $72). So it's expensive. Even a lamb costs five hundred (US$20). Merino lambs cost eight hundred to nine hundred (US$32 to $36). This week I brought one. I bring them regularly. They bring them from Peru. This man from Sak'eni always brings some. All the butchers, some twenty-five or twenty-seven, are from Sak'eni, except for one, Manuel Quispe, who is from Jank'o Amaya. But he is the only one from there. Then there are some who come to buy in Compi, but only rarely.

[I think that meat prices are higher in Bolivia than in Peru.] That's why they dare to engage in that business. Fathers, sons, and grandsons come and sell. [I buy] only from some of them. Some ask too much. They all know me, so they offer the meat. They say, "Why don't you buy from me?"

[Here I have my own site]. The *coordinadora* doesn't try to stop me because I am from the neighborhood. She doesn't ask me to become a member or pay money—nothing. I simply sell and everybody knows me. I am good to them too. All sorts of things happened this year: there was the revolution of Natusch and road blocks and things of that sort and I would help them. Since the house is nearby, they would bring their wares to the house for safe keeping. That's why they like me. The *coordinadora*, a *cholita* called Sara sells right on the street corner. Before that,the *coordi-*

nadora was Antonia Cachi. I think I used to talk to you about her, she was very much involved with the Movimiento Nacionalista Revolucionario (M.N.R.) party. Well, they got rid of her and this woman came in. She is a good person. When someone dies she stops me when I go down the street and says, "Sofía, this has happened, could you give me a contribution." I give her twenty or fifty. I also go to the parade. So no one says anything to me or fines me. She fines all those other people who come to sell there. They must say that I am from the neighborhood and don't just come to sell here for one day. Also, when I go home I always greet them. Then, when some president arrives or some mayor comes to visit and they prepare flower arches, I contribute poles. They already know [that they can ask me].

I charge people to store things. That money goes to my mother. Sometimes I earn seventy (US$2.80) on Saturdays, sometimes one hundred twenty (US$4.80). I look how much they have brought but don't charge them on the spot. Later, at eleven in the morning or two in the afternoon I go from site to site. For the low selling tables I charge them ten pesos (US$.40) per month. I collect the money at the end of each month for that. I don't know what the neighbors farther down the street are charging. They all keep things in their patios. Only the dance hall isn't an *agencia*.[3] All the other patios are full of selling tables.

We also charge for [bundles]. I charge five pesos per bundle. Others, who have brought trichinous meat, sell it right in my patio and the vendors from here come and get it in secret. I don't know how many times I have had run-ins with the police. I prevent them from entering the house at any cost. Recently, when the woman President came into office they changed the police. That day, someone left two bundles of meat in the patio. I already knew to whom they belonged. Well, the police came and said, "Oh you have an *agencia* here," and jotted down the number of the house. I became angry. I was really hostile. But they didn't pay any attention and entered the courtyard anyway. They were about to open the meat bundle when my brother came out of his room and shouted at them, "Why are you scolding her? She is the owner of the house." They answered, "Why did she call us *yokalla*? She didn't show us respect." But I made them run. "I have the right. This is my house. Why are you coming in?" "Oh let's go to the town hall," they answered. "The town hall nothing," I cried, I can do in my house whatever I want, this is no *agencia*. They insisted that it was.

One would have to open a store for it to be a real *agencia*. I told them that this was my house and that the people who were keeping things in the courtyard were my *comadres*. So now the policemen don't come any more. That's why the women take advantage. But when there is a lot of meat, my brother complains, "Why are you doing this?" The meat begins to smell. My sister-in-law tells me not to allow the pork vendors to enter the courtyard. "Why don't you approach the potato vendors. They will pay you per bag." I tell her, "Fine, fine," but I have already gotten used to dealing with the pork vendors. [I almost never sell onions any longer]. My mother planted some onions this year. [Generally] she hasn't been cultivating the fields any longer. She makes sharecropping arrangements with others. So, this year I did sell onions. I went to the Rodriguez during Carnival and didn't know where to sit. I was sitting there all day and sold very little. I counted the money: two pesos and another two. I had lost practice. I was accustomed to selling rapidly and counting the money quickly. I found it very strange. Everything had changed. Everybody had gone to sell in the upper part of the street, close to the Puente Abaroa, because they are putting in sewage lines. Also I didn't know anybody. So then I decided to sell the onions by the bag to the girls who were selling there.

Back to a Military Dictatorship (1981)

The military coup lead by García Meza, although less violent than that of Natusch Busch, also exacted its toll of human suffering. In 1981, Sofía recounted the case of the restaurant owner, Doña Betzabé, to whom she regularly sold meat.

Everybody in the Incachaca knows about that woman. She became wealthy. She owns two cars. [But] her only child died during the revolution. He would be twelve now. He died during the revolution of García Meza or Natusch. It must be a year ago. We were all worried that they would topple Lidia Gueiler and so all the people were up in arms.[4] The Garita was full of soldiers. There was gunfire, people blocking streets, soldiers who disappeared. . . . Several people [including Doña Betzabé's son] died in the Garita. A boy told the child's father what had happened. The child had left his home, had gone to the Garita and a bullet entered his skull, spilling everything. The child went straight to his death. Doña Betzabé was crying bitterly. The child's brain was a sad sight. Doña Betzabé's husband is a DIN sectional police chief. He lamented, "Why did this have to happen to my son? Why didn't they kill me instead? Aren't there enough criminals—thieves that deserve to be killed?" We buried him on the eleventh. We had to get a special permission, because the cemetery was under close surveillance. Then, suddenly, when we were entering the cemetery, a young man shouted, "Down with the military!" The soldiers began shooting and we all had to flee. I don't remember how we finally buried the boy. It was a sad funeral. The coffin carried a banner with the inscription, "Brother Ramiro: Assassinated." They killed him, a man and a woman. Doña Betzabé cried and cried, "Why did they do this to my son? They could have asked me for my money or for my jewelry but not my son!" The boy was bright. All his schoolmates came. I wonder why he went out on the street that day. They say that he was doing his homework. When they told his mother, she almost went mad. They took her to the health care center where the cadaver had been brought.

When Lidia was in power there never were any soldiers. But when they toppled her, they were all over because people were blocking streets and highways. They say that in the Max Paredes a señorita was leading a group of people and the soldiers beat her up and dragged her away. The soldiers advanced towards the cemetery shooting at people without mercy. Now no one can do anything because the military controls everything.

The Return to Democracy and Hyperinflation (1984)

[People were very happy when Siles came to power in 1982.] In fact, they were so happy that they celebrated a "second Carnival." We had free punch here [on the street], and bands played in every neighborhood. People were rejoicing because they thought that now that "El Papá" had come back, everything would be fine. The dollar fell in value and the merchants even reduced prices for their goods out of fear of the new president. You see, he had won the elections by promising that he would solve the entire economic mess within ninety to one hundred days. But he has been unable to solve anything. He has led us to ruin. Now the people [have turned against him]. They say, "That old traitor. See what he is doing to us!" I feel sorry for them. They had welcomed his return so eagerly. They thought that now there would be plenty of everything. Instead he raised the price of bread, sugar and everything else. So now everybody is calling for him to step down. My brother [hears about it in the Senate]. He is working there [as a private driver] for the president of the Senate. He says that even the senators are feeling the pinch. Even the wife of the senator [he is working for is worried about rising prices]. She is always asking, "How much is this worth? How much does that cost?" She complains that she can no longer hire a maid. She cooks and washes herself. I ask my brother, "What does 'El Viejo' plan to do?" [And he answers], "He does not want to step down. He does not want to relinquish his throne. No one else wants to leave office either. We are in a terrible mess."

Things are no better in the countryside. My mother no longer sells anything. Her store is empty. Peasants no longer eat bread because it costs too much. The store doesn't even carry sugar any longer. [However], I think that this government is planning to provide more assistance to the peasants. The engineers go [out into the countryside] and tell the people, "Make a river, clean the stones off the road," or "remove the rocks from the hill slopes," "repair this road" or "open a new road here" and after the people finish the task, [the engineers] give them a hundredweight of sugar or flour, or a can of cooking oil, milk, or tea.[5]

Apparently, they come from the city to distribute these things. They call themselves engineers. Some girls come as well. I asked one of them—a girl from the country who is *de vestido*—who had sent her. She answered, "The Urbanization Priests (Párroco de Urbanización) sent me to provide assistance." She established a women's union [in Compi], separate from that of the men. I thought that some ministry had sent her [but that wasn't the case]. So both men and women are happy. The men say, "When the military ruled we never received these things. Now the government is helping us." They are not complaining against the government. But, people here [in La Paz] are resentful. "We haven't received anything," they say angrily. On April 9th, when the M.N.R. celebrates its anniversary, peasant [delegations] arrived from every province. People here were very angry. They said, "Those people come here to feast El Viejo because they receive flour, sugar, milk, cooking oil, and even lentils that they (the peasants) feed to the pigs. But no one gives us anything." [And it's true, the peasants] do receive help. Now they say that they are going to build outhouses again [as the Peace Corps did in the 1960s]. In Visalaya they have already built them. They get assistance for all sorts of things.

I think that what is happening is that there are people from the UDP [party] out there who gave their support to the president and now they go to the government and ask for things [in return for that support]. But there are also people [from the government] who tell [the peasants] to do this or that. And people do those things quickly and they receive help. They gave things to my mother too.

Today, I am told, people were distributing flour among themselves. Each received a hundredweight bag of four and a can of oil—each can contains five liters—because they channeled the river—I don't know what river they were working on. My mother didn't go, but she sent soft drinks over. The person in charge of distributing [the staples] is the son-in-law of Pedro Quispe. He is from Huatajata. I found out about it today. I decided to stick my nose into the affair. You see, the truck driver who brought us here transported the goods. He says that some deal had been made [between the man who distributed the staples and the engineer]. The engineer followed the truck in a red vehicle to the place where the road from La Paz reaches the altiplano and they unloaded sixty-seven hundredweights of flour and nine boxes and an additional four cans of cooking oil. That means that they took out more than they needed. They must had entered into collusion and planned to divide the spoils between themselves. I am going to tell Pedro Quispe about it. They only wanted to give my mother half a quintal. If they have given her the flour already today, I am going to go there early on Sunday morning and ask them, "Why did you only give her that much?" I will tell about what I have found out. I will tell them, "Show me the bill (there is a paper with a list of all the assistance they received). You are colluding with the engineer. You made the truck driver unload sixty-seven quintals of flour and nine cases and four cans of oil." They take advantage. They must already have sold all those things . . . and they will give only a little to the peasants. That's what the truck driver told me. He told me, "Go ahead and tell him." What crooks! They take out more than they distribute and only the engineer and the person in charge of distribution know about it. The people [from the agency in La Paz] know nothing about what is happening.

Here in La Paz we don't get anything at all [for free]. Each street has its president and delegates just like the market unions. We hold meetings and gather money from everyone and we buy a five kilo bag or two of sugar or some cooking oil or noodles [from the authorities]. Right now they are holding a meeting in the meeting place of the street organization to discuss the purchase of cooking oil. There is none to be had in the stores. The stores only sell it [at higher prices] under the cover of darkness. That's how things are. Life is sad. Some time ago there wasn't even any meat to be had. Now there is an overabundance of meat, but there is no money to buy it. Now one can hear the vendors pleading pathetically, "Niñito, papacito, mamacita,[6] buy from me." Since there is no money, the market is full of [unsold] meat. They say that the banks aren't paying either the pensioners or the public employees. Now my brother went to stand in line at three in the morning in order to get his wages, so perhaps sales will start up again today. People can only consume when they are paid. When they have spent their wages, they have to do without. They can no longer eat. This morning everything was spoiling. Even the meat in the closed markets was smelling. Meat now costs fifteen hundred pesos per kilo (US$.75 or US$.44 at the official or street rates respectively). Many people can't afford that any more. On the radio they say that one should treat meat like a luxury item. Only those who have money can buy it. Most people are only buying eggs and cheese. People are under a great deal of stress. Neither kerosene nor gas can be had. One has to obtain it with one's neighborhood organization membership card. With that we can get five liters a week. People from our neighborhood can go to the gas station near the Said factory to get their allotment. Many smuggle the kerosene to Peru and sell it there. In Peru, kerosene has risen to two thousand pesos (US$1 [official] or US$.59 [street]) for five liters. People can't afford to buy it at that price. Now, they say that the Sol (the Peruvian currency) was devalued. Before that, the Peruvians would come across the border to buy potatoes, kerosene, bran, and whatever else struck their fancy at our fairs. But now the value of the Sol has decreased and they are no longer coming.

[All this happened] this week, when the last devaluation occurred. I saw women with tears in their eyes. They came to the market but couldn't afford to buy anything. Everything costs one thousand pesos (US$.50 [official], US$.30 [street])—peas, broad beans, everything. Everybody was desperate.

[I suffered too]. My capital amounted to two hundred thousand pesos (US$400 before and US$100 after the devaluation [official rate]). With that I bought pork. At that time a kilo cost twenty-five hundred (US$5 [official], or, depending on the month, US$.89 to 1.19 [street]). Then the devaluation caught me. I was bitter. But I said to myself, "What am I going to do now. I will have to borrow money. I will have to become a debtor." In order to deal with meat, I would have to have a capital of [1.5 million pesos] (US$750 [official], US$441 [street rate]). At present, I [only] have four hundred thousand pesos (US$200 [official], US$118 [street]). The devaluation caught my mother with an empty store. She had sold all her beer and soft drinks. So now she doesn't have the means to stock the store. Prices have doubled.

Thieves are working openly. If they see you counting money they come and grab it from you. There is a lot of theft now. Who knows what the future will bring! We are in a real mess. Both rich and poor are suffering. The poor are getting poorer. The government has fixed bread prices at seventy pesos (US$.04 [official], US$.02 [street]) for a [standard] roll. But sometimes we have to go without bread for an entire week. Bakers only bake when they receive an allotment of subsidized flour and those allotments don't last more than five days; after that we have to suffer again. We have to look all over the place for bread. Often we can't get any even for one hundred pesos (US$.05 [official], US$03 [street])! Now, if we manage to get a hold of some flour, we can't get yeast. During the Easter holidays, when I went to the countryside, there was no yeast to be had, so my sister-in-law used baking powder [to make bread]. The bread [she made] was awful." [In addition] we have to stretch the flour with bran and yellow corn flour in order to save. [My nephew] Teodoro, who lives here, has to do these things too. Things are very tight. My brother complains bitterly saying, "What is happening to us? We are ruined. And to think of how people supported [the president]."

Now prices are going down [again]. Even clothing is getting cheaper because business is so slow. But now, no one is interested in buying clothing. Why should we buy clothing, when it's so expensive. We are only interested in buying food. [I even make my own bread]. I don't like to pay one hundred or more and that's why I bake bread myself. Sometimes Teodoro's children come up here with their heads hanging and when I ask them what's wrong they say, "We want bread." Then I just *have* to give them some. Their father wants to limit them to one roll in the afternoon and one in the evening, but the children want to eat more. They crave bread. They stick around and when I ask them why, they say, "I want bread." It's sad to think about one's children. What is going to become of them? Even your father is upset. The other day I saw him in Tiquina. He was desperately looking at the buses arriving from La Paz. He didn't recognize me [at first]. When I asked him what he was looking for, he told me that he was looking for bread but couldn't find any. Fortunately a friend of mine had brought some. I scolded her in Aymara, "Sell him some. He will pay you well. He paid one thousand pesos or something like that for seven buns. That's when I told your father to write you that Pascual[7] and his wife had died in a terrible truck accident. I saw your father again the other Sunday in Tiquina. He was no longer driving himself. A driver was driving the vehicle. Yes, life is sad these days. One can't even drink, or dance, or celebrate a fiesta any longer.

Right now it's very dangerous to speak against Siles. [The government] has people put in prison and makes them disappear; or else they are found dead. That sort of thing didn't happen even when the military ruled. Of course we were under military law, there was the curfew, and they made us suffer with that. But I think that [Siles] has a secret militia that is listening [to what people are saying] and takes care of them. For example, a veteran of the Chaco War shouted, "Perjurer!" when Siles spoke in the Plaza Murillo. [The man] was taken away and was never seen again. More recently, they say that [Vice President] Paz Zamora went personally to the Rodriguez Market to find out about the prices, and the husband of one of the market women, a young man, insulted him. They took him away in chains. The women raised a big fuss about it, but he was found dead in the morgue.

The people can't stand it any longer. The demonstrators who take to the streets assault the stores of the Chinese[8] and the Manaco shoe stores. Doña Aida is complaining about it to the authorities. They broke into her kiosk, removed the door and took soft drinks. They can't get away with things like that down in the center of the city. They say that the police comes with tear gas to establish order. I wonder why [the demonstrators] are doing these things. The poor Chinese have to pay for everything. When something happens, the demonstrators go and ransack their stores. Last year (1983), at the end of November, when there was another devaluation, they also went on strike and blocked the streets. There was a terrible hailstorm. Groups of youngsters were roaming the streets. Then they suddenly broke into one of the stores of the Chinese stealing cloth, jackets, everything. They did the same thing to Manaco. They always target the Chinese stores and Manaco.

What are people going to do? They feel like dying. They say, "Let's just die. Until we get out of this crisis we will have to buy a lamb and dry it in the sun to make *charqui* and put a little piece of it in our soup." I think that all the women in La Paz are making *charqui*. High society women from Miraflores and Obrajes come to buy lambs here.

[Of course family members help one another.] For example my brother might ask me, "Give me some eggs." Then he pays me when he can. Then, when I don't have any, I tell him, "Give me some bread," and he gives some to me. We help one another. A few weeks ago there was no meat, so my sister-in-law and I shared a lamb. Then Teodoro looked at me sadly. So I went out early in the morning and was able to get a kilo of cow's head for two thousand (US$1 [official], US$.59 [street]). I brought him the meat and told him, "Here, cook it for yourself." I no longer want to quarrel [with my brothers]. And Teodoro has changed for the better as well. With all those problems (*tiradas*) around Christmas time, we thought that the end of the world had come. We decided that in times like these we shouldn't have family quarrels.

One can't put money away. Before [all of this happened] one did, but not now. When we get a hold of some cash we have no idea whether we [really] have made a profit or not. As far as I am concerned, I would say that I don't understand what it means to make a profit [anymore]. When I go on a [business] trip and I find that I have thirty thousand (US$15 [official], US$8.82 [street]) left over, I do something with it immediately.

Every time I come home with some money I buy some shawls that very day. Right now I have twenty shawls that I bought for ten thousand to twelve thousand (US$5 to 6 [official], US$2.94 to $3.53 [street]) a piece and I feel happy because they presently cost forty thousand (US$20 [official], US$11.76 [street]). [That means that] I do have a little something that I was able to rescue. But if I had stashed it away like my brother Pedro did. . . . Remember that he had a lot of money. He had one hundred thousand pesos from the retirement benefits that he received [when he left the factory where he was working] and he put it all on a bank account. When he withdrew the money recently, it was no longer worth anything.[9] I scold him, "Why didn't you go and get it [before]? Why didn't you buy something with it?" [The exchange rate to] the dollar was twenty-five pesos and he didn't want to buy anything. He would tell me that the sum was too large. I tell him, "You should have bought a bus with those one hundred thousand." Now only did it occur to him to withdraw the money. Before the devaluation he gave [some of it] to his wife and told her, "Take this, I will lend it to you." She had taken the money and had purchased beer from the brewery. In this way she was able to safeguard some of the money. But the rest of the money is no longer worth anything. That donkey of a brother is really stupid.

I wrap the [stacks of devalued banknotes] with this carrying cloth and with these rags. Even if a robber follows me, he won't notice a thing. Sometimes, when I go to Doña Betsa and she pays me, I protest, "Why are you giving me this chicken feed." We call the fifty and hundred peso notes *huallpa mank'a*. She gives me bundles this big. I have to wrap them carefully and enter a taxi. The other day there was a fellow who pushed me and lifted my skirt up. "What's wrong with you?" I asked. But he just continued, leaving me naked below. He turned out to be a robber. He had smelled the odor of the money and when I looked back he had stolen what the [bus] driver had collected from his passengers and was escaping with it. That time I was carrying six hundred with me. That's why I always carry the money in my carrying cloth.

My mother thinks that I have a lot of money. She says, "Uh! You have a lot of money. I never handled that much money." But all that cash is not worth anything. Once, Cosmi Condori, who is a butcher and sells in Miraflores, was coming along cheerfully carrying a whole flour bag with easily discernible bundles of bills. I asked him whether he was not afraid of being assaulted. He answered, "No, why should they assault me? It's not much."

The meat business is going well. Everybody is hunting for meat. One doesn't have to plead with people to buy, *"llevate niñito, patroncito."* Not any more. I don't reduce the price. People buy without bargaining. This is because of the devaluations. Everybody says that prices will rise, so no one has butchered their animals. They are hiding them. At least, everybody is chasing after mutton. You sell it in a moment. Here the best day to sell is Friday, Monday, and Tuesday. They sell in this entire area, very early in the morning. From here it goes to the fourth hand. Let's say that those of us who travel are the second hand, then the resellers buy from us—that is the third hand—and the fourth hand are those who retail it. People from Corocoro, Jesús de Machaca, Santiago de Machaca arrive in this place. On the other side are those who come from Oruro, Challapata, Wari. They arrive with truckloads full [of meat].

Speculation with food staples manifested itself in other ways too:

The bakers sent bread and flour to Peru at night. They say that they were also sending flour. But now that flour is cheaper in Peru it's the other way around. Flour is entering [into Bolivia] from there.

Marketing in 1981

You must have seen [the Peruvians] already. They bring the same things they bring to Huatajata: soap powder, matches, blankets, wool, picks, batteries, all sorts of items made out of plastic, even glasses—the things that the Peruvians always bring. Well, on the anniversary of the market, the people who sit in that row (there is a long row of them) decided to elect a *maestra* and have her sponsor the celebration. So now the Peruvians have their own *maestra*.

Meat has also become scarce again. Only a few of us are bringing pork [from Jank'o Amaya]. There are only six of us, where there used to be fifteen intermediaries who brought pork to the market . . . The supply of meat diminished progressively. Meat used to be cheap. So money flowed and those men bought up animals in Peru and provided the market with a steady supply. Now they say that that is no longer possible because the value of the Sol has gone up and our own currency has gone down and so they would stand to lose. Five of them are still coming with meat while the others have gone to work for companies.

The men are from Sak'eni and they go to Peru. [Those who have continued with the trade] prefer to sell to the middlemen in Batallas because they pay more for the meat. [They now take meat from Bolivia to Peru] because it's cheap here and expensive in Peru, they say that the middlemen from Ticuyu and Batallas are coming by truck as far as Jank'o Amaya in search of meat. There is very little meat. After butchering the pigs in Ticuyu, they bring them to La Paz where they sell the large ones to the meat stores and the small ones to the market vendors. But they [too] are saying that there are no pigs. It's not worth bringing a truckload for eight thousand pesos (US$320). Now there are no pigs in the countryside because a disease is killing them. The pigs die just like that and the sale of pork is highly controlled. They take the meat [from the diseased animals] and give it to the animals in the zoo.

[I brought four pigs last week.] I bought the largest pig for eighteen hundred pesos (US$72) and sold it for twenty-two hundred (US$88). The one I paid 1,500 (US$60) for, I sold for 1,600 (US$64) and the one I paid 1,650 (US$66) for, I sold for 1,650, without earning anything. I also brought one for 550 (US$22), which I sold for 750 (US$30). So I must have earned some five hundred pesos (*sic*, actually seven hundred [US$28]). [One can earn more]: fifteen hundred or one thousand pesos (US$60 or 40). But one has to deduct 20 or 40 pesos (US$1 or 2) for each round trip for the bus fare and the meals (during the trip: let's say a total of 120 pesos (US$4.80). Then the stevedore charges some ten pesos (US$.40) [per load]. Also [one has to] pay the truck twenty pesos (US$.80) because the pigs are tied to the side. That time, I sent the pigs by truck because they were heavy and I couldn't lift them. Perhaps [costs] amount to some two hundred pesos (US$8). That means that one still earns eight hundred (US$32).

[There was a rapid change in the supply of pigs]. There is a lot of pork now. They wanted to sell me more pork on credit. But I didn't want to because I might lose money and then the Indians will be crying to be paid. Before, I would obtain seventeen thousand pesos (US$680) worth of meat on credit. I would cancel my debt the following week, but if a client failed to pay me on time, I ended up looking bad. That is why I don't like buying [and selling] on credit. Doña Betzabé still owes me four thousand pesos (US$160). She owed me fourteen thousand pesos (US$560) and she wanted me to bring more pigs. [She paid off a bit at a time, but the debt continued to accumulate. I became impoverished dealing with her. I no longer had any working capital. Finally I scolded her telling her that, after all, I had to *pay* for the meat I brought. I don't want to sell meat to Doña Betzabé any longer. When I told her that I would no longer travel for her, she made a contract with another man. I told him, "Poor thing, she will do the same to you as she did to me." Everybody in the Incachaca knows about that woman. She became wealthy. She owns two cars.

The Strike of the Peasants against the Truckers (1984)

Hyperinflation in the mid-eighties brought with it considerable public unrest, which, among other things, disrupted transportation both in the cities and in rural areas, making marketing more difficult for Sofía.

[The protest was against the truckers and bus owners travelling] the route to Huatajata—I think that they call themselves Transporte Cooperativa Ltda. They travel [all the way to] Tiquina. Recently, the people from Tiquina rose in protest. They went on strike. They threw stones at the buses breaking the windows and let the air out of the tires because [the bus owners] had increased the fare to two thousand pesos (US$1 [official rate], 0.59 [street rate]). They broke off relations with the drivers on that route. They didn't want to pay that much.

They say that Torribio Navo (a man from Llamacachi) had betrayed them. He said that he and his brother would be ready to travel to Tiquina for fifteen hundred pesos (US$.75 [official], $.44 [street]), the amount that the people from Tiquina were willing to pay. But the people from Huatajata drove him away with stones. That's why this bus no longer goes to Tiquina. When they found out that the people from Tiquina had been successful in forcing the fare down, all the people from the area of Pacajes, Larecaja, and Achacachi held a meeting to bring down fares in that area as well. The people from Jank'o Amaya followed suit. They wanted to bring the fares down from the fifteen hundred pesos we had been paying to thirteen hundred (US$.65 [official], $.38 [street]). The drivers are refusing to do so. They went to the federation and held a meeting there and are very angry at Torribio. Those who travel in the direction of Larecaja want to beat Torribio up. Apparently, the Federation of Bus Owners and Drivers have thrown him out for breaking ranks with the rest of the membership. As a result, the day the bus drivers were supposed to sign a contract setting fares at thirteen hundred pesos, not a single bus driver went to Jank'o Amaya in order to avoid signing it. That day, there were no buses at all.

We would be willing to pay more because we suffer when there is no transportation; those who are unwilling to pay more are the people who live there, the peasants. They are the ones who block the roads to force the fares down. I think that the quarrel will get worse. In Tiquina they threw rocks. It was last Wednesday. There weren't any buses when I went [to the bus station] as I usually do. We heard that they had blocked the road in Tiquina and so they were afraid to travel there. The soldiers from the regiment stationed across [the straights] came to their assistance.

They had taken the minister of transport from here [to Tiquina]. Apparently they weren't even afraid of him. The people of Tiquina stood their ground. They have guts. Catari (a bus owner) from Huatajata asked to address them, but they didn't let him speak. They roughed up Vicente Suxo, a driver from Tauca, and even broke his glasses. They didn't want to budge. Now the people from Tiquina are suffering from lack of transportation because only two buses are going there. They broke ranks and betrayed the union. [I] came here in the cabin of a truck and the driver told me that the union was accepting new members who had been working on other routes. They claim that on the stretch from Huatajata to Tiquina there will be three scheduled buses: one in the morning, one at noon, and one at midnight. We will see what happens. We have to suffer. [The peasants] don't. I think that the peasants are going to come out on top and the price will be set as it should be set. The fare used to be 350 pesos (US$.70 [official], $.17 [street]). That's what it still was last February. Then it went up to 1050 pesos. What they are charging now—fifteen hundred pesos—is too much. The peasants, who aren't stupid, figured out how much it should really be and came up with 1050 pesos (US$.53 [official] $.31 [street]) as the right amount. [Gas] didn't increase in price at all. They shouldn't have raised fares that much.[10]

The Pig Fever Epidemic and Marketing Pork in 1984

I still send meat to Doña Betsa [who has a restaurant.] If there was pork to be had, I would earn well. But unfortunately this year it will be scarce. There won't be any pork for the entire year, because a disease killed all the pigs. So everybody killed them early, when they were still small. That's why there was a lot of reddish meat on the market. The disease leaves the meat an unappetizing red. They say that it can infect people (who eat it). Pedro Menacho says that he had 240 pigs—like a pig farm. But they all died and he was left with only four pigs.

The pigs get a high fever and lose their strength. Injections or vaccinations apparently don't help at all. He had all the pigs vaccinated earlier and the pigs became ill anyway. They say that this illness comes from the lake. There are tiny mosquitoes along the lake shore, lots of them, like in the Yungas and those mosquitoes climb up onto the bodies of the pigs. So this year there won't be any pork. The six of us who engage in this type of trade are forced to fight over each pig like dogs.

Last year [business] didn't go as well, but this year I have been lucky. I earned a lot because of the scarcity of meat. [She chuckles] Before that I was in debt a lot. I was a debtor and even a money lender (*sic*). Since last Christmas, things have been going well. My mother [and then my uncle] raised some piglets that belonged to me. It turned out that [a sow I had bought] had nine piglets—three females and six males. I fed them bran and potato peels and for Christmas I was able to take enormous pigs to La Paz. I sold the sow that had cost me seven thousand (US$35.71 [official], US$8.08 (?) [street]) for sixty-five thousand (US$130 [official], US$52.25 [street]), while I sold the piglets for twenty-five thousand (US$50 [official], US$20.10 [street]). That time they were looking desperately for pigs for Christmas. When the soldiers caught [a market vendor] with pigs, they would force her to sell them. They went like hot cakes. That time I earned a lot of money. I would go, come back here, and sell. I didn't even have to leave the house! They would come right here, knock at the door and say, "Doña Sofía, doña Sofía, sell me some pork." I would sell it to the highest bidder.

In contrast, last week things went badly. They no longer knocked at the door, so I had to send pork to Betsa. But then, sales were good again on Friday. To tell you the truth, I haven't taken any losses during the entire month. I had good luck with the pigs of Pedro Menacho; thanks to the pig disease. Don Pedro has someone who works for him called Julián, a pox-marked man, who gets paid a monthly salary. Apparently Pedro had a pig. One by one, the pigs began to die. One day I bought a reddish colored pork carcass at the fair, and when I asked from whom it was, [the middleman] said that it was from Pedro Menacho. "Well," I said, "I will pay you and you will earn money too, but if the pigs are dying don't just watch them die. If they are sick, butcher them before it is too late. Then the meat will still be white. If you kill them when they are about to die, the meat will be reddish and it will be no good. I told him to kill them and he sold them to me.

I earned well. I bought the [sick pigs] for forty-five hundred and sold them here for sixty-five hundred.[11] Pedro Menacho is raising pigs there now, but when the man told him [what was happening to the pigs] he exclaimed, "Let them all die, let them all die. We are no longer going to have a pig farm. I don't even want to hear about giving them medicine!" You see, earlier on, they had brought a specialist to vaccinate the pigs because with the certificate of vaccination he received he was able to buy bran, which was scarce. We had even wanted to form a cooperative to raise pigs and we were going to take a doctor there to vaccinate them, which would have enabled us to buy bran directly from the factory. We had had a meeting about it but then abandoned the idea. The plan was that, for example, my mother had six pigs at the time and we would have told him that she had twelve and we would have offered the 'ingeniero' some food and drink so that he would have signed the papers [correspondingly]. We didn't do it ourselves, but Pedro must have taken out bran in large quantities. So he told this Julian that they might as well give up raising pigs and start a dairy farm instead. He said, "Let's buy some ten cows and then we can open a cheese factory." He told me that he had some flat land and that he would buy lake reeds. He also owns some chickens.

[He has a store here and is also] the *coordinador* or [rather] secretary-general for all the stores that sell staples. His wife sells in the store and remember that he had a little daughter. She is grown up now. She married recently. Uh! My brother says that they had a wedding the like of which he had never seen before! I didn't go, but he said that it was a sumptuous wedding. Two rich men were competing with one another, because Pedro Menacho is rich and the father of the young man is wealthy. So, there were two orchestras; there were songs and panpipe music. And everybody had beer bottles by the dozen standing around them. The groom's family held the first day of the wedding in a luxurious hall in the Inglés Católico (a school) and on the second day, Pedro Menacho gave a feast in the Hotel Tumusla. What do you think of that? I wonder where they got the money from to celebrate such a marvelous wedding. Now the daughter and the son-in-law help with the business. The son-in-law has a car of his own, Pedro Menacho has a bus and two cars . . .

[This morning], when the bus stopped in front of Pedro Menacho's house [in Compi], [Pedro's caretaker] climbed into the bus and looked in my direction. I asked him whether another pig had died. He said yes and I told him that I would buy it from him. That's when he told me the story.

It's prohibited to sell meat like that. These old women sell [the meat] to those from Villa Cruz, Puente Topater, Puente Negro who cook meat in little frying pans and sell it on the street at night. One has to be careful. You know the ones in San Roque that call out "*chichicharrón, chichicharrón*!" they are the ones who buy [this kind of meat]. The drunkards who come out on the street eat it. The restaurants won't touch it. At least Doña Betsa won't. She has a lot of customers. Also, her husband used to be a detective. Now he is retired and helps his wife. He takes in the money. He might get angry. She has a lot of clients with the *chairo* (a stew) she makes. She serves large plates full. It's a very good *chairo* with vegetables. She makes it with white beets, carrots, chard, and peppers. To that she adds pork skin . . . uuh, even high class gentlemen come to eat. She would [never want to lose those clients].

[Once I went to the stand of a woman to whom I had sold trichinous meat].[12] She was selling nice golden brown chickens, pigs feet—a wonderful smell—and sausage. High class gentlemen were buying from her. "Sit down sister, sit down," she said. Men accompanied by their wives came up to her and asked for sausage sandwiches. They fell in love with her golden chicken—well that was passable. Handing me some sausage, she asked me, "How do you like my sausage, how do you like my sausage?" I ate it, even though I felt repulsed. "Why are you looking at me like that?" she said. But the sausage was, in fact, well prepared with cinnamon and everything . . . And the gentlemen were eating it . . . with trichinae. I laugh—the best gentlemen are eating trichinous meat! No, they really cheat people.

Apparently even the sausages are contaminated. Would you believe it? There is a factory in Villa Fátima, and they say that they buy trichinous meat. They grind everything up. I only want to eat meat from pigs that we have raised ourselves, not from strange pigs. I don't even buy from Betsa. She sells all this good food and I sell meat to her. But she might mix it with meat from sick pigs too. And how they all eat happily! Licking their fingers!

This illness has wiped out all the pigs. Now, when I go to the fair, I only bring back two or three. I used to bring back seven or eight. One could save! I used to tell my brother that I could buy a car for him. But now there are no pigs any more in this entire area, even on the Peruvian side. There probably will be some again next year, but this year we are suffering.

The Cheese Business (1984)

[As for cheese], for a time I could sell all the cheese I wanted. I asked my sister-in-law what I should do. I told her that there was a lot of cheese in Llamacachi. She told me to bring nice ones. She was sure that I would be able to sell them. I have a woman customer who sells doors and windows and my brother also buys cheese for the senators. I know the people from whom I buy cheese. The wife of Juan Navo in Llamacachi brings me cheese—very large ones for thirty-five hundred (US$1.75 [official], US$1.03 [street]). I don't want dirty cheeses. When I buy dirty cheeses, my mother scolds me. They are disgusting. People bring some that have sheep's dirt all over them. Now they are mixing the milk with the milk that the aid programs bring—they bring bags of ten kilos, my mother has ordered ten kilo bags. They put cheese made with that milk in the middle of the basket and arrange the cheese made with natural milk on top. So, it's very difficult these days to buy cheese. The people are distrusting too. They say that they don't want to buy "Cari" (CARI-

TAS) cheese. They say, "Since we know you, we will buy from you." No, it's dangerous.

[In Llamacachi], they started only recently because they have milk. Everybody has cows now. [Before] they didn't. For example Lucía has two cows. Sometimes she brings fifteen, sometimes twelve cheeses. [She sells them for three thousand pesos (US$1.50 [official], US$.88 [street]).] Today she only brought me seven. They are pure and clean. She is the only one who brings cheese now. The others don't bring any anymore.[13] All that started this year when the assistance came. They mix it in with the other milk [especially during the dry season when] milk is scarce because there is little grass.

I sell [the cheese] for thirty-five hundred (US$1.75 [official], US$1.03 [street]). Here in La Paz there is a lot of cheese. It's cheap now. One can buy some that are almost as big for twenty-five hundred (US$1.25 [official], US$.74 [street]). Since there is no meat, everybody wants to buy cheese. Half of the persons [I sell the cheese to] pay me, the others do not. I come back angry. I only finish getting the money from them on Wednesday. I sell the cheese on credit. There is no way that they would pay cash for it. I go to Doña Marta (Pedro's wife) and she takes four or so, Betsa takes two or so, Doña Teresa five, Doña Augustina another four. Then I go down to the *abasto* and sell another five there. After that I begin to collect the money. One woman might say that she doesn't have any; another that the vendor just left. [When one collects the debt], one always has to chat first. One doesn't just say, "Give it to me right away." One asks them how they are, whether sales are good. Then I tell them "give me the money." Then they might say, "Please wait, I haven't sold [the cheeses] yet." For example, [when I go to] Doña Agustina who sells baby bottles in the Max Paredes, I have to sit there till late to watch whether she is selling anything. Then only does she pay me. That woman doesn't like to pay. When the moment comes to pay, they become reluctant. [I often have to go twice]. Some pay up, but others drag their feet. For example, the other day Doña Marta asked me, "How much do I owe you?" I figured it out. It was thirty and something. She answered, "Right now I'm only going to pay you twenty." "You have to give me thirty," I countered,"you can pay the rest later." But she said, "Come back at six for the rest?" When I returned at nine, she had already left her stall. Then, when I went once more early the next morning, she again told me to return later. She finally paid me at noon. It's tedious.

With pork it's different. When I send pork to Doña Betsa I wait until Wednesday at ten or eleven. And she always pays. But I have a *casera* in the Uruguay market, she is called Doña Nativa, who pays half in cash and the other half on credit. I tell her that I want the rest on Sunday. She never brings it on Sunday, but she always brings it on Monday, Bolivian time.[14] She brings it here and calls out, "Doña Sofía." I immediately know that it is she. In contrast, I often suffer a lot because people don't pay for cheese. This morning I told my mother, "Don't buy cheese, don't buy cheese." But she bought lots of cheese anyway and only a few eggs. I had her bring half of it back again. I brought more than twenty.

I will take [these cheeses] to Doña Marta, Doña Justina, Doña Francisca. . . . Yes, the cheeses already have owners. They eat a lot of cheese. They are the ones who buy a lot and so I bring better and larger ones to them. Before, I had a regular customer who made egg and cheese sandwiches, but I no longer sell to him because he drinks a lot while his wife is not well. Now I am selling only to those who eat cheese themselves. I guess they eat it with their coffee. For example Doña Marta has a large family and so she always orders six or so. She makes coffee and eats the cheese with it as a main course. She makes cheese salad and noodles with cheese—things like that.

Doña Marta is Martita's *comadre*. She hadn't known that I brought cheese, but one day I offered her some and that's how it started. Now I bring her cheese every time. Then [Doña Marta] said that her landlady, Doña Delfina wanted some too. I send them the best cheeses so that they can sample them and that makes them want more.

The Llamacachi Store (1984)

My mother is losing her memory. She is no longer working. I have to go and cultivate the fields there. She is no longer minding the store properly. She is selling less. Even she agrees that its time for her to move to La Paz. She is afraid that people might assault her and kill her. But she says that she doesn't want to come to this house the way things are. There are always problems here. My brother quarrels with his wife. His children are already grown up. Things happen like the case of Marta that I told you about and she doesn't want to see things like that. She says that if she sees my brother being treated like that she will get angry and they may show disrespect towards her too, and then she might die of anger. That's why she doesn't want to stay here. I have my own ideas about what to do. I have given the little store [to my sister-in-law] for three years and I want to tell her that I want it back now for my mother. If she doesn't want to give it back then we should sell house. This room is empty. My mother can live there.

Selling Pork in 1988

Lately my business has gone downhill. People say that a fall is inevitable. Business is climbing a soapy wash board. One eventually loses one's footing and falls. It's like an illness. Right now I am suffering. There is a woman who owes me more than five hundred pesos[15] (US$210[16]). She hasn't paid me yet. That's how my life is.

If I am successful in collecting the money, I leave here at five or five thirty [on Wednesdays.] Then I go directly to Jank'o Amaya and sleep there. I arrive there at 8 p.m. You have seen how I buy on the next day and come back here. I arrive here at twelve. Then, on Friday morning I sell the pigs. I put my meat near Ruth's store. I pile it up there and they come and buy from me and I note it down.

[I have *caseras*.] [The woman who came] is one of them. Another one is my friend Vicky from the restaurant. Another one is Sabina. She owes me almost five hundred. Apparently she is in Pokota right now. Some private persons [who are not *caseras*] also come and buy. [I also have *caseras* in Jank'o Amaya.] We wait to see who comes. Whenever my *casero* comes, the others don't approach him. I run over to him and buy the meat. But whenever a "private person" comes then we all run and the first one who gets there gets the meat. We prefer to buy from the owners (i.e., the producers themselves). We have a scale that indicates too much weight in addition to one that indicates the correct weight. The one that indicates too much weight shows 1.3 kilos for every kilo.[17] For every three kilos it indicates one too many, that's [an extra] ten pesos (U.S. $2.65). That way we earn extra. We make a big effort and the one who has the most strength gets the meat. [When we can buy directly from a producer, we leave] the *caseros* [to one side]. All this for ten cents.

Before, when my mother was still alive, I always stayed with her [when I went to buy meat.] Then, I would wait for the bus from Huatajata—the one owned by Katari—at four in the morning, and I would arrive in Jank'o Amaya at dawn. I continued this practice even after my mother died, I am afraid to arrive there all alone. I prefer to rent a room together with my friends. I keep a mattress and blankets there. We pay fifteen pesos (US$2.38) a month. We take turns paying the rent. So, now I travel directly to Jank'o Amaya. We wake up with an alarm clock. We have to leave our room at 5:30 in the morning because the owners of the house arrive at that time.

[If my *caseras* fail to pay me on time,] I stay here, like I did the other week. They gave me only 150 (US$63) that time. What was I going to do with 150? I went and threw the money and the ticket I had bought at [the woman] and went home. Why go there in vain?

[Obtaining pigs is less of a problem.] Even when there aren't any, we always come back with three or four. When there are plenty, we come back with nine. We have won the lottery when we get ten. Then I feel happy. On those occasions, I cook a really good meal, because with ten pigs I can sometimes earn seventy (US$29.40). When I am really lucky, I can earn [up to] one hundred (US$42) with the extra weight I steal. But when I bring three or four, I only earn miserable sums: fifteen (US$6.30) or twenty (US$8.40). Nevertheless, it's better than nothing. No one is going to give me a gift. I have to earn something to maintain my household.

I think that I explained to you that the meat comes from Escoma .... Well, there are three kinds of meat: *carne criolla, carne cabaña* and [meat that comes from around the city].

The *criollo* meat comes from Jank'o Amaya, Escoma and Batallas, that's the best meat. And the *cabaña* meat comes from Villa Montes and Cochabamba. The meat from the slaughterhouse has a different taste. It is a type of meat that I don't like as much. You might go for meat that looks fresh and white and think that black meat is bad. I would like you to buy meat with black skin. There is a better guarantee of good quality. Once it was even on the television channel 4 of Carlos Palenque. They made us look bad and we lost money. Almost all of us were left without capital because we couldn't sell any longer. The people here in the city no longer wanted to buy pork when they saw on television what they had filmed in Llojeta near Sopocachi. There are hills in the back of that place where garbage is deposited. It turns out that people brought hundreds of pigs there. One person had three hundred pigs and was in cahoots with the big wigs at the town hall. They were rearing pigs on our garbage!

The *criollo* pig [also lasts longer. It] can last for as long as two weeks if one treats the meat with care, placing it on top of a table on white paper that one changes frequently. But the pork that comes from the valleys, from Villamontes already smells after two days. It turns green because it's kept in a hot climate and therefore does not keep well.

If they can't sell it on the first day, they store it away until the next day. If they still can't sell it on the second day, then they cut it up the following day. Perhaps they sell the legs but they might be stuck with the ribs or with the legs. One can never tell in advance. They take care of the meat and clean it with salt so that they can still sell it. If it begins to smell a bit, then they sell it on credit to the women who sell cracklings at night cheaply. They liquidate the meat by going around and hawking it. Let's say it costs 3.50 (US$1.47) per kilo when it's fresh, then a vendor might sell it for 2 when it's spoiled.

[I also earn some money from renting a room to the union]. For the union office I get sixty (US$25.20) and eighty (US$33.60) from the *agencia*. I get twenty (US$8.40) for each corner. Then I get money from the sales tables [people store in our patio]. Thanks to the meat display tables I can buy clothing for myself and for the girl. In total, I have thirty-five display tables, both small and large. I charge the same amount for them regardless of their size: Bs (the abbreviation for "boliviano") 3 (US$1.25) per month. Multiplied by thirty, that makes ninety pesos (US$37.80). Some people have told me that I should charge five thousand pesos. If I did, I would be a millionaire. But I feel sorry for the people.

With the money I receive, I buy meat, potatoes, sugar, or whatever else a household needs . . . even soap. If one doesn't sell and doesn't have the money, one begins to smell. That's how I support myself.

Sofía's description of her family's strategies (and mistakes) in dealing with the economic crisis of the 1980s reveals the turmoil and the existential fear most Bolivians, but particularly poorer ones experienced. It was a time when more usual strategies of saving no longer made any sense and when a person's capital could vanish in a matter of days or weeks through rampant inflation. The most extreme of the strategies engaged in by market women was to attempt to provide the basic necessities even in the midst of a coup attempt, risking their lives to fetch higher prices.

Most revealing is the Velasquez family's decision to drop outstanding feuds and to help one another instead. At the height of the crisis in the mid-eighties, even the most basic staples were often so scarce that only a wholesale mobilization of a family's social network could secure basic needs. Sofía's nephew and nieces begged her for bread which she, as many others, baked herself with ingredients mobilized through various contacts. Ultimately, as we shall see in Chapter 12, Sofía successfully mobilized a tie which had lain dormant for eight years, that with her former lover and father of her daughter, René.

Sofía's own marketing strategies in the 1980s had in many ways not changed from those she employed before. She continued to rely on caseras/os. *She continued to buy in Jank'o Amaya and sell in La Paz and to engage in tricks such as using the time-honored practice of cheating her suppliers with a* "balanza de compra," *or "purchasing scale," a scale that indicates less than the actual weight, and of selling meat from diseased animals. Even the commodities sold had not changed substantially since the mid-seventies. However, there were both new challenges and new opportunities. Democracy in 1980 and again after 1982 brought with it a reduction of the abuses suffered by the vendors at the hand of the authorities. On the other hand, it also permitted protests and strikes such as the peasant protest against increases in transportation costs, conditions that Sofía commented on with a mixture of annoyance at the inconvenience and sympathy for the peasants and the truckers. At the same time, the deepening economic crisis made sales increasingly unpredictable.*

There are seeming contradictions in Sofía's statements regarding her selling activities: long explanations of why pork is scarce are followed by assurances of her own business success. These contradictions are resolved when one considers Sofía's flexible response to each new crisis and to new opportunities. When pork became scarce, she made a killing on the sale of diseased animals that had to disposed of rapidly. When many families became too poor to afford meat, they became good customers for cheese that had become more available thanks to the efforts of development organizations to foster dairy farming and those of other development organizations to distribute surplus milk donated by the United States (which ironically ran counter to the logic of economic self-sufficiency implicit in the promotion of dairy farming). Then, when cheese became so abundant that intermediaries either had difficulty selling it, or could afford to antagonize their regular suppliers because they could easily find other sources, Sofía was able to remain competitive by selling cheese directly to consumers to whom she was able to guarantee a superior product. When the economic crisis—and the huge bags of devaluated bank notes that merchants had to lug around—encouraged theft, she and other vendors found new ways of hiding the money. Finally, she and her neighbors took advantage of the opening of the market in their street to rent space for storing sales tables and for holding union meetings.

The example of the cheese wholesalers difficulties in maintaining a regular clientele also highlights the vagaries of Sofía's relationship with favored clients and/or suppliers. There appears to be a tradeoff between ease of access to goods and the degree of reliability of casera *ties. Sofía's experiences with cheese in 1984 echo those she had in 1980 when her* caseras *for pork also demanded more and more credit and became less and less reliable in paying their debts when there was a sudden flooding of the market with pork. Hyperinflation added to the attraction of paying one's debts as late as possible, since the value of the peso fell daily. Such situations of unpredictable supply and demand which undermined* casera *relationships became increasingly frequent as the economic crisis in Bolivia deepened. In Chapter 4 we already saw how hoarding preceded rumored devaluations and how each devaluation was followed by periods when few had the means to buy more than the basic necessities. In this chapter, Sofía described how rampant inflation in Bolivia increased the relative value of the Peruvian sol, encouraging both legal exports and smuggling from Bolivia to Peru, and leading to the drying up of Peruvian supplies of pork. Government regulation of basic foods could also affect the supply of pork.*

Sofía's description of marketing in the 1980s shows the astounding flexibility and persistence of Bolivian vendors and small-scale producers. Depending on the circumstances, they continued established practices under new conditions, adapted these practices to fit new situations, or invented new ways of dealing with adversity.

Marketing in the 1990s

By 1994, the Bolivian economy had improved markedly. Small- and medium-scale productive and commercial enterprises appeared to have multiplied and, since the late 1980s market vendors had access to bank credit for the first time. However, the apparent boom may be deceptive. While the restrictive monetary and other "structural adjustment" measures adopted by successive governments beginning in 1985 to reduce inflation appear to have had the desired result, they did not permit a rapid expansion of production. As a result, large numbers of former miners and factory workers tried their luck in small-scale productive, transportation, and commercial enterprises, thereby heightening competition and probably reducing profit margins. Meanwhile, economic conditions in rural areas have not improved, adding to the flow of immigrants to larger cities and further increasing competition (see Arze et al. 1993 and Chavez Alvarez and Toranzo Roca 1993).

The economic deterioration in rural communities is apparent from the decreasing size of rural fiestas. As Sofía explains:

[The fiesta in San Pedro has deteriorated]. Its not like it used to be. The young people are no longer as fun loving as they were before. So, I don't want to go any longer. I say, "Where is the fiesta as I knew it?" There used to be seven or eight dance groups. [Now there are only two or three.] They came with brass bands from La Paz. It could be that people don't have money. The bands now charge in dollars: some US$5,000 to $10,000.

When the band from Oruro plays for the vendors here, they charge US$12,000. Where are they going to get the money from? People don't have savings. Everything is purchased on credit and with loans. People buy cooking oil, sugar, noodles, shoes on credit. I still owe Bs 20 (US$4.21) for the shoes I am wearing, and they are already old. The stores earn double that way. A woman sold me a sweater for 90 (US$18.95) with Bs 10 (US$2.11) down. When I checked in the Calle Tumusla, they were selling them for 40 (US$8.42). So she made Bs 50 (US$10.53) on the deal. That's why I think that there are no fiestas in Compi. I don't want to go any more. Also most of the older people have died. The last time I went I didn't know anybody. I couldn't find anybody to talk to. I was sitting alone with my daughter and felt like a stranger. So I returned. Before, people were polite. They would invite you to sit and chat. But not this time. I said to myself that the fiesta had deteriorated and I left in disgust. Its not like it used to be. The twenty-year-olds don't know anybody. Those who reside in the city no longer go either. Since it took place in the middle of the week, they couldn't go. They only see one another when someone marries. Recently, I went to a wedding here in La Paz. There we all saw each other as though we were coming from another country. But not there. All that is lost. When I go there, I go to my house and don't visit anybody. The same thing goes for Chua Visalaya. Times pass. You too, Señor Hans. So you went to the fiesta and came back all sad. Remember how you even danced in the *morenada* dance? They have all died.

In order to offset the effects of increasing competition, lower profit margins (and, as we shall see in chapter 12, the flagging support of her lover for her daughter's education), Sofía expanded her economic ventures to include selling cooked food. In addition, she was, for the first time, relying on bank credit to finance her business. Since the late 1980s credit has been more readily available through non-governmental development organizations and through Banco Sol, a formally constituted banking institution. The bank has followed a system of lending to "solidarity groups" introduced by the nongovernmental organization PRODEM, *an affiliate of ACCION International of which the bank, the first of its kind in Latin America to specialize in financing microenterprises, is also an affiliate. By 1992, Banco Sol reached over 27,000 clients and in 1993 it made 106,886 loans averaging US$507 for a total of over $54 million. In 1994, expansion was still progressing at a rapid pace. The bank requires no collateral. Rather, an individual's credit-worthiness depends on the solidarity group's loan repayment record. Borrowers are also required to make deposits representing a percentage of the loan*

> *into a savings account at the bank. Banco Sol charges about 5 percent per month, while commercial interest rates are only 4 to 4.5 percent (see Simone Buechler 1993 and Women's World Banking 1994).*

I now sell [both] meat and food at my sales site. I sell meat early on Fridays. I start selling at 6:30. Then I take out the food at 7:30. I serve until eleven or until noon. On Saturdays I also take food out. I used to sell on Mondays too, but this street is no longer busy. There used to be more people. On Tuesdays and Wednesdays it's empty. On Mondays I go out and, since I am the coordinator of [a lending group] of Banco Sol, I have to collect money from the members who all sell around here. Sometimes they give me the money right away, but at other times they ask me to wait until two. If they pay me early I go to the bank to pay in the morning, if not, I go in the afternoon. Then I go inside to cook with my daughter. On Tuesday, I go and collect the money that the women who buy meat from me on credit owe me. Often, they don't pay me on Tuesday and so I have to go out again on Wednesday. I used to travel [to Jank'o Amaya] on Wednesday afternoon, but now I only leave on Thursday at 3 a.m. I take a bus to El Alto and from there another bus to Jank'o Amaya, where I arrive at six. This way I don't have to stay overnight at the fair as I used to. The bus fare costs Bs 4 and each bundle costs another Bs 3. Each bundle contains three pigs. Sometimes, when we don't have money, [the bus driver] gives us credit. This time I owe him Bs 25. I usually go to bed with the chickens, at eight in the evening, while Rocío continues doing her homework until one or two in the morning.

I have been taking out loans from Banco Sol for a while already. Before, it was called PRODEM. Six or seven years ago I found out that they were making loans from my niece Marcela, who sells in the Uruguay market. I wanted to obtain a loan because one needs a lot of capital to deal in pork. I used to get loans from other people at a high interest rate. For three days they would charge Bs 5 (US$1.05) for a Bs 100 (US$21.05) loan. Sometimes, they would not give me a loan at all. At other times, they would ask for pawns. Often, I would pawn my jewelry. I had a friend called Caita who worked with me in the union, and I tried to convince her to come with me. She didn't want to. So I asked a woman called Hortencia who has died since. She said, "Let's go." So we went to San Pedro. They told us to make a group of five persons and bring our identity cards and they asked us where our sales sites were and things like that. Five of us, all meat vendors (most of whom buy their meat here) took out loans of Bs 300 (US$63.15) each. We were supposed to pay them back in eight or twelve installments. But we did not succeed in paying on time. We were in arrears three times. Some women would get lost and would reappear only after two weeks. That destroyed the group. The lady [at the bank] refused to give us a second loan. We didn't take out any further loans for three years. But then PRODEM became larger. They opened a branch in the Calatayud. So I became interested once more. I told them I was coming for the first time. I formed another group with some of the same women. We took another training course. They told us that if one of us became ill, the others would have to help. That group was active for almost two years. It was called Inti Karka. We were each taking out Bs 1800 (US$378.95). They wouldn't increase the amount because we would fail to pay on time. Finally we quarreled among ourselves and I left the group. At that time, Nati was the coordinator. [When one of us couldn't pay], we would have to lend her money. I often had to come to Nati's assistance and lend her or some other woman money so that our group would get a star. A group earns a star when it never fails to make any of its payments on time. Such a group is acclaimed and receives the right to double the amount of its loans. But if the group pays late twice, it gets a square. If it has a more serious fault, it gets a black circle. Nati would often not gather the money until Tuesday, when the money was due on Monday. There was also a time when I couldn't pay and [the other women in the group] refused to lend me money but went to tattle on me. That's how the quarrels started. They [told] the young man at the bank that I was away on a trip and that they couldn't pay on time because of me and the young man would appear at my doorstep with the police. So I became angry and told the young man that I hadn't paid late and that I was retiring from the group. That group continues to this day. I told the young man that I would stop taking out loans for three months and then I would form another group. And I did form another group.

The new group I formed is called "Las Ch'axtitas." Doña Cloti gave it that name. She says that money was called *ch'axtitas* in earlier times. We were four members. But Doña Cloti became difficult. I had to come to her rescue again and again, every Tuesday. Then, once she let me wait for two whole weeks. I continued to lend her money, but then I went to the woman [at the bank] and we dropped her from the group. Now another woman has taken her place and she too fails to make her payments on time. I am going to drop her too. But [in general] this group is working well.

Not everybody does the same thing. I sell meat. Marcela sells innards. Juana sells mantas. Alicia doesn't have a sales site. She buys the heads of animals. But people have to be responsible. If a member isn't responsible then the group suffers. I am taking out larger loans than the other group members. I am taking out three thousand (US$631.58). They discount three hundred (US$63.16). Of that, 150 (US$31.58) goes into a savings account. The rest is for papers and things. I can take out more because I have more seniority. Perhaps its also because of the house. At any rate, they give me more. The people with whom I formed the group say that I should be the coordinator. They don't want anybody else to do it. So I have been coordinating the group from the start. Marcela is taking out fifteen hundred US$315.79), Alicia, one thousand (US$210.53) and Juana six hundred (US$126.32).

I use the money to travel for meat. However, sometimes, when sales are bad, I lose part of my capital. When that happens, I have to borrow some money or sell something I own to make the payment. When I have finished paying off the loan, I have to wait for another loan to come through. Then I start travelling again.

I also get loans from Procredito. Don't tell Banco Sol. They control such things and [if they see that a client is also borrowing from another bank] they refuse to give another loan. They told me that one didn't have to form groups at Procredito and so I went. A señorita asked me all sorts of questions about whether I had a fixed sales site, whether I had gotten loans elsewhere and why I had stopped going there. She asked me for my address and she told me that the analyst would pay a visit. Some had told me that they often didn't come and that one had to remind them. But I was lucky. I made the request on Friday and [a young man] came to see me on Monday.

He was very nice. He asked me whether that was my own sales site and the woman who sells coffee across the street confirmed it. Then he asked me to see the house. Once inside, he asked me how many rooms I had, with whom I lived, whether Rocío's father gave me any money, how much I had to pay for Rocío's school, and with how much capital I was working. I told him the truth. Then he asked me what else I owned. I told him that I had a plot of land in Compi. Then he asked me what objects of value I had. I named the television set, the cooking range, the gas tank, the radio, the blender, a typewriter. I told him that was all I had. He didn't want to know about jewelry. He also asked whether I owed money to any bank and I said that I didn't.

He told me to wait for a week and then to phone him. I phoned again and again. First he told me that the computer was not working, then that they were just having a meeting about my case. Finally I told him to tell me one way or another and he said that there was going to be a loan. So I went and took out five hundred (US$105.26). Then he doubled it to one thousand (US$210.53) and finally further increased the amount to fifteen hundred (US$315.79).

I was going to get three thousand (US$631.56) the next time but then they changed the young man and a young woman, Patricia, took his place. She told me that I was no longer on the list of clients and that she had to come to look at the house once more. She asked me whether I had bought something more. I answered that how could I have purchased anything with life as difficult as it was. I was just earning enough to eat. The señorita said that I had to buy something. I answered that that was impossible, so they reduced the loan amount to six hundred (US$126.32). They slowly upped it again and now I am taking out fifteen hundred (US$315.79).

They tell us to buy things. A person who has a telephone can take out more.[18] [In contrast] they never ask about things like that at Banco Sol. I paid late ten times recently and the señorita asked me why I had failed. I answered that February and March had been bad months. "I know that all your clients have told you that sales were down." [It was true]. There were no sales at all. It seemed as though money had simply vanished. I bought pork and lost half of the capital every week. That's why my business was failing. So, after I repaid the loan, I stopped for two months. But now I have taken out a new loan.

Oh, and there is something else. Before, I could take out a loan just like that but this Patricia asked me to come up with a guarantor. She told me that I was a single mother. I told her that my daughter could act as a guarantor, but she said that she was under age. So now [my niece] Marcela is the guarantor. I have to take her along every time I take out a loan. It I had a husband, he would act as a guarantor.

The interest rate is lower than that of Banco Sol. At first it was 2 percent, then 3 percent and now it's 4 percent per month. It's really cheap. And they only discount Bs 10 from 1000. For four months I pay Bs 140 (US$29.47) in interest, that's all. In the Banco Sol it's more expensive. Everybody says that its high. I can't figure it out and they don't tell me, but one of my friends says that it comes to 15 percent a month. Now I have to deposit eighteen installments of Bs 168.

The problem is that in this Procredito I can't take out larger loans because I don't have objects of value. If I had such things as a refrigerator, a video recorder, or a large radio I would take out loans of five thousand or ten thousand (US$1052.63 or US$2105.26). People are taking out loans like that. In that case, I would no longer take out loans at Banco Sol. But there, if we pay back on time, they double the size of the loan and they never ask for guarantees. That's why I continue to take out loans there.

Now I have been in arrears twice at Banco Sol. I was taking out three thousand (US$631.58) and they would have doubled the amount. But now they will only give us the same amount. I would have liked to take out at least Bs 10,000 (US$2105.26) for Christmas. I will have to make every possible effort not to be in arrears during the next loan period. One of the arrears came because I went to Compi for the fiesta of Saint Peter. And the other was because I took a trip somewhere and left the money for someone else to pay and she failed to deposit it on the day it was due.

The loans have permitted me to bring more meat. I don't have to bother anyone for loans. Banco Sol and Procredito are "my husband." We have a relationship of trust. I also buy things for Rocío with the money or I buy a bag of sugar. The rest I use as capital. That's why Rocío helps me make the payments.

I always had a notebook where I note down how many kilos of meat I bring and how much I pay for it. If one kilo of it spoils I can figure out how much I lost. For example, I recently lost Bs 20 (US$4.21) from one pig. [After I started to take out loans] I became more careful about giving credit to women who might cheat me. I have to deal only with women who are reliable because I have to deposit the earnings in the bank. Before, I did give credit. For example there was a woman, Catalina Miranda, who died owing me Bs 1800 (US$378.95). She would stay at home for long periods and I would try to find her there. Then one day I found out that she had killed herself with a knife. She owed money to everybody. Some say that her husband killed her. . . . I have to take great care because the money I handle doesn't belong to me. I no longer give credit easily. I prefer to sell for cash even if I have to take a loss. I have to measure my expenditures. Before, when I had money I would go out to eat. I have to tighten my belt because the money belongs to the people. When I earn a lot, I tell Rocío, "let's buy this or that." When I don't, I tell her, "no, we have to go without. I have to make a deposit on Monday." She doesn't say anything.

Now I bring eight or nine pigs. I began to sell food since 1988 after my mother died. I have to pay back loans in two places. Also, I have more confidence in cooked food than in selling pork. I know that I will earn selling food. I sell the small pigs without cutting them up. The large ones, I sell per kilo. People don't buy entire large pigs any longer. Everybody buys by weight. The men who bring me the pigs also all have their own scales now. One can't cheat them any longer. Instead, they cheat us with their scales. I have two scales, one that is accurate and the other that indicates too little. When I use the latter, they protest and take out their own scale. So I buy from the owners of the pigs. And the customers ask for a pig of so and so many kilos. They buy per kilo.

For Christmas I want to take out a larger loan because on December 29th and 30th sales are better. Even poor people eat pork that day. We have to pay our *caseros* a week in advance to secure meat. At that time we go to their communities of origin and pick up the meat going from house to house. We earn some two thousand or three thousand (US$421.05 or US$631.58). While I sell meat, Rocío sells cooked food.

In the future, I would like to work with only one bank rather than with two. Also I would like to rent a sales site and sell wedding gifts and things like that on weekends opposite the fiesta hall. Another plan would be to sell the house and open a store. I would work only with Procredito. That bank is growing as much as Banco Sol. They make a lot of adds on television that if you have jewels they will give you low interest loans on the spot. [If we sell this house and I buy one of my own], I would have the house as collateral. However, I won't give up selling food. I will always come here to sell cooked food. I will also continue selling meat. After all, its only one day a week.

We don't make any profit. We just earn enough to eat and for the bank. I don't count on making a lot of money. If I had been earning, I would have a lot of things. Rocío has all sorts of dreams. She would like us to have a living room, a video recorder and all sorts of other things. But I don't know where to get the money for things like that. With the present government, life is more difficult. There is no work. So those who don't have work have all gone into commerce. There are more men now selling things from carts or small cars. They compete with us. Most sell fruit. But there are also butchers who come. There is a lot of competition in everything. For six or seven years I have had a sales site in the Garita for Christmas for a week. I got the site when I was union leader and I have kept it since then. I pay fees to the municipality for it. I sell crèche figures made out of gypsum. There, competition is also strong. I still have a lot of merchandise from last year. People who don't have any sales site come and sell on the side walk. I have another site, that I also obtained when I was secretary-general where I sell masks and things like that before Carnival. But there too there is a lot competition, especially from men who carry the things around with them. There are more vendors than consumers. If we get stuck with too much merchandise we have to sell at cost. So there is no profit. I sell things that others don't sell because I have been working for the last four years with a man from Tembladerani whose figures are very pretty. He makes new kinds of figures every year. So my things are unique. I have to go early and leave him an advance because his wife mostly sells his goods in Santa Cruz. In addition, I have gone to the Feria de Alasita in January and saw some small pretty things. So I have asked for the address and have made orders for next Christmas. In this way, I will vary the goods I sell even more. People like small, fine and novel things to add to the crèche each year. If I sell the same goods every year, no one will come to buy. The same thing is true for Carnival. [I don't sell miniatures in the Alasita fair]. If I go to sell during Alasita, I will go with food.

[Even though we work with more capital now], earnings haven't changed. From meat one earns twenty centavos (US$.04) per kilo. Before, one earned more. One hundred kilos cost 700 (US$147.37) and I sell them for 720 (US$151.58) earning 20 (US$4.21). But from that I have to pay Bs 8 (US$1.68) for my fare and then I have to pay for the transportation of the meat. So there is nothing. That's why I don't want to leave food. The food is what sustains me. From a pig that weighs ten kilos I get thirty-five servings. At Bs 5 (US$1.05) per plate, I get 175 (US$36.84). My costs are say Bs 70 (US$14.74) for the meat, 20 (US$4.21) for the *chuño* and the corn, 5 (US$1.05) for the *ají*, let's say 100 (US$21.05) all in all. That leaves me with 75 (US$15.79). I earn most from fricassee. I have prepared all sorts of dishes, and have decided that fricassee is the most lucrative. I also earn well from a mixed *saxta* (a hot dish). I net fifty (US$10.53). In contrast, if I cook tongue, I only earn Bs 20 or 15 (US$4.21 or US$3.16). The people who buy the food are passers by. At first I served the vendors who sell in the street. My daughter used to go from sales site to sales site to offer the food. But then they would eat and wouldn't pay. So she refuses to continue doing that. Now we attract people who come by by giving generous servings. Before, I would sell the food on credit and they owed me a lot of money. I no longer do that. Now everybody buys on credit. Everybody from the Alto on down is getting credit from the Banco Sol. Even the women who sell drinks from a pail and the unemployed men who sell from their carts take out loans. These days, there is a lot of unemployment so they get loans and work with them.[19]

6

THE *Supernatural as a Tool of Control*

Sofía often resorts to magic in order to improve her luck. She herself has considerable expertise in magical practices. and she regularly consults a variety of experts in various forms of magic to further her business and to thwart her enemies, whom she suspects of engaging in sorcery to impair her business success. Various talismans protect her La Paz door from intruders.

Because I am alone and have so many enemies, I don't want them (i.e., their spirits) to enter. It is as though [these things] were acting as guards. That's why the knife is there. [It signifies] that I am standing there ready with a knife. That's why nothing happens to me. Then I have palm fronds, both on this door and on the other one.

Sofía also owns several gypsum figures she has purchased at the annual Alasita fair, a fair where miniatures of desired objects and goods are sold, representing market vendors selling the goods she has specialized in at various periods during her life:

First, when I was selling in the Rodriguez market, I used to sell tomatoes, peas, broadbeans, corn, and onions. So I bought this [figure] thinking that I was going to stick to vegetables. Then, I advanced to buying eggs in Jank'o Amaya, so I bought this one [representing a woman selling eggs]. Finally, I moved to the Incachaca and began selling pork, and I bought this one [representing a pork butcher]. I have continued with the

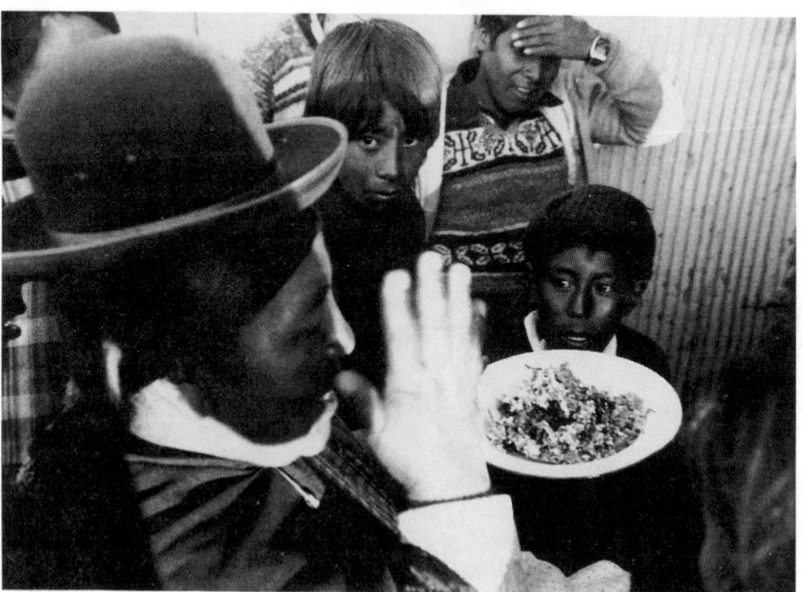

Sofía divining from the configuration of molten lead (El Alto 1981)

occupation of selling pork. One buys the figures on the 24th of January, in the fair of Alasita. For example, if you want to become a physician or a mechanic, there are figures [for that too]. One has to buy them with a lot of faith. So, when I had the desire to sell pork, I bought one of these [gypsum figures] because I had faith in them and now I am a pork vendor. Every year during Carnival one has to give them libations, throw confetti and paper streamers over them, and put them [in a prominent place]. I continue with all my three activities. Sometimes I bring eggs and cheese; when my fields produce in the country, I bring peas and beans; and at the same time I sell pork. Since I engage in these three activities, I have these [three figures]. Other women, engaging in other work, have corresponding figures. I have seen [figures representing] *empanada* (meat turnover), sausage and french fry, soft drink, and vegetable vendors, as well as beef butchers. That's about it.

In addition to applying her own knowledge of magical techniques, Sofía relies heavily on a variety of magical practitioners to help her in her commercial ven-

tures. In this, she follows her mother's footsteps, often consulting the same specialists as her mother.

As far as business is concerned, I always consult them when sales are bad. That means that I have been bewitched. So I have to go to someone. In particular, I go to Sra. Nieves. She tells my fortune from [tarot] cards.[1] She tells me that I have been bewitched; that my friends who sell next to me have taken business away from me. Then she tells me that she will smoke some cigarettes for me. She smokes four cigarettes for me and she charges twenty pesos (US$1). She tells me that now I will be able to sell again. She instructs me to sprinkle a little bit of the ashes of the cigarettes that she has smoked. I go off and sprinkle some on my produce and I always sell again. . . . Well, not for the whole year. After two or three weeks I go and see her again. Sometimes, after looking at the cards, she tells me that she can do nothing for me. She only tells the fortune from cards and smokes. [If she can't help me] she tells me to go to someone else.

For those occasions [when further measures are in order], we have two persons we go to: my mother's cousin, Isidro Parra, to whom my mother has gone for many years, and Manuel Llave, whom I know.[2] He is the one who has three skulls. I ask Sra. Nieves to read in the cards whom I should consult.

In 1988, Sofía elaborated on the nature and background of the various types of magicians she has consulted:

There are two types of *yatiris*: those who have made a pact with the devil and engage in black magic, and those who believe in God and who were either struck by lightning or have had twins. We go to the *yatiris* who, like Juan, have had twins or were struck by lightning.

[The *yatiris* who have a pact with the devil] speak to the devil and have more power than Juan does. Those *yatiris* have the power to take a person's life through witchcraft. They say when a person will die and the person dies on that day.

[There are both men and women *yatiris*]. For example, Rosita, the woman who died recently, had a pact with the souls of the cemetery. She would always pray to them. She would call them, saying, "Female and male." And she would libate in their name and she would say that such and such things would happen. And they always did happen.

I became acquainted with Juan because he sold meat to me. Although we are not related, he calls me "sister." He brought meat and I bought from him and so we got to know each other. For a long time, I didn't know that he was also a musician. When I became a market leader at the rural fair for the second time and had to sponsor and organize the market fiesta, I told him that I needed a musician. Then he told me that he was a musician himself, and he came to play in Jank'o Amaya.

[There is no problem engaging in other things at the same time as being a *yatiri*.] Juan helps himself that way. He would not have enough work as a magician. He only does it for persons he knows because he is doing it in secret. The people of Jank'o Amaya don't know that he is a magician. He is afraid that if they found out they might become envious because he is young. He says, "I don't want them to know, only my close relatives know about it." Most of the time he seeks work as a musician and he butchers meat. To ask for permission to become a curer, he went to the Jipi (a prominent mountain behind Compi). He had acted as a magician for many years before he told me about it. He does go to other communities to cure, but he doesn't like to do it [in his home community].

I only found out this year (1988) that he was a curer. His wife told me. She noticed that I was despondent. So I told her about my troubles with my lover, René, and with my business. I said, "I am close to financial ruin. I am becoming more and more indebted and I have had to pawn my valuables. I am unable to extricate myself. I am paying interest in U.S. dollars and can't keep up the payments." She told me, "My husband is a curer. Don't tell anyone. He will perform magic for you as though you were a sister, because you are a good person. He will prepare a *mesa* (burnt offering) for you." So Juan came here and read my fortune in the coca. And what he divined about my troubles and about my past was all true.

There are [other curers in Jank'o Amaya]. Another one, called Simon, is almost his age too. They do not recognize one another as curers. Juan is a magician because he has twins, the other because his son was struck by lightning. They are not of the same type.

Juan's wife, Satuca, tells me that he never learned from anyone. She had twins, a girl and a boy. Both are living. They are called Emilio and Emiliana. They are 18 years old. The girl lives in El Alto, and the boy is doing his military service in Tarija. When they had the twins, Juan was inducted into the army in Tiquina as a musician. Satuca didn't want Juan to go, because she thought that soldiers were philanderers and he might abandon her for another woman. So she had him quit the navy in Tiquina. However, Juan continued to play in brass bands, and he would sometimes lose control over himself and say crazy things. Sometimes she had to tie him up because he was screaming. She wondered what was

Juan, the magician, burning incense during a magical séance for Sofío and Rocío (Llamacachi 1988)

happening to him. This happened even when he wasn't drunk. Also, sometimes their animals would die for no apparent reason. So, Satuca went to her uncle who is a magician. He told her that it was because they had twins and that the Lord had chosen him to become a curer. He said, "If you don't cure him, your Juan is going to go mad." Juan didn't want to hear anything about that. He refused even to read the coca leaves. But then another cow died. So Satuca told him, "You must do it. Even if you only do it for our relatives. No one needs to know about it." They pleaded and pleaded with Juan until he gave in. The uncle took him to the mountain himself, so that he could receive permission [to become a magician]. From then on he has been able to divine. He sees things directly and even catches thieves.

It's not necessary [to learn much]. Even I look at the coca to see how my luck is going to be. Juan only had to go up to the mountain to ask to be ordained, just like priests are ordained.

In 1975, Sofía continued her story about consulting magicians.

If Sra. Nieves divines that I should go to Isidro, then he is the one who does it for me. He asks me to bring a bag with a *dulce mesa* (sweet *mesa*), wine, tufts of colored llama wool, llama fat, and *wira qua* and he prepares (the offering) for me. First he reads my fortune in the coca leaves. He always says that someone is jealous. Then he divines what mountain he should (take the offering to)—either Jipi or Concachi (two mountains near Llamacachi). If he says Concachi, he has to bring it there. Then only does he prepare the *mesa* on a white piece of paper. He calls all my *caseras* and says, "Let Sofía sell. Let her sell. Let no one envy her." He says this while he is cutting up the fat into small pieces "naming" each item.[3]

There are two little [tablets] that form part of the *mesa*, with little figures [molded] on them. There have to be two of them. Sometimes, they turn out to be a little car, the Virgin Mary, or a snake. There are all sorts of figures that can turn up. Isidro removes these and examines them. That time, I had drawn [a tablet with] a truck, so he said that, in the future, I would own a truck. The other had the figure of the Virgin, and he said, "All your fortune is fine and you will prosper." Then there are two sweets in the shape of bottles. He says that they represent beer. He names things as he proceeds.

[The "beer" is] for the *achachilas*. Isidro places them [on the offering] and divines from the coca leaves once more. He tells me that my luck is good in this or that respect.[4] After he has finished preparing the mesa, he hands me the wine and I have to name the street where I sell and my clients, while I sprinkle the wine [over the *mesa*]. I name them drop by drop. Then he hands me the cigarette and again tells it to indicate my fortune. My mother follows suit. When everything is properly named, he wraps [the *mesa* with some of the colored wool and places it on a plate. Then he tells me to go outside at midnight to raise the incense burner [to the Holy Trinity]. I go out with my mother. We do this to ask for pardon from the Lord. Isidro lights the incense and has us kneel on the ground and he [holds it up] as though he were offering it to the Lord. He asks the Lord to give us our daily bread and to forgive us our trespasses and asks Him to [protect] us from evil persons. Then, he tells us to ask for pardon from one another. We give him a hug [too], and we go back into the house. After that, he requests some [dry] cow's dung as fuel [to burn the offering], half a bottle of alcohol and matches, and he goes off with that. The white llama wool yarn, [he also uses], is for good luck.[5] He calls the *coraje* and the *ánimo* and "ties" them [to me] with it. He also calls all my *caseras* and ties them too. He gives me the yarn and I carry it in my bag. Then he goes to Concachi (Mountain) and burns the thing up there. It isn't big, its just a small [offering].

Isidro [also] tells us to dream. If we climb in our dreams that night, that means [the magic] has worked. If we don't climb up, then it has not worked. If I climb carrying potatoes, my mother says that our luck will be good. That we will earn well. From that day on, I sell a lot. My *caseras* seek me out. I don't even have to call out [to potential customers]. They come on their own.

I make [an offering] on New Year's day for the entire year and once in August, also for the whole year, and I also go whenever sales are bad. I always sell well as a result. I believe in it. I can't deny it, I do. Even my mother tells me, "If you believe in it, you must believe in it until you die." Quite frankly, my mother taught me to believe in it. I have faith in it, and it gives me hope. What can I say? When I don't sell—when I get stuck with my produce and have to run around like mad—it means that someone has done me in.

Sometimes I dream [about the reason why my luck is failing]. This *brujo*, Isidro, has told me that I should dream. When I see chickens in my dreams, it means witchcraft. If I handle guinea pigs, it also means witchcraft. Or, I might dream that my sister-in-law or someone else offers me a dish of food or invites me to eat. That too means witchcraft. If I descend in my dreams, it means perdition. The same is true if I go to bed and go to sleep in my dreams. If I dream that I am going to the bathroom and wet the bed, that is bad. It means that I will lose all my money. When I fall in my dreams or dirty myself with excrement, that [also] means perdition. I lose something then, or break the eggs I am carrying. That's how it works. It never fails. The *brujo* instructs me to tell my dreams to my mother right after I wake up, because she is a widow and can [therefore] counteract [the impending misfortune].[6] So, when I get up, I tell my mother what I have dreamt. My mother tells me to take care. When I don't tell her, because I am worrying [too much], then I am sure to break one hundred or two hundred eggs. When I have dreams like that, I have to go to the magician right away and tell him what I have dreamt, and he tells me that we have to [make an offering] immediately.

[He prepares the offering in the usual manner]. He always names one or two things so that nothing happens to me on the road and don't become involved in a truck accident. And up till now, nothing has happened to me on my trips. In addition, following his counsel, I carry a tiny little bottle of alcohol, and he tells me to sprinkle some alcohol surreptitiously on my merchandise in the name of Pachamama and the Tíos,[7] so that they will give me [money]. As you know, they say money is a thing of the Tíos. So I name them. And I say, "Pachamama, I am giving you this small [offering of] alcohol so that I will sell today and that all my *caseras* come to me. And if envious persons have done something to me, or someone who sits next to me has bewitched me, then you, Pachamama, must take charge of the matter." I make a cross with [the alcohol] (*con un* (*sic*) *cruz pongo*). I sprinkle it on the floor and then I sit and begin to sell. You see, I reckon that if, after that, the persons next to me don't sell, it means that they must have [tried to] do something to me.[8] The *brujo* tells me to do the same thing, when I am going to the countryside to buy eggs together with Marcela and one other woman. So, in order to do it, I have to leave at four in the morning to get to Jank'o Amaya at five before the others get there. I go with my mother. [I invoke Pachamama], "Either Marcela or the other person who sits next to me has done something to me, Pachamama, you must deal with the matter." And, [sure enough], either Marcela or the woman who sits on the other side can't obtain eggs that day, and I get them all. When that occurs, my mother tells me that Marcela must have done something to bewitch me. When I carry the cigarette [ashes] with me, Marcela is incapable of buying while I can buy more than I need; but when I forget to bring them along, I only succeed in buying two or three. That's how it is. I do all this following the advice of the *brujo*. I used not to be able to tell who had cast a spell on me, but thanks to the *brujo*'s advice, I am now able to tell that they have bewitched me. When I can't sell, or I become sick, or don't earn well, or my earnings disappear, or people scold me without cause, I realize that someone has bewitched me. That's when I dream about chickens and guinea pigs, or about food. I see chickens in the room. Then, I say that it must be witchcraft—that someone has cast a spell on me. Then, my mother will wonder who it might be. I have to force myself to dream. I want to know exactly what is going on. In my dreams, either Elena or the person who sells next to me invites me to eat a plate of food—something delicious to eat. If I eat it, it means that the witchcraft has already had its effect; if I refuse to eat, it means that it hasn't affected me yet. For example, once I quarreled with my sister-in-law, Elena. I don't remember what we quarreled about, but we didn't speak to each other for almost three months. Oh, it was about the sales site in the Avenida Montes [when I was selling onions there]. Elena went away crying and told me, "Fine. I hope that your sales site will serve you well," [meaning just the opposite]. [For a while], I continued to sell normally. But suddenly bad luck struck. I no longer was able to sell. My clients refused to buy from me, and the money that I had, that is, my capital, vanished. I ended up being in debt. I wondered what was happening to me. I hadn't thought about it, but, in my dreams, I went to visit Elena in Río Seco. In my dream, we went to the house next door where a *de vestido* woman served me some very good food, which I ate. When I woke up I knew that Elena had bewitched me.

Following my mother's advice, I went to see Sra. Nieves. Sra. Nieves told me that Elena had bewitched me out of anger. She willed my ruin. Elena's *bruja* is a woman. Sra. Nieves asked me, "Didn't you dream about a woman?" "Yes," I answered. "Well, it's a woman who did it," she said. I didn't believe her. [So I asked my friends about it]. Everybody has friends who can give advice. One of my friends—she is *de pollera*—asked me why I looked so sad. I answered, "I don't have any money. I even had to pawn my jewelry. I don't know what's happening to me." My friend said, "Well, let's go to the Señor de la Sentencia. Perhaps something has happened to you—perhaps someone is jealous and has bewitched you."

[The Señor de la Sentencia is] in Villa Armonía. One has to go there on Fridays. Lot's of people go there on Fridays. Why don't you go there once? Some people even go there barefooted. *De vestido* women go too. It's a church of the Señor de la Sentencia, who is thought to do miracles. So I went there one Friday. There were lots of *brujos* and *brujas* there, both *de vestido* and *de pollera*. They were doing their thing, burning incense. People were standing in line for them to raise their incense burners [on their behalf]. I didn't know whom to ask, so I chose a young, tall and hefty *bruja* who was *de pollera*. I bought a peso's worth of incense and another of copal and approached her. She asked, "Is it for your fortune?" I didn't tell her anything. I didn't tell her what had happened to me, nor what I had done, or even why I had come. I just said that it was for my luck, nothing more. I knelt down and she asked my name, whether I was married or single, where I sold—I said that I sold in the Avenida Montes—my mother and my father's name, and that's all. She began to raise the incense burner, looking intently at the smoke and praying all the while. Suddenly she said, "Ah, poor thing. With whom did you quarrel at your sales site? You quarreled at your sales site, and the woman you quarreled with has bewitched you so that all this would befall you (*para que andes así*). That woman lives in your house. She is a relative of yours." I told her that she was my sister-in-law and she replied, "Her foot is hurting her." It was true. Her foot is always hurting her. She also told me that my father would be all right and that I should do something quickly [to thwart the witchcraft]. I believed her and I consulted Isidro and he did it for me.

They always blame a person [for bad luck in selling]. We know that there are days when there are no sales. [That is normal]. But it has happened to me that my sales were bad on the first and fifteenth of every month. Everybody else would sell all their wares and I was the only one who got stuck with my produce. The evidence was clear. My *caseras* would walk by and I would call out, "*Casera*!" but they would walk right past and go to the other vendors. I would watch with amazement as they would buy from another person. Then, other *caseras* would come and they would look straight at me, but they too would buy from my neighbors. Then, when I asked them why they hadn't bought from me, they would say that they had[n't] seen me. They would act strangely. That's how I became aware of the fact that something [bad] was happening to me. Normally, my *caseras* make a beeline towards me when they see me from afar and say, "*Caserita*, I have come." But [on those days], they would pass by and buy from others. The same thing happened when I bought eggs. For that, I have my *caseras* too. When I would say, "*Casera*, sell some to me," they would refuse and go to the next egg dealer. That way I know that that dealer has taken my sales away from me. On the other hand, if sales are simply bad that day, things don't happen that way. [No one sells.]

Dreaming

We dream more [when we are bewitched]. We wet the bed in our dreams and we become covered with mud. The *brujo* I have in Alto Chijini, the one who has the skulls, told me that I should continue to dream, because I do in fact dream [about things like that]. [If something good happens in my dreams] I am not supposed to tell anyone, because if I do, it will not come to pass. He tells me that God has given me the gift of being able to see things that will happen in the future in my dreams. I believe in it, because when I dream, *trán*, it happens.

[For example], before my father died, I dreamt that I lost my shoes and the sun suddenly went down, it became dark and I went away crying. I dreamt that it was San Pedro (the major fiesta in Compi/Llamacachi) and I wanted to dance and I had to dance without shoes. I wondered what I should do. I was afraid that people would criticize me. So, holding some potatoes in my apron, I went to the Compi cemetery crying bitterly. Then, I told my mother what I had dreamt and wondered what it could be about. A week later, my father died, and I went to the cemetery crying, just as I had in my dream. See? I firmly believe in all this.

Now, if something is going to happen, or has already happened, I will see it [in my dreams]. For example, a month ago I encountered my sister-in-law, Ruth, in the street in a dream. She was wearing her best clothes. In my dream, I asked her why she was angry at me, even though we hadn't had a quarrel. She excused herself (*sic*) and laughed at me. We fought and I tore a large patch of her hair out. [The next morning], I told my mother what I had dreamt and remarked that I was afraid that Ruth would get sick or something would happen to her. Why was she talking to me like that [in my dream]? And why was she wearing her best clothes? Wearing nice clothes means illness, Señor. So, I said [to my mother], "I know what's going to happen. I tore hair out. You know, mother, that when one does that, that means that a person will lose his or her honor." She told me that I was a fool. But less than two weeks later, I learned that Ruth had been admitted to the Hospital Obrero. Apparently she was pregnant by this young man she had met and had taken something to abort the child. As a result, she had hemorrhaged so badly that blood was running out like water from a faucet. She couldn't even speak any longer. For a while, she was between life and death. I was at the fiesta of San Pedro [in Compi], and I learned about it only upon my return. When I went back to Llamacachi, I told my mother that my dream had come true. "Now Ruth has lost face because I have taken her honor from her. I knew what she had been up to." As far as we are concerned, she has lost face entirely. As you can see, what I dream actually comes true (*por eso me sueño efectivamente*).

Some time ago, I saw my brother Moises sleeping in bed in my dreams. The next day, I asked my sister-in-law whether my brother was all right. "Yes, he is," she answered. "He is working." "Does my brother have money, or doesn't he have any?" I persisted. It turned out that he had not been able to draw his salary, poor thing. I told him that I already knew because I had seen him asleep in my dreams which meant that he didn't have any money. See? I already knew. Now, when someone is going to die, my dreams say so directly. Then, a truck appears [in my dreams], or a car, or a bus. I tell my mother, "Mamita, in this community someone will die." "Why?" she will ask. "It's going to be a woman," I continue. [Once], I dreamt that a truck was coming from over there and a small car from the direction of Copacabana. The little car stopped at the bridge [near our house], while the truck entered the soccer field and stopped there. It was a large truck, like an International. It was an International, while the little car was a little black taxi. And I told my mother, "In Visalaya a young fat man will die and then a small old woman will die soon after." I know that a man called Kamiri from Visalaya died. He was well and he died all of a sudden from the *qarisiri*.[9] But mark my words, Señor Hans, one of the female teachers will die too or perhaps one of the men from the construction crew [that is working on the road], because I recently dreamt that a tree fell there, and when a tree falls, that also means that someone will die.

[The trucks and cars are coffins]. One has to distinguish them according to size, because there are all sorts of cars. A very small car represents an infant. A woman is always [represented by] a little car, while trucks and buses are always men. For example, before Doña Aida came to live in our house, I dreamt that I was in my little room and a very long bus came out of the storage room under my room. It was light blue and brand new. New means that a young person will die. Well, a brand new bus came out. Imagine that! Through that narrow passageway! There were passengers in it and I waved it goodbye from above here. The next day I said to myself, "That was a coffin. Who is going to die? It's a tall person and young." So I went to my renter Alberto, who is widowed. He lives [in the room] facing the street. I said, "Alberto, are you ready for this?" He already knows that when I dream that something bad will happen, I have to tell him. "What is it, what is it," he asked. "Tell me." He quickly took out some coca and began to chew it. I told him my dream. "It's a coffin. And they will take it out of there. But who can it be? There is no one here who is young and tall. Neither Pedro nor Teodoro are tall." "Well, let it be for nought," he proclaimed. He chewed his coca and spat the liquid into a nightpot, saying, "Let it be for nought, let it be for nought. Let it be in vain." And nothing happened. But if I hadn't told him my dream, something would have happened. Two months later, I rented that room to Doña Aida. Doña Aida asked me to give her electricity, but I am not in charge of the electricity, Pedro is. He has even taken it away from me and Moisés connected me [to his meter]. I said that I would get her room connected, or perhaps we could get ourselves a line of our own, since I did have an identity card. Aida agreed. They said that we could get connected in May. That was this year (1975). The months passed and the woman was always entering the room with her little candle which she often lost. Perhaps you have seen a tall young man, who recently got married. That's Doña Aida's son. Well, one night, the Señora told her son, who at the time was not yet married, to go to sleep. It was just a month before the wedding. The young man entered the room and turned on his tape recorder. Then the stupid man lit a candle on a little plastic plate and placed it on top of the tape recorder. He must have been listening to a tape while he was eating and he must have fallen asleep without blowing out the candle. It was 10:30 or later. When I climbed the steps to my room I saw that the room was brightly lit, but I didn't realize what was happening. I closed the door and went to sleep. All of a sudden I heard Pedro's son, José, who lives in the room next to mine cry "Papi, papi." I jumped out of bed while Pedro ran down the steps like crazy. He knocked on the door and shouted, "Young man, young man, open the door. Fire, fire!" The room was on fire, and the young man was asleep. He would have died from the smoke. So, that was what the dream had been about—the dream [whose prediction] had been averted. I told Doña Aida that I had dreamt that a large new bus came out of her room. "That long bus was your son. He was saved." She was so happy that she took the day off and drank. She said, "Sofía, if you hadn't countered the dream, I think that my son would have died." See? My dreams almost always come true (*casi fijo me sueño*).

Now, someone is going to die in my family. Perhaps it will be my brother, Pedro, or someone else. You will remember [what I said]. I will write you a letter that someone has died in my family. I am dreaming again, [this time] that I am pulling out all my teeth. I have had that dream three times already. This death will be through treason, because, in my dreams, I look at myself in the mirror, which means treason, and it will come out of the blue. I ask my mother, "Who could it be?" Sometimes I also look at my mother in my dream. So I wonder whether my mother will die. That's why this *brujo*, Manuel Llave, tells me to continue dreaming. He told me to keep it a secret. He tells me that they will cease to work if I tell about my dreams. So our Lord has chosen me that I should dream and that I should know what will happen through my dreams.

[Another way of divining is with tarot cards]. I had a friend. Well, she was not really a friend . . . I was selling in the Avendia Montes two years ago (in 1973) and was very sad because my father had died and my mother and I were all alone. I felt that I didn't have any luck anymore and was very preoccupied. Then, a blonde and blue eyed *de vestido* woman approached me and asked me whether I wanted her to read my palms. I agreed right away. I am not afraid of those things. However, I did tell her not to tell me about my death. I told her to hide that. So the woman sat down beside me. It turned out that she was from La Paz. She asked me to stretch out my hand and she began to pray the Lord's Prayer and invoked the name of the Señor de la Sentencia and Santa Elenita. Then she began reading my palm. She said that I was hard-working and single. And she was right. She also told me that I had a boyfriend with whom I had not spoken for seven years and that now I had another one. Again, she spoke the truth. Then, she told me that that young man was good, but that he had disappeared and that I was sad because of that. "But, be careful, he is spying on you in secret. He wants to know what kind of a woman you are. He wants to catch you. But he is the jealous type. He is going to treat you harshly (*de punta*). There is also another man who is watching you in secret. People are jealous of you because you sell well. Your mother is fine." She told me all those things, and they were all true. I paid her, and, since I was curious, I asked her if I could talk to her in private at her home. She gave me the address—it turned out that she lived in Villa San Antonio—and she told me that she knew how to cure people and do "little jobs" (*trabajitos*). ["Little jobs"] mean witchcraft. I don't know how she does it, but she uses dolls. I didn't have her do any of that.

I went to her home. She lived with a young daughter. She told me that she knew how to read the coca leaves and so I told her about my business activities and then about my mother. She told me that everything was fine, but that I should let her cure me. I [did want] to have myself cured of all maledictions. [But] when I asked her how much that would cost, she told me 120 pesos (U. S. $6). In addition, I would have to provide all the necessary items. So I didn't have her do it. I told myself, "Why should I?"

People also pray to the Saints. They ask Santa Elena to help with her three nails. She is a virgin who is in the Santo Domingo church. You should go and see her. She is a young virgin and she holds three nails in her hand. They say that she is especially good for matters concerning love. Nieves prays to Santa Elenita and also to Saint Anthony, the saint for lost things and for finding a mate.

When Nieves was single, she says that neither her father nor her mother were *brujos*. She says that after her divorce she had to support her mother, her sister, and her two daughters and so she went to work as an assistant to a Chilean woman who was a soothsayer. The Chilean taught her how to read the tarot cards.

She must have been a society lady and that's why Nieves went to work for her as a servant or an assistant. Nieves says that she received clients in the evening. In addition to teaching her to read the tarot cards, she taught her how to smoke cigarettes. Nieves helped her in her work, but the Chilean prohibited her from engaging in this activity in her own house. She did it anyway, and she was successful. She has a lot of clients. I only go for my business, but she has more clients who come to her with love problems and problems of women who are quarreling and are separating from their husbands. *Cambas* (people from Santa Cruz) go to her and prostitutes as well as "better" women. When I go there I always meet some. You see, I have to wait for my turn, and I watch who comes out. So, the *señora* tells me, [for example], that that *camba* has come because her business is not going well.

I found Nieves through a friend. Do your remember Carmela, Señora? When we were up there? She is black. She knew Nieves. I got to know her when I lost my earrings. They were just like the ones that I have on. I didn't know where they could possibly be. My mother had given them to me as a present. I had the ones I am wearing made according to a drawing I made [of the ones I lost]. Carmela told me that we should go and see a woman who reads the cards. She would be able to find out how I had lost them. When we arrived there, an old woman came out. Two *cholas* were sitting there already, so we waited for our turn. We entered, and she asked Carmela, "Who are you, daughter?" Carmela answered, "Don't you remember my mother? She is Viviana who used to come here." She is from Yungas. "Yes, I remember her," said the soothsayer. "So you are her daughter?" "Yes," replied Carmela, "and this is my first cousin." That's how I got to know Nieves. She told me that I had lost my earrings on the street and that it would be impossible to find them.

That time, Señora, I had to pay her three pesos for a divination. Now a smoke costs twenty pesos. When she smokes, she takes four cigarettes and places them in her mouth all at once like a panpipe and begins to smoke. Huu! The smoke it makes! She smokes and prays at the same time and she throws the ashes into a can. The cigarettes have to be Astoria cigarettes. It can't be just any brand. She used to smoke Inca cigarettes, but that brand no longer exists. She smokes looking carefully at the ashes all the while to see whether I will sell or not. I also had her smoke to find out how things would turn out when I went to sell fricassee at the folklore festival in Compi. She called my clients and told me, "There won't be a bone left for you to taste. Mark my words, not even a bone." And she was right. I didn't even have a taste of a bone. People came and bought half a side. They called for more cracklings. They bought everything. I don't know how she does it. She moves her feet while she is smoking. Anyway, she is always right.

Nieves's story is long. She does the same thing for the *cambas*, so that their business prospers. For example, Sra. Nieves told me the story of one of the *cambas*—she confides everything in me; she acts as though I were her daughter. She told me, "Do you know why that woman comes to see me? She got involved with a millionaire and the millionaire left for Argentina." That man paid good money every time he came to be with her. Now the millionaire is gone and the *camba* is sad because no one else pays like that. She says that the *camba* was her best client and I think that Sra. Nieves made the millionaire come back. She does things like that. She always rejoins spouses who have separated or who have had a quarrel, or where the man has gone off with other women.

When I go there during Pentecost, she prepares some very nice *sullus* (llama fetuses). She buys them in the Calle Linares. She adorns them with gold and silver [foil] (*quri t"ant"aja* and *qulqe t"ant"aja*). But they are very expensive. This year (1975) she was charging two hundred pesos

(US$10). [As a result] she lost money on them. She only sold four *mesas*. She prepared them for the trucks. She makes beautiful *sullus*. She says that those who offer (*waxta*) them will be able to obtain another vehicle during the year. That's why people come to see her. But this year there were few takers. I thought to myself, "Why are you charging so much? People are poor." But she is a good person.

Now that Nieves is old, I wonder whether her business will fail. I am sorry for her. She can't see well any more. I don't think that she can see the signs on her tarot cards properly. [I noticed because] I know the meaning of the different signs. Once, when we were alone together, she began to teach me their meaning. She told me that the goblet was the house; the spades, the road; the white flowers mean that one is expecting a child or will become pregnant; a wedding is a large spade wrapped in a banner. . . . But when I went to see her about my luck concerning my brother, she looked at the cards but was unable to see them. She just said what came to her mind. So I told her to her face, "Doña Nieves, it seems that you can't see." "Yes," she answered, "I am tired." You see, I had already seen my fortune. I asked her, "Where am I?" And I saw my sign, the spade, to one side. But she was still looking and mumbling, "Where are you, where are you hiding?" I told her, "Here it is," and took it out for her. It's from all that smoking. But, thanks to her business, Sra. Nieves owns two taxis. She even pays taxes on the earnings from her work.

Manuel Llave is the *brujo* of the brother of the godmother of Marcelino, who sold us the house. They are *compadres*. Manuel Llave works differently. He requests that I buy four packs of cigarettes, candles, white wine, pure alcohol, and things like that, just for a regular consultation. He makes his clients sit on a chair, while he sits on the floor, and they tell him that they have come for a consultation about their luck. One shouldn't tell him right away what has happened. One should only say, "I have come about my fortune." Only then can one know whether a person is a good *brujo*. I said, "I have come about my luck." "Fine," he answered, "hand me a candle." The candle was for the skull. Another candle was for me and yet another for my mother. After lighting them he said, "Cigarettes!" I gave them to him and he began to cut them up and he wrapped one in a little piece of paper, lit it, and placed it into the skull's mouth. So the skull was smoking cigarettes. Then he said, "Pure alcohol!" and he made the skull drink it. Finally he said, "Coca!" and I handed him the coca which he placed on the skull's head (*sic*). In the meantime we talked. He was telling me about his clients. He said that he was a well known *brujo*. "I am the *brujo* of Korilazo (a bus company), of Papaya Oriental and of Rafael Mendoza of the Copacabana bus line."

"How did you get to know them," I queried. He answered, "They already knew about me. They are wealthy because I have contacts with the devil and I ask him for money—the money of the devil." "How much do you charge them," I continued. "Huy, one has to get money out of them because they are rich. I treat poor people as poor people and the wealthy as wealthy people. [But] I [also] help the poorest of the poor." He said that he was sixty-five years old, but he looks much younger. It turns out that he has had twelve wives. Imagine that, señor. What a *brujo*! When he didn't like one of them, he bewitched her *trán, trán*, and she would die. If a wife got involved with another man when he went out to work, he would also bewitch her and she would die. Because he was young, he could attract and marry any woman he desired. Finally, he stayed with a woman whose name is Nicolasa. She is young and has three children. I asked him why he had stayed with that one. He answered, "She respects me and she knows what I have to do and knows everything about me." Then he told me that his other wives had been *cochabambinas, tarijeñas, orureñas*, [and women from many other places].

He told me that he had travelled all over the place in connection with his witchcraft business. He is from Achokalla. He says that no one taught him. He said that his grandmother had already been a witch and she had passed [the trade] on to his mother, and when she died, she had passed it on to him. "And how did it occur to you to make a pact with the devil?" I asked. "I wanted to be more powerful than the other *brujos*," he replied. He said that his grandmother had already had a pact with the devil, while his mother was a *bruja de Dios* (a witch who believes in God). His grandmother would bewitch people and make them die. He said, "Sofía, if something should happen to you, I am on your side. When I [cast a spell], the person dies within three days. Do you want him to die in a car accident, or as a result of a fight, or through an illness? I do whatever you want." I told him that I would come to see him some day and thanked him. He said, "You are a good person. I would like you to be the godmother of my child." And I will be, because his wife is expecting a child.

Then, he started to divine from the coca leaves. But he did it differently. He threw the leaves into the air and smoked a cigarette and took out the leaves to tell my fortune. And he says the Lord's Prayer but all wrong. He doesn't say,, "Our Father, who art in heaven." He says, "Our Father, give us the power," or something like that to the devil. It's a very strange prayer. He prays, "Oh Lord give me the power. I want to say the truth to this woman." And then he addresses the skull and asks it to give him intelligence. He says that the skull belonged to the best, most famous sorcerer. This sorcerer had died at the hands of thieves. He had been travelling with llamas and was taking along a young woman, when he was accosted on the road and killed. Its an interesting story. He calls the skull Juco Manuel Condori. Juco Manuel was the most famous sorcerer of the Indians, that's why he calls the skull Juco Manuel Condori.[10] He dug [the skull] out. He says that he used to work as a mason. He dreamt where the skull was located, and then he unearthed it. From then on Manuel Llave had the power. That's why he loves that skull a lot.

After he asked the skull it to give him intelligence, he told me that I was fine and so was my mother. He also said that my father's death had been inevitable. He even told me correctly that my foot hurt. How could he have known that? He told me everything. The *brujo* [also] said, "Let her pick up a fortune and let her earn well." And I did. I earned well by smuggling sugar. Manuel Llave must be a good *brujo* to be able to do all that.

[That *brujo* says that all money comes from the devil.] He says it's from the devil. He says that God was poor and didn't have any money either. So one has to ask the *Tío*[11] for money. He says, "If you don't ask the *Tío*, you won't have any money." He gave me a little thing that is like a companion. And nothing bad happens to me. It's a secret, I am only telling this to you: what he gave me is specially good for commerce. If my carrots just won't sell, I take the thing out and place it underneath the carrots and its as though I was speaking to that person. I tell it that it should cause everything to be sold and the carrots begin to sell. I carry it in my little bag and it's always in there—I don't have it with me right now.

I also own a magnet that this woman from La Villa gave me. It's in a little bag and one can't show it to any stranger because the person might die just like that. I don't look at it myself either, I just handle it. I have been carrying it around for almost five years now. I think that the woman put [something symbolizing] money, a *huayrurito* (red and black seed), a fist [carved out of stone clutching money], and I don't know what else into that little bag. I carry that in my purse as well. So I have two "persons" in my bag.

Sofía's comments about when she employs magic in connection with her work and when she does not is reminiscent of Malinowski's (1922) observation that the Trobriand Islanders did not employ magic in familiar conditions which were regarded as controllable through human mechanisms but reserved it for dangerous, more arbitrary, and risky conditions and endeavors. Thus, when sales were low for everyone, there was no cause for supernatural intervention. It was only when she felt singled out for bad sales, that she suspected supernatural causes. Unlike illness, where a spirit could intervene directly, in the case of commerce, human agency was always considered to be involved in the mobilization of supernatural forces. This reflects the highly competitive nature of marketing.

Magic and Specialization

Sofía's description of her own and the specialists' practice of magic reveals the degree to which magical knowledge is universalized and the degree to which it is specialized in urban as well as in rural areas. Much of the knowledge a magical specialist requires to engage in his or her trade is regarded as widely disseminated. Sofía learned from her mother, who was not a specialist herself. Juan, the magician from Jank'o Amaya, learned his trade not from other specialists but by experimenting with coca leaf divination in the context of his work as a musician. However, the efficacy and empowerment to engage in magic is regarded as an endowment bestowed by the supernatural, often mediated by established specialists. Certain unusual events are indications that such a talent, or, indeed, onerous charge, has been bestowed on an individual. The nature of these signs (such as giving birth to twins or being struck by lightning), and, concomitantly, the kinds of supernatural forces involved and the nature of the magician's relationship to these forces, can vary. Not everyone endowed with the gift of manipulating the supernatural employs it professionally, i.e., regularly and for a fee. Sofía herself has clairvoyant dreams but has never used her skill professionally. She regards this gift as god-given. However, magical practitioners can also confer limited supernatural powers on their clients. Thus, Manuel Llave gave Sofía a piece of the powerful skull in his possession which enabled her to control her family's and other persons' behavior. And Nieves and other practitioners gave her special cigarette ashes and other ritual paraphernalia to improve her sales on her own.

The Semiotics of Dreaming

In an analysis of the semiotics of Quechua dreams, Mannheim (1987) argues that, unlike ritual and myths, in which the context of other signs and interpretation are crucial elements in the generation of meaning, southern Quechua dreams are interpreted in terms of the semantic relationship of a set of conventional (i.e., widely shared) individual signs taken out of their context. In other words, the dreamer looks for particular signs: in the case of Sofía, objects such a potatoes or motor vehicles and actions, such as carrying potatoes uphill or going downhill, bedwetting, or tearing hair out, each of which has a specific referent: prosperity, death, quarrels, and so forth.[12] *In Sofía's interpretation of at least some of her dreams, the interpretation of dreams is not quite as atomistic as Mannheim claims it is for southern Quechua myths: thus, the meaning of being served a plateful of food during a dream is modified by the dreamer's acceptance or rejection of the dish. With this qualification, Mannheim's thesis is largely applicable to Aymara dreaming. Sofía does, indeed, ignore most of the contents of her dreams.*[13] *Unlike southern Quechua dream predictions, predictions in Sofía's dreams are not limited to the day after the dream has occurred, but may refer to events in the more distant future. It is further noteworthy that in both Aymara and Quechua dreams future events are rarely referred to directly. Instead, the signifiers often seem arbitrary. In this, Aymara and Quechua theories about dreaming and those of many other native South Americans share a feature in common with Freudian analysis, which also postulates that "dreams contain disguised meanings requiring interpretation" (Basso 1987: 86).*

7

BECOMING *a Union Leader*

A shrewd understanding of the economic conditions and magical intervention (discussed in the previous chapters) are not the only means Sofía uses to control her economic well-being. She also actively involves herself in the politics of the market by assuming leadership positions in market unions.

I continued to [sell onions] in the Avenida Montes on Saturdays. From a *feria franca* it became [a street market governed by] a market union. Apparently they had a meeting one day—I wasn't there at the time. . . . Señor Hans, do you remember that I told you how [my brother] Pedro didn't want me to sell because he said that it was unseemly for me to do so, and that his friends would criticize him? Well, God is great! His wife started to sell in the Avenida Montes just like me! His present wife is *de vestido* and so I ask myself, "Why don't his friends criticize him now that his wife is going to sell?" She has been selling there for almost a year. She has had a fixed site ever since the *feria* opened and—would you believe it—she is selling onions! I laugh at him. He used to scold me so much and now his wife Ruth is going out to sell. Now, all of a sudden, it's nothing to be ashamed of.

[The reason I am mentioning this is that] my brother would, on occasion, go and see Ruth there and, since my brother was well known as a *movimentista* (M.N.R. supporter), militia chief and all that, [the vendors knew that his wife was married to a well known man]. At the time, they were forming a union to defend themselves against the abusive police. They also wanted the market to live eternally. And it does, in fact, live on to this day. Well, both Julia Monje and Ema Cruz wanted to become secretary-general and they began to quarrel about it. Ema Cruz knew my brother by sight and she told him, "Don Pedro, I would like your wife to hold an office in the union." My brother answered, "I can't allow my wife to hold an office. Someone who has the time should do it. Why don't you ask my sister instead." That's how it came about that they asked me.

I didn't know anything about unions. My brother called me into his room one night and told me that they wanted to nominate me and I had him explain [what this would entail]. He told me that I would hold the office of standard bearer. When I asked what I would have to do as standard bearer, he told me, "You will just have to carry the standard during official parades and street demonstrations and you will have to get the vendors in line. In addition, you will have to attend union meetings. Now, in those meetings you should be outspoken and become involved in everything. You should have an opinion about everything." He really instructed me in detail. So I accepted and the leaders were sworn in. Ema Cruz had already gone to the labor ministry with our names and she had collected money from all the vendors for the inauguration. That first inauguration took place in a hall in the Calle Max Paredes facing the church of Gran Poder. I didn't know how one did inaugurations, and so Pedro told me about that too. He told me, "You have to wear your best clothes and you will take an oath of office."

So we went to the hall, and some men from the labor ministry came as well as some officials from the town hall. They were the guests of honor. And Ema Cruz had ordered someone to prepare cocktails and had even bought champagne. Champagne is a must for these occasions. For dinner, she had ordered roasted suckling pig. They had selected someone as *madrina de cohetillón*[1] and had hired an orchestra. They paid all this with the money they had gathered from the vendors. At that time, things were cheap.

That's how I was inaugurated in 1966. I have an official certificate and everything. Someone, I think that it was a man from the federation [into which the unions are grouped], called out the names of all the *secretarias*, some ten all in all—I don't remember all their names—and then they called my name. We gave our pledge by kissing the cross and being asked, "Do you swear to fight for the union?" and things like that. Then the people came, hugged us, congratulated us, and threw confetti at us. We all looked like couples who had just come out of church after their wedding. Then the fiesta began. We danced with the guests of honor and everyone else and drank until eleven o'clock. But I myself didn't drink at the time. Don't you dare tell anybody that I drank that night! I just saw to it that people danced with everybody. From then on I was *porta estandarte*.

The way in which Sofía remembered her nomination as a market leader in 1975 was quite different from her reconstruction of the same event in 1967, a year after it occurred. Then, she constructed the event, which she wrote down for us and titled redacción,[2] *or "essay," in more democratic terms. Perhaps, the authoritarian nature of the military government that came into power in 1971 led her to remember and emphasize the more manipulative, hierarchical, and paternalistic aspects that were also apparent in previous regimes. In contrast, as we have seen earlier, even during the less than fully democratic presidency of René Barrientos, union leaders, and members alike stressed the democratic nature of the political process, at least within the unions.*

An Essay (Redacción) by Sofía about Her Nomination (as Standard Bearer)[3]

The following happened when they elected (*nombraron*) me as standard bearer: I was selling onions at the free fair in the Avenida Montes on Saturdays. Then one day a group of *cholas*, the vendors who sold there, got together and talked about forming a union. Afterwards they passed the word that there was going to be a union in the Avenida Montes. The women vendors discussed it among themselves and agreed that there should be a union, and so a meeting of all the vendors of the Montes was announced for that Monday afternoon in August 1966.

One hundred fifty eight women came to the meeting and talked about struggling against the authorities of the municipality. Then they nominated the executive committee. The members nominated two women [for the post of] secretary-general: Ema Cruz and Julia Monje. Then the two women fought to become secretary-general. The members did not like the fight. So a general election was held which Ema Cruz won with 124 votes while Julia Monje had 15.

Then Ema Cruz, who was [now] the secretary-general, appointed her directorate. I was the only onion vendor who knew how to write and read. I was also the one who spoke up most frequently, and discussed things at the meeting in favor of the onion vendors. So then they nominated the secretarias and they named a *cholita* called Juana Chavez as standard bearer. The members were not in agreement with this choice, and so *Señora* Ema Cruz asked the members who could be a standard bearer. She said that it had to be an unmarried woman who was intelligent, astute, and who knew how to fight for the union. The members looked at one another and discussed the matter in hushed voices. Then one of the onion vendors cried out that Sofía should be the person. The members looked at me and also shouted that I should be the one. Then Ema Cruz called me and said, "The members have nominated you to be secretary standard bearer. Are you willing?"

I didn't know what a standard bearer was and told her to give me three days to discuss it with my brothers and my parents. Then my brother Pedro told me that a standard bearer had to carry the standard during parades and attend meetings. And he told me many [other] things about unions. So I accepted and the members were in agreement. I was sworn in on August 12th of the same year and, together with Ema Cruz and her secretarias, I gave a sacred oath to fulfill my duties in front of the minister of labor and many other authorities.

In 1975, Sofía remembered her subsequent rise in the union organization as follows:

[I continued as a standard bearer] until the power struggle between Ema Cruz and Julia Monje, when I sided with Julia Monje. Now I am secretary of organization. This entails organizing people: when they fight I have to tell them to stop. I have to impose order and discipline. I became *secretaria de organización* in 1968 and continued until 1972 when the union became less active. Then, in 1972, I was supposed to enter the federation as the delegate of the Avenida Montes. There was an election with green and white ballots [for the two slates of candidates]. I was of the green ballot and we lost because we lacked the support of the vendors. No one wanted [Ema Cruz] any longer. She found herself isolated. Ema Cruz was too negligent. Julia was very active and knew everyone. She wasn't afraid of anything. For example, when we had a demonstration against the police, Julia shouted, "Down stupid ones, down stupid ones!" while Ema didn't say anything. I think that she was afraid. Then one day she no longer came to sell. I don't know what had happened to her. Once Ema came to the house. She knew where I lived because at first we had our meetings at my house because the union had only recently been organized and we didn't have any money to rent a hall to hold our meetings. At that time, Julia Monje was already working against us. That's why we held the meetings in secret in my house, which had a large patio. We would distribute citations on small pieces of paper with my address on them. At any rate, she knew my house. And one day she came and said that she had to attend a fiesta of someone who was being inaugurated in the Federation of Food Vendors and didn't have new shoes. I told her that I had some, and it turned out that we had the same shoe size. So I told her that I would sell them to her. She asked me to sell them to her on credit and she left and never paid me.

We held meetings whenever some federation leader was inaugurated, and they would ask the market union leaders to bring beer or something else, and we would have to collect contributions from the vendors. We also had meetings when someone died or to help someone. We had monthly meetings to inform people of what had happened.

In 1988, when, as we shall see later, Sofía had advanced through the ranks and had become secretary-general of the union of the market in the street where she lives, she elaborated for us in greater detail what the functions of the various union leaders are.

I was sworn in with eleven other persons. They were the secretary-general, *relación*, treasurer, organization with a replacement person, conflicts—also with a replacement, press and propaganda with a replacement, standard bearer and her replacement, minutes (without a replacement), a spokesperson, and the secretary of sports. Sra. Clotilde became secretary of sports because she likes to organize soccer matches. Last year (1987) there was a soccer championship on the fourteenth (of July?) in which four teams of the Garita participated: Tumusla-Garita, Tumusla, and Incachaca. Garita won and Tumusla was the sub-champion. The game was beautiful. It took place [in the soccer field next to] the Uruguay Market. All the market women were playing. I had to select the players among the younger ones.

The secretary-general must act like a mother: she must take care of the membership, see to it that they are disciplined. She is just like a mother. She has to go wherever she is needed, including downtown when the authorities call the market leaders. She must know what is happening in the city of La Paz and what needs to be done with the mayor. So the secretary-general must get things going and know about everything. Then, when there are problems, she must decide, again like a mother. Now, when the secretary-general is absent or is sick, the *secretaria de relaciones* steps in and takes over these duties.

The *secretaria de hacienda* administrates the money. She must know when and whether to invest it or whether to hold it in reserve. For that task, a serious person who knows how to think must be chosen. The *secretaria de conflictos* has to take care of lawsuits and quarrels. She takes the persons involved to the union office. The *secretaria de organización* watches over the sales sites. She observes whether people are selling or not and whether they are properly seated or are encroaching on some other vendor's site. The *secretaria de beneficiencia* has to assist the members who are sick at home or in the hospital. If they are in the hospital, she has to visit them and talk to the doctor to find out if they need assistance. If they do need help, she comes here and we discuss it and she has to gather a quota from the entire membership. If a person should die, she also has to gather money to bury her and to carry the coffin. The *secretaria de prensa y propaganda* is the woman I ask to notify everybody about meetings or to inform the members when something has happened. She must make propaganda [for the market], go to the radio station or carry messages to other places. The *porta estandartes* are two girls who have to participate at parades or assemblies and carry the standard. And the *vocal* has to go to the federation or confederation to find out when meetings will take place.

[Most of the *secretarias* are women, but] we have a man as *secretario de actas*. Before that, he was a *vocal*, and he advanced because my *secretaria de actas*, a *de vestido* girl, had a terrible handwriting. She didn't even know how to read. When I asked her to read something, she was incapable of doing it and everybody would shout, "Let Doña Sofía read it."

Sofía's entry into rural fairs and her success in finding a site to sell her produce in urban weekly fairs and permanent markets is regulated by the vendors themselves who hassle "outsiders" and call those who have gained admittance to comply with ritual obligations, and by elected officials known as secretarios\as generales (secretaries-general) who arrange and lease sites in village plazas or in designated streets and empty lots in La Paz. In La Paz, an elected mayor[4] who, depending on the person and the times may favor market traders, or seek to circumscribe their activities, controls markets indirectly through a market superintendent. Both of these officials, in turn, are dependent on three levels of union organization—the union local, the city-based union federation and the regional confederation—for political support and to carry out their directives. Specifically, the superintendent regulates market facilities, appoints or hires tax collectors for stall taxes and a special market police, who, as the narrative shows, often act to control sanitary conditions, and disputes. Parallel to this organization, some regional fairs, urban markets and tambos (wholesale market depots) have retained the traditional organization in which a maestra mayor *responsible to the city administration was appointed by her predeces-*

sor and was then assisted by an aide or two.[5] *This system was modified during military regimes.*

From Sofía's accounts it also becomes clear what qualifications were deemed crucial for leadership positions and how the M.N.R. government tried to recruit persons like herself from peasant or other non-elite backgrounds. She also admits that the union ideals of mediation, political communication, and cooperative projects were undermined partially by the actions of the leaders themselves and by internal factions like those led by Ema and Julia on the Avenida Montes. Rifts did not only occur on the local level, but were commonplace in the federation and confederation as well. The complexity and nature of union meetings are also revealed by the account.[6]

8

THE *Demise of Market Unions*

As we saw in chapter 5, the regime of General Banzer was highly repressive. The measures that affected Sofía most directly included the prohibition of union activities, and indeed of most public gatherings.

Since last year (1974), the president and the mayor decreed that there shouldn't be any unions anymore, only coordinators who would take charge of union matters. In the Avenida Montes there is now neither a coordinator nor a union. Do you remember the secretary-general of the Avenida Montes, Julia Monje? Well, she has neglected the union entirely—she has abandoned it. Instead, she has gone to sell in another market, San Miguel in Calacoto, where there is a market on Fridays. She also sells at the Bosquecillo and that's all she does. There was a parade, but she didn't do anything. Then there were popular rallies, and again she did nothing. As a result, fewer and fewer people [are selling in the Avenida Montes]. But most of all, people stopped selling there [because of the government decree].

[After the decree, meetings were] prohibited totally. After my father died, in 1973, we had only one meeting—about the standard. Now we have our own standard. Then they held another meeting about a loudspeaker [to advertise the market, announcing that our prices were low] so that a lot of housewives would come and buy, because sales had dropped.

So, one day I met Julia. I asked her, "What's going on with the union? You have forgotten all about the union and about us. You are neglecting us." "I haven't forgotten you," she answered. "It's just that my husband doesn't want me to be involved with the union. He is very jealous. He thinks that I am having affairs with the leaders. That's why I don't want to be involved any longer. *He* is preventing me. Also, whenever I call the people here for a meeting, they don't come; they don't heed me. So what else can I do? Leave them be." So that's how things stand. Everybody has gone off to sell in the Camacho Market.

If Julia had been the kind of woman who didn't forget people, I think that she would have become the coordinator of the Montes. All the other markets like the Graneros, the Uruguay, and the Rodriguez have coordinators. They work in a manner similar to unions but there are no meetings. It's prohibited. Also a state of emergency has been declared and everybody has to be home by 10 p.m. At first, they said that the state of siege would only last a year, but then there was a new coup attempt and they decreed a state of siege again. It is prohibited to have meetings. The coordinators have the sole charge of getting people to attend rallies to support or to greet the president. Then, when there is some vote, they have to tell the people that they must accede. Or, when there is a parade, they have to force them to attend and threaten them with a fine if they don't. It's no longer like before, when we had meetings every Tuesday. As for me, I am in agreement with what the government has decreed, because in 1971 and 1972 I was getting into the habit of drinking. We would have meetings every week, we would call the people together and we would gather quotas, some three hundred or four hundred pesos (US$15 or $20), but we didn't use it to benefit the Montes. Rather, Julia would take it and say, "Let's go to a restaurant." And we would all go and drink and eat. [The government] was right [to stop that]. We did other things like that too. For example, if there was a parade for the sixth of August or the sixteenth of July, we would prepare little slips of paper and distribute them, and if the people didn't march in the parade, I would gather fines from them. They always asked me to do it because I have an energetic character. If a vendor didn't pay, I would return with a policeman. I would give him a wink and he would understand right away what it meant. You see half of the fine would go to him and the other half to Julia and me—just the two of us. [The government was right] when they said that the union leaders just drank, celebrated their fiestas, stole, and hadn't done anything for La Paz. It was true. The Montes has gone downhill. If Julia had been a well educated person, she would have wanted to do something for the union. She would have wanted the Montes union to be better than the others and to have everything complete: a standard and a banner some twenty meters in length to march in parades with. We gathered money for these things but we didn't use it for that. We just drank it all up. [Both Julia's husband and my mother did not want us to go to the federation meetings and drink.] They thought that the women there would lose their morals because there are mostly men in the federation and they would do bad things with the women. That's why I didn't go any longer.

The same persons who were secretaries-general before now have become coordinators. In addition, there must be some chief coordinator at the town hall. They hold meetings there. If there are quarrels in the market the police intervene. Neither the union nor the coordinators or the *maestras mayores* have anything to do with that any longer. The *maestras mayores* of the markets have continued but they no longer organize the market fiesta. Before, the *maestra mayor* and the *alcalde* would gather quotas to celebrate the market fiesta on the 15th of July. Now they say that the *maestra mayor* and the *alcaldes* have to spend too much of their own money. That's why they haven't sponsored the fiesta this year (1975). A woman whom I know well who sells in the Buenos Aires told me that there was only a band playing and that people didn't decorate their stands as usual because the vendors said, "How can we light our stands if we haven't contributed a cent for the band or for drinks? What will the *maestra mayor* say? Let's just go home."

[I think that the town hall organizes things now because when Banzer took a tour [of the markets] with his wife the palace must have sent a telegram to the town hall who notified the police of each market and they in turn must have told the *maestras mayores* or something like that. At any rate, the policeman of the Uruguay market talked to Julia, who apparently is *maestra mayor* there, and soon after that, she was telling the women that they had to welcome the president. It's not as it used to be.

[At the Rodriguez market union] they used to be strict and attendance was obligatory. Then a woman called Feliza—she is *de vestido* and sells fruit—held the office and everyone was united. When some policeman took some woman's vegetables away from her, they acted together. They would go and hold a protest rally and everything. During the last two months, I have seen her running all over the market. When the policeman takes away someone's onions, she runs and scolds them, telling them that they are being abusive. I think that, in secret, she is an agent herself, so I was surprised to see her side with a market vendor.

[Now], when there are quarrels, the police has to intervene. The DIC or 110[1] police are in charge of us. They control prices and cleanliness. That's all there is now. Also, when the President travels somewhere or something, we get called through the radio to appear at some place with our standards.

Frankly, [even before Banzer abolished the unions], the leaders spent more time drinking and taking advantage of the money for their personal gain. Maybe they already guessed that there would no longer be any unions and they took advantage of the situation. Anyway nothing got done at all. They didn't provide for housing either as they said they would. They even went to Río Seco [where the union members were supposed to receive land] for a celebration. But no land was distributed. Instead, the people from Huatajata bought land there. The people had already paid for half or one fourth of the value of the land and it seems to me that Gallardo (the secretary of the federation of market unions) and another man stole all the money. He doesn't seem to be around any more. Maybe they banished him to another country. They had wonderful plans but nothing came of them. All they did was drink.

[There is little one can do about it]. We have to do what the government decrees. But maybe when the government changes again we can do something once more. Earlier on, I was toying with the idea of establishing another union together with a man who now sells in the Mariscal Santa Cruz. He sells perfumes, powder, and things like that. He told me, "Why don't we establish another union including all the vendors of the Avenida Montes and hold an inauguration? The market has deteriorated badly." And he is right. The market is dead. We are not selling the way we used to sell. Before, I used to sell fifteen or twenty bundles of onions and I earned two hundred or three hundred pesos (US$10 or $15) and now I barely sell a single bundle even if I sit there from nine in the morning till nine o'clock at night. Even to do that, I have to do everything possible, including lowering the prices. Before, when sales were lagging, we would quickly collect money and advertise over the radio, and we would hire a car and drive around the city announcing that we had a large market with low prices. That would attract people even from down here [in Calacoto]. Now, no one is coming. Only the people from the neighborhood come to buy. So this man wanted to form a union and beat Julia in the elections. He told me that I had at least eighty girls coming to sell onions and that we could easily win. I didn't want that because I was afraid that Julia would be angry. But then he told me that Julia had gone off to sell in San Miguel. She has some position in the union there now, but no longer as secretary-general. All that happened last year (1974). Now this man's wife has died, and he is no longer selling.

[At first], I think that there were some [clandestine unions]. But now there are none. People are afraid. No one wants to take the initiative. I would like to organize the Montes, but I am afraid. They might arrest me and say that I am working against the government because it is prohibited. I might even land in jail for no reason at all. I will give you an example. The first days when I came down here to work in one of those green microbuses, a policeman stopped the bus and asked the driver for his license and permit to drive a bus on that line. The driver showed him the license but told him that he didn't have a permit because he belonged to the Litoral union and he showed him his union card. The policeman shouted at him and began to swear, "What union? There haven't been any unions for some time now." The driver continued to insist that there was a union [which made the policeman even angrier]. Finally, he took away the driver's license. The policeman didn't even want to hear the word union. Apparently, the three bus unions were merged into a single entity directed by a single coordinator. All the buses [of the different lines] are all mixed up now. Even during the time when the unions still existed, there were Barrientos and Banzer supporters among the members. They must have become the coordinators now. They are everywhere now. For example, in the judicial system, in the tax office and in the town hall I see lots of *cambas* (people from Santa Cruz). They pronounce "*pues*" as "*pue*." I think that Banzer's wife is a *camba* or from the Beni. He has placed his people everywhere. There are *cambas* even in the national police force. They don't know anything about being policemen but they are working there anyway. That's why people are unhappy with this government. They complain that the government says that there will be no more politics and yet they place their people into every office. People think that there could be a revolution at any moment. Two or three days ago, I heard that one had been planned but was uncovered. Another one was supposed to take place in Oruro. Also, I am hearing rumors that prices could rise again and that it is better to take advantage and buy as much as possible. And I said to myself, "What am I going to do? I don't have any money." We *paceñas* are trembling of fear. We no longer say "Long live Bolivia, long live the government." Before, when we were drunk, we would shout, "Long live the Movimiento, down with Falange." Now everybody keeps quiet. I am sure that if someone called out something like that, the 110 would take them away. Even I am afraid of the little white Jeeps with their red lights. When something happens, for instance, if they go after a thief, they go by with their sirens screaming. They grab anyone. Even women with small children. They just beat them, force them into the jeep and take them away.

Then, as you must have seen already, there are policewomen now who are also controlling us. It doesn't have to be a man any longer. A woman can do it too. They always work in twos. Even *cholitas* are becoming policewomen. The newspapers announced last October or

November that a *cholita* had become a policewoman. They are mean, these women. They even become involved in matters like the pricing of onions. Its not just the municipal police who deals with these matters any more. There is a new law which allows the traffic police to take us to the police station too. All the authorities have joined forces: the municipality, the *guardia* (*guardia civil*, or national guard), and the traffic police. For example, if there is a quarrel here and there happens to be no *guardia* around but a traffic policeman is present, he will take us. So we have to respect all the authorities.

Now the people are commenting that we are returning back to hacienda times [when poorer people had no rights]. Peasants are hated nowadays. Before, peasants commanded respect. Now, in order to sell at a high[er] price, we have to plead with the police chief of the area, who is in charge of the market and he extracts [a bribe of] one hundred or fifty pesos (US$5 or $2.50) from us. That's how much we have to give him. [Then] he surreptitiously passes by several times [without saying anything]. But if a *guardia* catches us, we are sunk. We have to sell at the price set by the municipality and the 110 takes us to prison.

It seems to me that sales have gone down [as a result] and that one doesn't earn as much because there is a lot of control. Even women in street dress are coming to control. They seem harmless enough until they take out their pads and say that they are from the town hall. That's why people are afraid to sell and so many women have switched to working in their homes. For example, one woman, Adela, who sold next to me, is travelling to Desaguadero [to buy contraband goods]. Another woman is making and selling *chicha* (corn beer) at home. Still others are sewing clothing or aprons at home and selling them on credit. It is impossible to earn money because they won't let us. Anybody may turn out to be a police agent, so we can't raise our prices. There is also as rumor that they won't allow women to sell on the street any longer but that they all will be concentrated in markets to be built in each neighborhood. They will be like supermarkets. So everybody is afraid of what will happen. They say that the capitalist women, those who sell in the Rodriguez, the Lanza, and [covered] markets like that have complained that they can't earn a living because anyone can just sit down on the street with ten oranges. The women from the countryside often buy twenty or fifty oranges and sell them at a lower price or give a little extra. So they don't want these women to sell. They want to force them to obtain a health certificate, wear a white apron, and have everything in order. Apparently, there has been a decree from the town hall to this effect already. In addition, the housewives from Miraflores have said that it is a bad thing that people are selling just like that. They claim that it is dangerous because many women are sickly and may spread disease by handling the produce.

We already have to buy price lists in a city office facing the Camacho market for two pesos once a year. The list has to have a municipal seal stamped on it. Otherwise they won't allow us to sell. I think that we are just lining the pockets of the authorities. [Prices have risen a lot since then]. But when a policeman comes, we can show him the list and when he leaves, we hide it again and sell the onions for double the posted price. A few customers insist on paying only the list price but most understand and pay the asking price without complaining. They know that onions are scarce and so they join in the protest against the police. It seems to me that the middle class is more understanding than the high society customers. We don't even want to sell to them! They will say, "Why is the price so high? I don't think that is the correct price," and they will call the police. So when these people come along and they ask, "Whose onions are these?" I tell them that they aren't mine. Or I tell them that I am only selling them by the piece, not by bunches of twenty-five. But the middle class and even poor people pay what we ask. They will say, "I feel sorry for you. It must be difficult for you to earn a living," and they pay without saying a word. Because of all of this there was a fight between the people from down here [in Calacoto] and the vendors in the Rodriguez. When the vendors saw these women, they hid their onions and began to shout obscenities at them. "We are not earning anything while you earn in dollars," they shouted. The society women would answer, "Thieves!" And the market women would cry, "We haven't stolen anything from you!" Frankly, we were not stealing at all. We only wanted to earn some money. Why do they accuse us of stealing? The prices have risen and the owners [of the products] also raised their prices. So, in order to earn something, we have to buy at the prices they are asking. I *have* to buy and sell. How can the housewives say that we are stealing from them?

So all the retail vendors hated the housewives, especially the ladies from Miraflores, Sopocachi, and Calacoto.[2] They no longer wanted to sell to them. If a policeman forced to them to sell onions at the posted price, they would say, "I hope that you will die eating these onions." They had a big fight. Even I feel hatred. I would like to see the police control those wealthy people, I have even told the policeman as much. [The wealthy] are the ones that make prices rise. When onions are scarce, one just has to buy without protest. For this reason, I only sell to a few trusted *caseras*. Also, I am on good terms with the policeman in the Montes. He is a fat, pleasant man. I give him ten or fifteen selected large onions every Saturday. He comes to my site and says, "How about it?" And I tell him,

"Give me your newspaper," and I wrap them up for him. He never says anything to me when he makes his rounds.

He has to live from something. What are we going to do? So we say, "Poor thing," and we give him something. Now he must miss me because I haven't been selling in the Montes for two Saturdays in a row. I was the only one who gave him onions. It hurt me to give him those large onions, they cost some two pesos when they are that large, so I must be giving him twenty pesos (US$1) worth. But he does me a favor by not forcing me to sell at a fixed price like the other vendors. Only when other policemen come around do I bring out my price list. [These days] one has to be very careful when one is selling.

The Market Organizations in 1976

Do you remember, that before you left [last year], I told you that there was no longer a market union there or anything like that and that all the people were abandoning the market and going elsewhere? Well, there was no one to lead us any longer. The police committed a lot of abuses. Then one day—I don't know when it was, but that day I had not gone to the market—a patrol of some twenty soldiers came in pickup trucks from the town hall and chased everybody away from the top to the bottom of the avenue. They said that they no longer wanted anyone to sell there and they herded everybody away. The people didn't know what to do; on one side, next to the Guaqui railroad station, is Challapampa. They have a separate union. And on the other side there was another union. So they had no other recourse but to go to Challapampa and join the union of Mr. Onofre. He is a small dark man. He has always been market coordinator or market leader. He came and offered people sales sites. And so they went to the Calle Vicente Quino, next to the Guaqui station. There was a big fight over sales sites. So when I arrived at the market the following week, I saw that all the [good sites] were already occupied, and I had to sit all the way at the end, near the door of the naval barracks where there is a lot of automobile traffic. We had already been selling there for seven Saturdays, when we arrived to find that the market had been abolished. They said that the military didn't want us to sell there—that it was very unbecoming to be selling in a military zone and that we were leaving the street very dirty. So we returned to the Avenida Montes—it wasn't all torn up as it is now. But then, three weeks later, we couldn't find a place to sit. They were making the super highway to El Alto, and everything was in ruins, with dirt piles everywhere. Again we didn't have a place to sell. So we insisted on selling in the Calle Vicente Quino once more. They let us sit, but the next Saturday the street was full of well armed police from one end to the other. We didn't know what to do. So we went to the other side, next to the beer brewery. Then we decided to name coordinators so we could defend ourselves and no longer have to move from one place to another. We said, "Let's sit somewhere and stay there." So [some of us] went to a meeting of the federation in the Calle Yacuma, the Federación de Alimentación. Most vendors are now affiliated to that federation: the Rodriguez market, the Lanza, Camacho, Alto and Villa Victoria—everybody. Even the photographers are affiliated to the Alimentación. So this Onofre called us together for a meeting. I didn't go, but others went. They appointed the leaders at that meeting. Perhaps, if I had gone, they would have appointed me. They appointed an elderly woman, Angelica, as coordinator and another *de vestido* woman and two others. This Onofre is principal coordinator of the entire *feria franca*. He asked for a quota of ten pesos (US$.50) from each vendor and they got two thousand (US$100) and something together. We are almost 240 vendors, and we are united with the Challapampa and Montes markets. Then, they called us together once more to present our documents either to the Navy barracks or to the townhall, so that we could again sell in the Vicente Quino. Well, it turned out that the townhall wanted us to sell inside the old customs building, where we were sure that there would be no sales, and we refused. No one would go in there. People always buy when they are passing through from once place to another. They wouldn't enter somewhere specially. Instead, we wanted them to let us sell in the Plaza Antofagasta. The townhall didn't want us to do that either, so we decided to stay where we were, and we (the four coordinators and Mr Onofre) brought presents and everything for the mayor.

Camilo Morales [from the federation], a fat, small blond man who is a tailor [came along]. He is a leader in the Federación de Alimentación. Then there was a Mario Laura from the Max Paredes, who is the international (*sic*, departmental?) coordinator; he helped us too. So we stayed where we were and, on June 8th, the leadership was finally officially installed. Before that, they went to the townhall, but they wouldn't talk to them because they said that we weren't recognized. They knew only about the *feria franca* of the Avenida Montes. That's why they had the formal installation ceremony. They invited the coordinators of all the markets and they all came with their standards. The installation ceremony took place in a large hall in the Max Paredes. There was an orchestra and the municipal band, Eduardo Caba. The hall was packed.

There were seventeen or eighteen standards [belonging to visiting unions]. Now [the market] is working fine. They say that we will have to pay an annual permit of fifteen (US$.75), the tax for the university and I don't know what else—some fifty pesos (US$2.50) all in all—but then they will never bother us again. So now we are in that street, and it's no longer called the Avenida Montes fair but the fair of the Calle Vicente Quino of Challapampa.

If the municipality engages in some sort of abuse or other, [the coordinators] don't intervene. Well, there *was* a case that I saw in the Rodriguez three weeks ago [where one did intervene]. There, the coordinator, Doña Gregoria, a tall woman who had acted as leader of that place for five years, had died. It was Mother's Day and the mayor had made a small fiesta and had invited the coordinators from all the markets to a barbecue. This woman had gone there too, and she was expecting a child. She must have drunk a lot, and she must have done something, and that night she died in the Clínica América. At least that's what people told me. We heard about it the next day. It was a Saturday. So they buried her on Sunday. Everybody from the Rodriguez went. I passed by there and they asked me to come along too. I said I would come but I didn't. Then, on Monday, I passed by there again—I don't know why . . . Oh yes it was the 27th of May and they named me godmother of beer for the inauguration of the union on June 8th. I said that I had spent too much money already. If they wanted to ask someone they should ask all the onion vendors and we would gather money jointly. So we gathered thirty pesos (US$1.50) from each of the seven onion vendors.

[At eight the next morning I went to the Rodriguez.] But when I got there it was all clean and clear. There wasn't a single vendor. I was shocked. I wondered what had happened. There was no one around to ask. On a whim, I decided to go to the townhall. There I saw a large agglomeration of people. They were all from the Rodriguez. They had gone to protest. Apparently some twenty soldiers had arrived at the market and had not allowed anyone sit down at their sales sites. What awful people these people from the alcaldía are! When they saw that there no longer was a market coordinator, they immediately began to abuse them. So the entire market went to the townhall together.

They said that no one would be allowed to sell in that street; that we had to sell inside the market and that the women who sold in the market were protesting. Under that pretext, they didn't let us sell any longer. So the women all went to the townhall led by Feliza, a woman my age who sells coffee. She was a classmate of mine in the Sagrados Corazones school and a former coordinator. She and a woman from Cochabamba took the initiative to go to the townhall. The mayor refused to see them and so they held a meeting right in front of the townhall and decided to elect a coordinator in order to stop this type of abuse. Now they are sitting [in the market] undisturbed.

Sofía's analysis of the demise of market unions is a curious mixture of acquiescence and resistance against government intervention in the market union movement. On the one hand, she accepts the government's reasoning for the abolition of the unions and blames the union officials of corruption on both the union local level (which includes herself), and on the federation level. On the other hand, she demonstrates how the government abuses its power, tries to take advantage of any power vacuum for its own ends, and terrorizes the market vendors. More generally, she feels that conditions are going back to where they were before the 1952 revolution. As we shall see in later chapters, the vendors resistance in the face of such abuse paves the way for the rapid reemergence of the unions, whenever conditions permit.

9

MARKET *Organizations in the Eighties*

The Rebirth of the Unions in 1979

[The unions] are becoming more powerful again. Now there is also a departmental[1] coordinator, Mario Laura. He is the godson of my brother. Yes there are a number of new people, but many of the old ones are still there too.

In 1981, Sofía rented out a room to the market organization of the Callejón Incachaca and neighboring streets. Before they moved in, the market coordinators, gave a burnt offering to the spirits during Carnival. Such offerings, or at least simpler ones in the form of alcohol, paper streamers, and confetti, are offered by many La Paz households at this time, but they are particularly appropriate when moving into new quarters.

[The renters do this] so that they will have luck; so that nothing will happen to them; and so that they may find something.[2] For example, that woman [who lived in the room before] left it in a filthy mess. That's why [the coordinator] said that she would come to *saumar* (literally "burn incense"), so that Pachamama would harm her rather than us. She said that [Pachamama] would punish the woman because one should never do things like that to the owner of a house. One should always leave the place clean and orderly. "We will come this afternoon," she added. Two women, the coordinator and the subcoordinator, did come last evening around nine thirty. They sell in the Incachaca. That

Inaugurating the market in the Inca Chaca street where Sofía lives (1981) (reprinted from Buechler and Buechler 1992)

woman doesn't know how to write. She is illiterate. She was appointed because she is an older person. The president (President García Meza) wants the coordinators to be experienced older persons and not young girls. Before, the coordinator of the Incachaca was a *cholita* who was only twenty-eight years old. All of them were very young. Now they are more senior persons. The other one is Constancia Rodriguez, a school friend of mine. She knows how to read and write and could be the coordinator herself, but she is still young and so they named the other one to be the coordinator.

The younger one [has experience as a leader too]. I think that Constancia held an office in the union before and so has her sister. Constancia sells mutton and pork. She doesn't travel for meat. I think that the sister has an *agencia* (wholesale market) in the Calle Exaltacón, where people come to sell meat from Escoma, Puerto Perez, Charaña and Caquiaviri. That's where Constancia gets her meat. Both she and the coordinator are from La Paz.

They were not selected by the members. Their names were published in the newspaper. The federation or someone else down there [in the city] must have appointed them. They don't get into these positions easily. I think that [the two women] must have gone down there to talk to someone so that they would be appointed, otherwise how would they know their names? A long list of all the leaders of all markets appeared in the newspaper. . . . I think that they were sworn in at the *intendencia* (market intendent's office). When they came back, the people welcomed them with beer. But they didn't have a fiesta or anything. They decided that it was necessary to have a headquarter for the union because the union owns a loudspeaker and strings of light bulbs to decorate the street on July 16th and if one leaves them in just anyone's house they get lost. They had approached me about it and I had told them that I did not have a room available, but that one would become free soon. They asked me how much I wanted and they gave me twenty-four hundred (US$96) as a deposit and they had the patience to wait for six months until it became free.

They came yesterday at nine thirty. They were waiting for me in my brother's room. They gave me fifty pesos and asked me to buy two bottles of beer. I thought that they wanted to invite me for a drink and I went to buy some. When I returned, they were already cutting up pieces of cardboard to *saumar*. Then they asked me for a basin and a poker. I have one to *saumar* in Espíritu, in August, so I brought them that one. Then I asked them whether they wanted some wood and we put it all in the middle of the room. I didn't see what they had prepared. They brought it all ready, in a little package. The magicians prepare these things. It seemed to me that the coordinator knows about things like that. She told me to sit, and I handed her the beer and sat down in a corner. She took off her hat and her shawl, and, before lighting the fire, she took out a little bottle of alcohol and, mumbling something, she sprinkled alcohol over the *misa* (offering). Then she got up and sprinkled (*ch'allar*) some more in every corner of the room. She must be a witch herself. Then she told me to *ch'allar* too, and I exhorted Pachamama not to harm my new renters. Finally, she lit the fire. Then she told me to open the beer. I didn't know how to do the *ch'alla* (libation), so I did it according to my own criteria. I filled a glass with beer and poured it on the floor near the door. Then I served the two women and myself. The two women were talking to each other and then the older woman mumbled something again while she stared into the fire. Then she said that Pachamama was ravenously hungry and was accepting the offering. I left for my room at 10:30, but my brother Pedro said that [the offering had burned so completely that] only white ashes were left. The smoke entered my room and so I have a headache now. I don't know whether they will come again today.

They say that they always give offerings in order not to become ill. They say that some places have been struck by lightning and make people ill. I didn't tell the women anything about it yesterday, but this room has a history too. I only told them that a number of renters have lived in the room already. But before, when my father was still alive, this room was always used as a storage area. [My parents] hadn't lived there for a long time. Earlier still, when the house had only one story, my mother slept there with my father. However, she had nightmares. She dreamt that a man was approaching her and she would scream. She said that he was a priest. He would not let her sleep in peace. So my mother sought a *brujo* to find out whether there was something in the room. So the sorcerer (*ch'amakani*) said that there must be something buried there. He dug and found a skeleton. My mother says that the previous owners must have committed a crime and must have buried the person there. The skeleton had blond hair. So my mother had the skeleton removed and a ceremony held to stop the nightmares.

They did it with some yarn. They sent the skeleton off. I don't know where to. My mother says that from then on nothing further happened. She was able to sleep in peace. Later, they had a second story built and they lived there and the room on the ground floor was used as a storage room. But the place still scares people. Last night, even my sister-in-law was scared. [Although] I know the room's history [too], I go in and out. Why should I be scared?

In 1984, when union activity had regained its momentum after a period of dormancy under successive military regimes in power between 1980 and 1983, Sofía was not active in union activities. In the meantime unions (and indeed all sorts of organizations including neighborhood councils) had gained a new function, namely to distribute bread and scarce, rationed, government-subsidized staples.

It has been a year now that Siles has come in as President. The meat vendors are holding meetings again. They have held meetings to determine monthly quotas They have also had meetings to buy sugar. They ask everybody whether they want to pool money and then they arrange to buy sugar. [The union] buys it from the corporation. It presents a written request and then picks it up. [They sell it] for the old price, fifteen hundred (US$75 [official rate], US$44 [street rate]). We only pay what it costs the union. Before, a bag cost only nine hundred.

The last time they had a meeting to discuss the statutes and they asked for money. The people have elected an elderly woman who sells at the corner, [as their leader]. She is a good person. Her name is Cloti Chura. She is active. At one point, she was a leader of the pork vendors in the Calle Tumusla. Before that, Constancia Rodriguez was our leader. She is a school friend of mine, a dark-skinned woman. She entered because of politics during the time of the military. She stayed in office for two years. She would stay away for months and even owed me rent [for the room the market leadership rented in my house]. She owed me a lot of money: almost two years' rent. That's why the people got together and elected that other woman. There were two persons who stood for election, one represented by a blue ballot, the other by a white ballot. Her ballot was white, while I was the delegate of the blue ballot. We ended up losing. She was sworn in that very moment [after the election]. There was no fiesta or anything because the woman is a Protestant.[3]

They [also called a] meeting for Mother's Day, because it was the anniversary of the founding of this street market. They were thinking of celebrating the occasion, but they didn't do anything [because there was not enough time to prepare.] I was listening to the union leaders discuss the matter downstairs where the union holds its meetings.

They are paying two thousand a month for rent. Apart from that, they pay my brother for the electricity. They gather a monthly quota from the membership and then give it to us.

Rising Through the Ranks in the Incachaca Market Union (1988)

In the later 80s, Sofía had become active as a market union leader once more. As a veteran vendor with more education than most of her peers and owner of a house in whose patio the vendors regularly stored their selling tables and bundles and from whom they rented a room for union meetings, she was an excellent candidate for a leadership position.

The market in this street was founded on the 27th of May, 1959: twenty-seven years ago. Two years ago they celebrated its silver anniversary. Antonia Cachi founded it. She was an enthusiastic follower of the M.N.R. party. She negotiated with the neighbors and the market was opened. It has been in existence for at least the past thirteen [*sic*] years.[4] Sara made a coup and took over [from Antonia]. She remained in office for three years and then was replaced by Constancia Rodriguez. She is a school friend of mine. She barely lasted a year. She did just what the others had done: stealing from the members, and so she too was turned out of office. But, thanks to her, the *orureñas* came to sell here. She moved them from the Rodriguez to the Tumusla. She also accepted the women from Jesús de Machaca who sit next to the door to my house into the market. She was overthrown by the woman I introduced you to, Sra Clotilde de Chura. She held the office for four years. I was the *secretaria de actas* under her leadership.

The women who work in this occupation come from Jesús de Machaca, Santiago de Machaca, Batallas, Escoma, Patacamaya, Eucaliptos, Tabla Chaca. The largest number comes from Escoma and Ticuyu.[5] Some are also from La Paz and two or so are from Cochabamba. There are some three hundred persons if one includes the *ambulantes* (i.e. those with no permanent sales site who carry their wares around with them). Sra Clotilde both inscribed and reinscribed people. We inscribed at least eighty persons. They paid thirty to eighty (US$12.70 to $33.90) depending on the kind and amount of merchandise. [They sell] mutton and pork. Those who sell wholesale pay eighty. Those who sell heart, intestines, head or *bofe* pay thirty.

First I was [secretary of] press and propaganda of our union which is called Asociación de Comerciantes Minoristas de Artículos de Primera Necesidad de las Tres Calles: Tumusla, Garita e Incachaca. Then I advanced to minute taker and from there to secretary-general. The members choose someone who knows how to read and write. When I was Secretary of Press and Propaganda, the secretary general saw that I knew how to write because I corrected the young man who used to take the minutes. So they got rid of him and promoted me to *secretaria de actas*. As *secretaria de actas* I had to read the minutes of the meetings, the correspondence, the agenda and "sundry matters." Well, I read with a clear and loud voice without making mistakes. So the members said that I should be their secretary-general.

There are two kinds [of leaders]. There are persons who become secretaries-general because of their government contacts. They become [leaders] for political reasons. They know how to use their contacts (*saben manejar*). They have contacts in the labor ministry or the federation. But I don't know persons [in the government]. I was urged [to become a leader] in spite of the fact that I had no experience. I am not involved in politics. I simply knew how to speak, read and think. The members told the woman [who preceded me], "Don't worry. [Sofía] is young. She will learn and will gain experience." I didn't know the people at the federation [either]. [But when] I went down there, I found out that they knew me. I also went to speak to the labor minister as well as the market superintendent. The only person I haven't spoken to yet is the mayor.

Right now, the major problem that I have is with persons who are trying to harm me and don't let me do my work. They are complaining about not being able to sell here. They are not members of our union but come from other unions, especially the daughter of Clotilda Chura who has her sales site in the Tablada. They say that that woman used to be a leader. Apparently, she was removed from office because she likes to fan the flames and then is unable to extinguish the fire. So they expelled her and she is now selling next to her mother. That person is now trying to harm me. She is inciting the persons I am leading according to the statutes against me.

[That] woman, whom we suspended for three months as a disciplinary measure, is ill-mannered and disrespectful. She has a bad tongue. I told her that she couldn't hog two or three meters of selling space for herself, explaining that there were other women who were asking for sales sites. A second woman with whom I had an altercation has [also] become my enemy. She tells me that, in time, she will topple me. She occupies almost two and a half meters of space. I even went to see the authorities in order to force her to use less space. She refuses [to budge]. According to city ordinances, each site is supposed to be only ninety centimeters wide, [but] from the day I became secretary-general, I observed that [some have larger sites than others]. At the lower end of the street, some occupy 150 centimeters and others have [very narrow ones]. The fat one that threw meat at you has two sales sites. There are quite a few women who sit in the middle of the street because they don't have a [proper] sales site. They are women whom Sra Clotilde inscribed. [But] they all pay the same. That's why I said that I would present a writ to the townhall to ask them for an inspector to remeasure the sites and give everyone the same eighty centimeters. [That way] the women who sit in the middle of the street could have their own sites. They are, after all, members of the union [too]. But right now I am unable to do that.

In another case, two women were quarreling. One of them wanted me to take her side. I can't do that. I have to be just and punish whoever is in error. That's why she is against me. The woman who [just] went out has a daughter. That daughter is not a member of our union, but she was a leader of the market union of La Tablada farther down. One day, I got very angry at her and shouted at her, "Why are you getting involved in the affairs of our union? Mind your own business." So she had the police take me down to the central police station. From there, I took her to the market union federation. There we came to an agreement. Five persons had gotten together to try to remove me from office. But the membership doesn't want that. They say, "You should be in office for four or five years. Why should those women be our leaders?" [Those women] said that I had gotten the members involved in [party] politics. The woman even wanted to hold a meeting without my authorization. This morning I told the woman, "You will have to give proof of what you say at the meeting. One has to be able to prove what one says. You can't just say things without evidence. You have to go down to the meeting and speak in front of the press. It should be apparent with what party the union is affiliated." She didn't say a word after that. [Earlier], she had said that I should provide a written accounting of the union funds. I told her, "I will furnish that to the outgoing secretary of the treasury but not to you. You were in office during four years and you only gave me the accounting for 1987." That's when she told me that I would have to testify about my political involvements. She said that a woman had told her that there was going to be a meeting at my house and that they would vote. I don't know how they can engage in such shady business. I said, "How is that possible? I have to announce a meeting to all of you. Then I would have to ask you whether you wanted to support such and such a party. How could I make a secret of such a thing?"

[At the moment we have no problems with the town hall.] I have spoken with the market superintendent. He is a kind person. He even gave me his home telephone number, something he has apparently not done for anybody else. Once we went to a restaurant and ate together.

[We used to have problems with the police] because of speculation. With the present crisis, speculation is no longer possible. Now sales are no longer regulated. They figure that you have to liquidate your wares as quickly as possible, even if it means taking a loss. So there is no control [over sales]. The townhall's function consists of collecting daily fees for selling on the street, stamping meat, seeing whether the meat has trichinosis, and watching over hygiene by making sure that no one's sale site is dirty.

Organizing Market Rituals: Becoming a Maestra Mayor of the Jank'o Amaya Fair (1980)

This year I am *maestra* [of the butchers who sell at the fair in Jank'o Amaya]. I must have a mass celebrated for the Virgin of Candelaria and bring a brass band. I have to prepare some dishes of food for the butchers who bring the meat [we buy]. They have a *maestro* too. Last year

(1979), I saw that they came with potatoes and mutton to give as a present to the *maestra*. So, some twenty of us held a meeting the Thursday before last. I represented the butchers, then there was someone from those who bring pants and things like that. The bakers, banana vendors, rubber sandal vendors, everybody has a *maestra*. I asked the Neighborhood Council whether the fiesta was going to be on April 3d or April 10th. We decided to hold the fiesta on April 10th and not during Holy Week, because that's a holiday and people might not come. The neighborhood council told us to inform the people that the new leadership for the following year would be installed on Thursday, April 3d. I notified the girl who is supposed to succeed me, but she told me that she didn't have the means to sponsor the fiesta. Instead, she said that she would do it the way I had, two years [after accepting the nomination]. You see, I have been *maestra* for two years already. Last year, I couldn't do it because I was expecting a child. They handed me official notices and even sent the police after me, so that I would accept. So I had a writ rendered by Mr. Quenta—you knew him, didn't you?—explaining that I couldn't do it because I was not feeling well and that my daughter might die if I did too much. I promised to act as *maestra* the following year instead. [They accepted]. However, the council told [my successor] that she couldn't postpone her turn [the way I had]. It was her turn. So she will have to do it. They had to force her the way they pressured me with the police. They told her that if she didn't accept the office, she couldn't come for meat any more. Remember, I told you that we were six persons selling. The first one to assume the office was Modesta, or Candicha, the pockmarked one, then Julia, then it was my turn or that of Julia's sister. So, since her sister had just passed and it was unlikely that Julia could pass the office on to her sister,[6] they forced me to do it. Last year, when I was selling meat, they called me.

It is very expensive, the beer. . . . I am afraid to pass. I am going to make a simple fiesta. They already know my situation, because the woman who passed the office on to me, a *cholita*, is a close friend of mine—although recently we have had some problems: we have even gone to the police with this woman. It was just a matter of something between friends, it wasn't anything serious. She is a good friend, but when she assumed the sponsorship, she said that she spent twelve thousand (US$480) because she had a mass read in a church in the neighborhood where I live here in La Paz. I won't [do that]. They know [that I can't]. You see, the woman who preceded me bought meat in large quantities during the period that she acted as *maestra* mayor, while I don't. They see that I buy [only] four carcasses or so, and I have to be stubborn to be able to do that. For example, when we had a meeting of the neighborhood council of Jank'o Amaya, I told them that I had a formal promise from these persons [to allow me to buy]; but, in spite of that, they don't give me the freedom to buy as I please. So, I will assume the sponsorship according to my own criteria. "Yes," they answered, "you can do as you please." I told them that I would pass [just] so that they couldn't say that I hadn't fulfilled my obligations. [In contrast, my predecessor] had celebrated the fiesta renting buses, hiring waiters, an orchestra. . . . She must want to display her wealth or something like that. Perhaps she thought that people might criticize her if she [didn't do it like that]. I think that she invited all the women who sell in the Garita and took them to Jank'o Amaya. I don't see how she did it myself. I escaped [from the fiesta] because I was pregnant. They told me I shouldn't escape, but I did it anyway in order not to have to pass. I used my pregnancy as a pretext. My plan was to come in the evening and I told my mother that I would present the *maestra* with a case of beer. The fiesta was held in the *local* (dance hall) next door to our house [in La Paz]. So I entered together with my nephew, Teodoro, and with my daughter's uncle, [René's brother], who also happens to be a friend of that woman. They were all drunk. Well, they had me sit down and they pinned [the little flag symbolizing the new sponsor on me]. They presented me with four bottles of beer, but I didn't want to accept. They took photos of me, saying that it was as a souvenir. I just laughed. Nobody actually saw me—one has to take the oath of office in the *feria*—but later, [in Jank'o Amaya] they made me take the oath in front of everybody. So I could no longer shirk my obligation, as I had originally intended.

Since I don't earn what they do—I think that they earn five or six thousand (US$200 or $240) during every trip[7]—I said that I would invite my relatives from Llamacachi and celebrate the fiesta there. I will invite the elders from Llamacachi, the *corregidor* (judge) from Compi, and people like that to accompany me, because I can't celebrate the fiesta alone. I asked the musicians from Chua to play. We agreed on one thousand pesos (US$40). At first they wanted fifteen hundred (US$60), but my mother said, "How can you charge me that much?" So they reduced it to one thousand. I am going to hire Tiburcio's truck. He probably will charge me one hundred fifty or three hundred (US$6 or $12). I will have Nicolás Nacho [who is a deacon in Compi] hold the mass. He always does. He even held mass in Compi for the Inca [dance group]. He holds wedding ceremonies, baptizes . . . he is just like a priest. The bishop of La Paz has authorized him to do this. He celebrates holy communion and everything. I didn't see it, but my friend says that one has to invite people to eat *lunche* consisting of cold cuts, cheese, and things like that, and one has to serve [a good meal and drinks] to the incoming sponsor for the following year. Then, so that they don't say that I am not spending enough, I want to hang flags everywhere in the fair, and after the mass, I will have to prepare a table near the site where we sell and set up a figure of the Christ Child. I don't know where I am going to rent one. One has to go there holding the figure of the Christ Child in one's hands. My friend rented one here in La Paz. She said that since I was alone, I should name a 'godmother' to accompany me during the fiesta. So a friend will accompany me. I plan to serve a *lunche* first. Then I will serve two rounds or so of beer. After that I want to give them more white rum so that all those people can get drunk. I have already asked a woman who has the site next to me in the Tumusla to help me. Then I am asking my nephew to collaborate with *colitas*.[8] I saw that [my predecessor] did that when I went to the fiesta that evening. Then, at four in the afternoon, I will serve a lamb stew—I don't have the means to pay for chicken.[9] Then I will return to Llamacachi with all my followers. I will do only that because I can't afford an orchestra—they charge nine thousand (US$360) per day. I will follow my own criteria. You see, last year (1979) I saw the [*maestra* of] the bakers dancing to brass band music. And since there was no *maestra* last year, we celebrated all alone. Only the person who had sponsored the fiesta during the previous year came with a case of beer and two gallon jugs of cocktail. There was no food. However, the butchers had brought cooked produce in bundles and they poured that [on long cloths] in front of us. There was fish, cracklings, potatoes, *ocas*, and *habas*. They said that it was for all of us, but the selfish [former sponsor] took it all for herself [and her followers]. I watched her without saying a word. The butchers were accompanied by Luribay[10] music and so we danced to their music. We arrived here in La Paz loaded with meat[11] and totally drunk. That's what it probably will be like when I pass too.

When we returned the next year (1981), Sofía had undertaken the sponsorship and had passed the charge on to the next person in line.

The two Espinosa sisters [one of whom passed on the sponsorship to me] are my enemies now. We used to be close friends. They used to leave their meat here in the courtyard. But one day when I was away in the country, a pig carcass got lost . . . so now we are no longer on speaking terms. She did, however, pass on the *maestra* sponsorship on to me. I accepted the charge and invited her to the fiesta. She was amazed how well I did it. I had food and drinks to spare.

At present, the *maestra* of the butchers is from Huarina. She came to buy on the market for the first time last year (1980). She only comes to buy a pig or two to make *chicharrón*. She is not an intermediary. She sells *chicharrón* across the street from the traffic police station. Originally, two persons were supposed to sponsor the fiesta together. Then they forced her to do it, because [the woman from Tiquina] had trouble with the village authorities. They said that she works for the naval base. In reality, she only cooks food [there]. So now Fermín (the village authority) [told the woman from Huarina] to undertake the sponsorship.

Now six women from Huatajata are coming to buy lamb. They buy the first-quality animals, the large fat ones that cost five or six hundred pesos (US$20 or $30), while I buy those that they reject for 180, 200, or 220 pesos (US$$7.20, $8, or $8.80). (The authorities) told them to assume the sponsorship. They refused. Because (the authorities) scolded them, no one from Huatajata came to buy lamb last Thursday. They are no longer welcome. It is their obligation to become *maestras*. On the anniversary of the foundation of the fair everybody has to participate. If they don't act as sponsors, their trade will fold. That's why *we* will have act as sponsors [representing the mutton dealers]: we don't want them to return. We compete for mutton and if they come [again] there will be quarrels.

Problems of Organizing Market Fiestas in La Paz

While the role of urban market leaders is not exclusively, or even principally, ceremonial, as it is in the case of maestras mayores *in rural fairs, ritual obligations loom large as well. The pitfalls of organizing a fiesta are many, as the following examples show: the first was a fiesta to celebrate the founding of the Inca Chaca market and Mother's Day, and the second one was to celebrate the founding of the city of La Paz.*

We named two persons as *padrinos* of *salteñas* (meat turnovers). And we bought an additional 150 *salteñas*. Then I talked to the woman over there—she is the treasurer—how we could get a priest to hold a mass. I wondered whether we would have to present a written request to the bishop of the cathedral. A woman who has recently started bringing pork from the slaughter house [overheard our conversation] and asked, "Are you looking for a priest?" "Yes," we answered. "I will get you one," she continued. So we arranged for the priest to be there at 10:30 to hold mass at noon. We prepared arches and everything for the mass. But the priest didn't arrive. The people were getting worried. It was already one o'clock and everybody was wondering when the mass would be held. I was in a pickle. We quarreled among the union leadership. Then the *secretaria de relaciones,* who always wants to know what we are doing with the union funds, asked, "Where is the money that you collected? Haven't you nominated *madrinas* for that very purpose?" So we ran off to fetch another priest at the Chapel of the Rosary in the Calle Illampu. The priest there, a thin man, told us that he didn't have time because it was Mothers' Day and he was going to the cemetery to hold a mass there for a deceased mother. I pleaded with him to hold a mass for us too, and he said he would come when he finished the mass. But then another man who has a cut in his face presented himself and said, "I am the priest." We asked, "How much?" And he answered, "sixty thousand (US$2.40). Give them to me right away." The *secretaria* gave him the sixty. When we reached the corner, the real priest was already waiting for us. The one that the *madrina* had asked to come is from the Augustinian order—I think they are Americans. When he saw [the real priest], the "priest" [whom we had given the money] tried to escape. I held on to him and told him, "Even though you will not be holding the mass, we would like you to bless our sales sites." He promised to return but vanished with the money. Later we investigated at the cemetery who the man was, and it turned out that he was some poor fellow who assists the priests. Ever since then I am suspicious. A man who says that he is a musician comes each month and asks me to give him an advance, [promising that he will bring a band to the fiesta]. I doubt whether a real musician would be so insistent. He came yesterday and the day before. He comes to see me every day. How am I going to give him money?

The problems Sofía had organizing the mass to commemorate the day of the inauguration of the market union in the Inca Chaca street pale in comparison with the problems she was to experience organizing the annual fiesta held in all La Paz markets on July 15th, the eve of the Day of La Paz, in 1988, a fiasco which was all the more embarrassing, since it was captured on video tape.

The fiesta, which has at least a semi-obligatory nature, as its observation is decreed by the mayor of La Paz, consists of decorating all La Paz markets with flower arrangements, strings of light bulbs and colored paper cutouts hung across the market streets and trimming each sales site with paper lanterns, and drinking, eating and dancing to the sound of a brass band or flute ensemble throughout the evening. Sofía and the other market leaders had been involved in making elaborate preparations for several days before the event. Quotas had to be gath-

ered from each vendor to finance the fiesta, flower baskets had to be purchased, the strings of light bulbs and paper cutouts taken out, the anthropologists and the filmmaker appointed as "lightbulb godparents" to buy light bulbs to replace the broken ones, cooked food sellers asked to prepare dishes to serve to members of the brass band and to the market leaders, and, most important of all, a brass band had to be hired to provide music for the occasion. At first, all went smoothly, but the happy mood was dampened when the musicians had still not arrived by 10:30. When they finally did appear, only half of their contingent arrived, for they were still participating in the longer than usual parade the ambitious mayor has organized downtown. When we visited Sofía, the next day, she was disconsolate and ready to give up her position as secretary-general of the Inca Chaca market.

I am going to present my resignation during the next union meeting because there is no understanding among us. Now with this problem of the contract with this band it will be worse. The people will say that I am not doing things well.

[The woman who is your enemy[12]] was sitting at the street corner. I threw confetti on her head and told her not to be angry with me. I told her that it wasn't my fault. The brass band was a military band. She answered that it was quite logical, that they always came only after the parade.

The one who [was most angry at me] was the secretary of relations, Cristina. Later, after you left, I had a quarrel with the secretary of conflicts too. She called me all sorts of names. She shouted at me, "Daughter of a whore, who signed this contract?" I countered, "Why weren't you there at the time?" Then her predecessor, who sells near the door [to my house] confronted her and said, "Why are you scolding the woman. She is conscientious. She is a good and reasonable woman. Who do you think you are? At your age, you should know better than to talk such nonsense. I am your junior but even so I was a better leader than you are." The two women almost came to blows. At that point I went into my house. They wanted me to go down to the entrance of the movie theater, but I refused and went home. The brass band was supposed to play down there and then go up to the corner performing a snake dance. But I said to myself, "How am I going to go down there with three musicians? I will lose face."

I thought about getting a *sicuri* (panpipe) band until the musicians arrived, but I had no idea that the parade would be so large and would last so many hours. The parade has taken place every year since I was a child and it always lasted only until 7:30 or 8:00. Now its too much. [The mayor] forced all the neighborhoods and the markets and the factories [to go]. All the military bands: the police band, the navy band, the city band. When [our] band finally arrived, the people had gone. Some eleven musicians came. Eleven plates of food were served. We had the cook prepare chicken. We wanted to serve them the food when they came. But then the hours passed. . . . The rest of the food was supposed to be for the leadership. Some stayed. They served twenty-two plates all in all. Thirty had been prepared.

I will have to show the people the contract with the amount I gave as an advance payment. I am not going to pay the balance. That way, I think, the membership will be satisfied. I will keep the money I have in the union treasury. I don't want the members to say that we are trying to cheat them and demand that we give the money back,

I will convert this money and the money we have from small fines I gathered when some women didn't want to go on the protest march against the mayor's office—I gathered five thousand from every woman who didn't go—into something for the union hall when I leave office. I am not going to give the cash [to my successor]. When I took over the office, the treasury was empty too, so I can't pass the funds on, I prefer to invest the money in something. That's my plan. I will stop renting the room for the union. The union had it's office in that room for five years now. I prefer to rent it for a rent in U.S. dollars. I need money. I have debts. Let the union find another place.

The Influence of Women

Hans Schlumpf, with whom we were filming Sofía's life, asked us to request Sofía's opinion about the role of women in Bolivia. In general, we did not ask such abstract questions, but we include her response here because it reveals the female centeredness of her world view. She replied:

With respect to the power of women in Bolivia I can say that their power is connected to their work. In these times of unemployment it is the woman who leaves the home to work. She is the one who works while the husband stays at home taking care of things there. Now, in the market, a woman may have power over the membership of a union if she has the character [to be a leader]. For example, I am a leader and they tell me to force the women to respect me. However, I don't have it in my character to scold them. I have a heart and feel compassion for them. When I see that a poor stranger needs a place to sell, I don't scold her but find her a spot where they can offer their wares. But when they quarrel, [then I must react differently]. In this market, [such quarrels] don't occur very frequently, but there are three small cliques of bad women who don't have any respect for others. For example, I punished Paulina Huanca by suspending her right to sell in the market for three months. She is a fat woman who sits next to the kiosk. I had the authorities punish her for three months to teach her to behave, but even that didn't work.

[Women do have other vendors as friends.] [Outside the market] I have a close friendship with the woman who owns a restaurant and to whom I sell meat. But I also see friendships between women sitting next to one another. They become friends or *comadres*. I frequently see them talk to one another or go and drink together. They lend one another money and they are concerned about what is happening in each others lives. For example, the woman who died last year, Ventura, had a friend called Máxima. She always knew what was happening to Ventura. She knew whether Ventura had a lover or not. The day Ventura died, Máxima cried. She said that Ventura had stopped talking to that man and that's why the man had killed her. The other neighbor knew to whom Ventura had sold meat on credit. It was just because they were selling side by side. I myself don't have any deep friendships [with other vendors in the market]. They respect me and I talk to them kindly and help them but it doesn't go beyond that.

[Sometimes friends assist one another against abusive men.] If a man is mean they might be angry against him. If a man beats a woman they may commiserate with her. That's why they came to the union office with Ventura—the woman who died. The man had beaten her badly and we became very angry about it. We called her husband but her husband told us that she didn't deserve to be a mother or a wife, because she had a lover. It turned out that the lover was a client of hers. He bought [pig] heads from her to make *enrollados*.

The union members didn't know about all this. Only her neighbors did. But the union leadership asked those who knew about it not to talk. The deceased woman also held a leadership position. We dealt with the matter, but the man killed her anyway, by beating her.

My secretary of organization, Rosa Espinosa, was [also] beaten by her husband. One day, I called her husband and told him that I didn't like the fact that he was beating his wife. I told him, "Your wife doesn't have any lovers. She doesn't cheat. Since I am a leader, I see with whom the woman is drinking." There are women who perhaps have problems at home. My secretary of organization says that her husband works in the Said factory but that he never brings his pay home. He will bring her twelve or thirteen pesos, or sometimes nothing at all. In contrast, she comes here and makes big sacrifices to provide bread for her household and clothing for her children. She can no longer cope with the burden, so she goes out and drinks with an elderly woman who [also] likes to drink beer. When her husband sees her [drunk] he beats her thinking that she has gone out with men. But I told him, "I have never seen your wife drink with men, only with Señora Nieves. And you must be aware of why she is drinking." [These instances are rare].

Seniority and Its Costs

The organization of rural fairs and urban market sites has technical, economic, political, ceremonial, and moral dimensions. With age and/or seniority, persons like Sofía are pressured to assume increasingly demanding and sometimes onerous obligations that generally include the organization and sponsorship of costly rituals. These sponsorships are usually associated with governance. They culminate a year of leadership service. As mentioned earlier, the relative importance of ritual versus leadership obligations varies. In rural fairs, the maestras mayores' *obligations are mostly ceremonial and are demanded of everyone. As a result, they serve to eliminate those vendors without a long term stake in the market and to legitimize and bestow prestige on those who do. In that respect, markets are similar to rural communities, where—at least in the past—all household heads were required to hold a series of civil and religious offices (H. Buechler 1980). Although associated with a specific group, in this case the butchers and, in a broader sense, the vendors of the entire fair, these groups merely form the anchorage point for the set of individuals who are invited to participate by the* maestras mayores. *For example, in the case of Sofía's predecessor (and rival), the guests included the market vendors of the street market where the* maestra mayor *sold. Such sponsorships usually also include a large number of kinsmen, friends and neighbors (see H. Buechler 1980).*

In at least those urban markets organized as sindicatos, *or unions (unlike the* maestreríos *of the still traditionally organized covered markets), only those individuals with obvious leadership talents tend to be selected for top leadership positions. A lower proportion of the economic burden falls on the sponsors, and the members contribute a larger share, but the responsibility still rests predominantly on the principal leaders. As the chapter shows, we had a hard time comforting Sofía for what she perceived as a failed fiesta.*

Leadership Qualities

Judith-Maria has discussed the notion of female empowerment in Bolivia using case material from Sofía and a female artisan elsewhere (in press). In this context, we wish to stress the way in which Sofía constructs her identity as household head and leader. Both roles require that she command respect, but exercise her authority and power with compassion. She is aware that leaders are apt to—in fact expected to—act in an authoritarian manner and to use their power for personal gain. In a previous chapter, she admitted and decried her own complicity with a leader who extracted fines and contributions for her own purposes. She sees the importance of the strong leader, but strength is here defined as the power to impose the just distribution of resources in the market and to mediate quarrels in the market and sometimes the households of the members.

In chapter 7, we discussed the political involvement of union leaders. Such involvement has always been the source of potential schisms within unions and union federations. Perhaps as a result of this fact, or because political activism was long proscribed during military rule and continues to have a negative connotation, or because different market vendors (or their spouses) could potentially belong to any of a plethora of political parties that have emerged (or re-emerged) with democracy, union leaders have to be more careful about involving their unions in politics. Union and federation leaders made claims of political neutrality in the sixties too. However, at least at that time, the temptation to side with a particular presidential candidate and to reap political awards should that candidate be elected constituted a powerful temptation to break with avowals of eschewing political partisanship. Given her family's history, Sofía's rival's accusations of political partisanship can hardly be taken at face value. Rather, they are indicative of the countless intrigues discussed in chapter 7 which pervade market unions.

10

CHANGING *Identifications*

While individuals representing a relatively wide range of the social spectrum engage in marketing, positions of power in union locals and the more traditional, guildlike marketing organizations are often held by women who identify themselves narrowly in terms of dress, rituals and, to a degree, lifestyle. Not surprisingly, Sofía, had to come to terms with this issue. In 1977, Sofía decided to change from the more modern European style of the chota chola *to the* pollera. *She found that she was more readily accepted by other vendors and was less likely to be bothered by men while selling. Her decision was thus intimately related to her occupation. Sofía made the switch when she danced in the major fiesta in her community. For that occasion, dancers dress in color coordinated* polleras *on the eve of the saint's day and early in the morning of the saint's day itself. Thus Sofía had a special incentive to purchase the expensive clothing and jewelry of the properly dressed* chola. *Sofía had begun to plan for the switch several years earlier. In 1976, she had made up her mind. She told us about her decision in the context of the career alternatives she felt were open to her. One of these would have been a career associated with the Catholic church.*

Mother Chantal, sister Ann, and the priest would arrive in a jeep and hold mass last year (1975). They always used to come. That's why Nicolás was put in charge [as deacon], because the nuns couldn't come all the time. . . . A young man from Chua is learning to become a priest.

Nicolás took a course and went all over the place. He was studying in Peñas for almost a year. He talked with Mother Chantal and she helped him and they have made a large meeting hall in his house. They hold workshops and meetings there . . .

Mother Chantal told me to go [too]. I met her in Compi one day. She had found out that my father had died. I was cultivating the land in Compi. I have some land there that my father had bought recently. The nuns were taking the pupils from the Sagrados Corazones School on an outing, and when they saw me, they called out to me and asked whether it was true that my father had died and whether I was married now. When I told [Mother Chantal] that I was not, she scolded me, "Why haven't you married? Why have you remained single?" I answered, "I can't. I don't like it." "Even the little birds have their companions," she countered, "You should find yourself someone. How can you remain all alone?" . . . Then she asked me what I was doing and I answered that I was tilling the soil like my father had done. Then she presented me to the mother superior, telling her that I had been the best pupil at Sagrados Corazones. Thereupon [the mother superior] told me that I should take classes. She said, "You are better than Nicolás. He didn't know anything when he started and now he is a priest (actually a deacon). You could be just like him. There would be a position for you."

I answered that I would think about it and she told me to visit her at the school. I never went—I didn't want to because my mother is all alone. She has just become a widow and she could easily become ill remembering my father. Now she has forgotten my father, [but only] because I entertain her. I can't leave her alone.

There have been other occasions when I could have worked for the nuns. People even told me that I should work as a teacher at the school in Chua. Last year, the director of the school, Yolanda, told me, "You have studied in the best school and you express yourself well. Why don't you teach religion or sewing." If this Edmundo Gutierrez, who knows nothing, can be a teacher, [you could do it too]. I told her that I would think about it, but decided against that too. Instead, I cooked for the teachers. . . . I made good food and there was always some left over for me. That's why I did it.

[I am not planning to become a teacher]. Quite frankly, señor, since I am alone and I don't want anything to happen to my mother, my plans are to sell this house and buy one directly on the street and open a grocery store like Menacho has and, at the same time, change to *polleras*. What do you think about that?

My mother tells me that I should do that. She says, "It's not proper for you to be travelling. It's ridiculous. Set yourself up in business as soon as possible." So I plan to bring my mother [to La Paz] from there and work with [a lot of] capital. I want to set up a large store and continue with it until my mother dies. I could work as a teacher, and I would like to, but it would not be convenient. They might place me in school in some far away place. [Also], to tell you the truth, I have seen what the life of a teacher is like, when I cooked for them. I didn't like what I saw. I used to like the idea of being a teacher, but I no longer do. People look down on you when you say that you are teacher. I have seen a lot of vulgar things. So I said to myself that I wasn't accustomed to behave like that. I am a woman and prefer to remain who I am. Now, as far as being *de vestido* is concerned, I could continue dressing the way I am dressing now, but then I would have to find some white-collar employment or public (formal) employment. For example, Pedro wanted to find me a job in the Manhattan factory [where he works]. I didn't want that. Then he suggested working in Inti (a pharmaceutical company) and I didn't want that either.

I am doing well in business. In the Manhattan factory, those who sew collars onto shirts earn three or four thousand (US$150 to US$200) a month, and those who cut, earn more than that. Those who check for faults apparently earn eight hundred (US$40) or so. My mother must be earning over one thousand (US$50) and what we eat comes from the store as well. At the same time, our capital doesn't get lost. My mother can buy lambs whole and so we can eat well. She buys more now than when my father was alive, perhaps because he used to control her spending. But she is not fat, like she used to be, she is thin, after all the grieving for my father.

Well, anyway, I am thinking of wearing a *pollera*. I already wanted to make the switch on New Year's Day, but I lacked shawl pins and [other] jewelry. I have some golden ones that I wear, put I want to buy gilded silver ones. I am having some nice *mantas* (large shawls) made. I have made myself *polleras* [already]. I own twelve *polleras* and I have a *manta*; I have a hat and *chola*-style earrings. I am having all this made for myself because I want to dress really well, not like those other *cholas*. Some *cholas* dress very well and that's how I want to be dressed too. Then I want to go into business.

A woman who is *de pollera* can sit wherever she wants without having to be afraid. Someone who is *de vestido* is afraid to [sit in the street] and can't sell as easily, because the [social] differences are more pronounced. Even the customers don't buy as readily from a *de vestido*. That's why when I go to sell, I have to wear a *manta*.

I would stand to gain [by switching to *polleras*]. You see, [European] dresses are cheap, the entire outfit is cheap. But if one want's to dress well as a *de pollera* [it costs a lot]. Even Sra. Judith must not be spending as much money on clothing. The best *polleras* cost two thousand pesos (US$100) and a vicuña *manta*[1] costs eight hundred pesos (US$90). That makes thirty-eight hundred (US$190). A borsalino hat costs fifteen hundred pesos (US$75), adding up to, say, five thousand (US$250). Then come the earrings. I had a pair made for three thousand pesos (US$150) and the shawl pin costs eight thousand pesos (US$400). Now, while a pair of street shoes costs only 120 (US$6) or so, a better pair of shoes costs 350 (US$17.50). A well made shoe immediately signifies a good *chola* who dresses well. I still need a small hat pin in the shape of a butterfly for my hat. Those pins cost one thousand pesos (US$50). I figure that to dress well, a woman has to spend between eighteen thousand pesos (US$900) and twenty thousand (US$1000), or, perhaps fifteen thousand (US$750). In contrast, a *de vestido* woman doesn't spend that much. The best clothing costs us [only] five hundred (US$25).[2]

That's why Banzer said on television that the *cholas* who wear all that jewelry are really wealthy. He said that [even] the upper class (*clase*

Sofía and Rocío assisting us with fieldwork in La Paz (1981) after Sofía had made the switch to chola *dress*

buena) didn't dress like that. He said that he didn't want to see women wearing *chola* outfits any longer. He said that, in time, they should switch to dresses. He felt that they were spending too much on their outfits, that they had too much money, and that he didn't know where they were getting all that money from. That's why he has declared war on the vendors using the police. He thinks that we earn a lot when we sell and resents us for it. They say that we will have to pay a tax on the clothing we wear.

[The *cholas* must have a lot of clothing]. I know that they do. When I see them in their outfits, my mouth drops open because I know how much it costs. Perhaps jewelry was cheap when they bought it and they were able to take advantage of that. Now they are well off. A *manta* made out of American polyester alone costs five thousand pesos (US$250). I am sure that they didn't have to pay prices like that when they bought theirs. That's why I am hesitant about switching. I would have to work hard to dress well.

Our first discussion with Sofía about dress and ranking was for Judith-Maria's dissertation. She and other vendors explained the minute distinctions of shawls, skirts, hats, etc. (J.-M. Buechler 1972). We had many other conversations with Sofía, regarding her switch to chola clothing. One of these took place in 1975, before Sofía actually made the switch. We were buying chola *outfits for our eight-year-old twin daughters. The hat, we learned, had to be light gray, to correspond to the latest* chola *fashion, the crown had to be high and the hat size relatively small, so the hat could be worn at a jaunty angle and with the combed back hair showing above the forehead. On another occasion, in 1981, when we were engaging in research on small-scale industries, Sofía explained the attributes of the ideal* pollera *for a fiesta. Such a pollera was made from a thick, textured, acrylic velvet, named "chinchilla" (presumably because it imitated the fur of the Andean rodent). Because of the thickness of the material, such a* pollera *had to be sewn by hand with three, rather than the more usual four, pleats. At another time, we were initiated into the intricacies of* chola *jewelry including the heavy, pearled earrings with floral motifs, which, in addition to their decorative and prestige function, also serve as a longer term investment. Interestingly, Sofía's friend, Yola, had made the switch to chola clothing a few years before Sofía decided to do so too, as the following conversation, recorded in 1975 shows. Yola's example highlights the multifaceted nature of the considerations involved in the decision to wear one or the other style of clothing: beauty, and social status within the market and vis a vis the world outside the market.*

Now [Yola] is selling cloth in those kiosks in the Calle Max Paredes. I don't know if that's how Yola came to know her husband. But I do remember that once, when we were fourteen or fifteen years old (in 1959 or 1960), we asked Mother Chantal for permission to celebrate a small fiesta. We wanted to invite boys to it too. Mother Chantal accepted and we celebrated the coronation of a class queen. They nominated me as madrina de cohetillón and Yola *madrina* of soft drinks. We were taking sewing classes at that time and the prettiest girl of our class was Maria Luisa Vargas. She was crowned as beauty queen. There were two *cambitas* who knew how to prepare fiestas well. We didn't know how to do it, but they organized it. We celebrated it in the Hotel Siglón in the Prado. It doesn't exist any longer. It was a nice small house. We collected quotas of fifteen pesos from everyone. We even had an orchestra. And there I saw Yola with this young man. Before that, I hadn't known that she had a boyfriend. Well, she had invited the young man to the coronation and danced with him. I think that her mother liked him because she was there too. She was sixteen then and she married him when she was seventeen. And one year before she would have gotten her degree, Yola married that man. She stopped selling produce and began to sell cloth at a site where her parents-in-law sold. Her mother, [Clorinda], and [her mother's friend], Saturnina, continued selling produce. Clorinda took over the daughter's business and her sales site. Later, the two "mothers" stopped selling produce when [the authorities] only permitted the sale of clothing. Yola still sells cloth.

Yola earned so that her husband could study. He studied to become a lawyer at the university. At the same time, he liked politics. He was a *movimentista*. He became a notary public in the Avenida Buenos Aires and was the head of the militia of the zone. He was very involved [in the party]. Yola no longer is *de vestido*. She is *de pollera*. She was very pretty when she was *de vestido*. She is also very pretty *de pollera*. She is light skinned and thin. It suited her to become *de pollera*. I think that she was the prettiest *chola* in La Paz. Once, when I was nineteen or so, there was a dance. At the time, Victor Paz was president. My brother Pedro was *jefe de comando* (militia chief) and Yola's husband was *subjefe de comando* (militia subchief). Well, there was a social event in the palace in the Plaza Murillo. I went too. I have been in the government palace! I entered with my brother. Yola was dressed very nicely with a white embroidered shawl (manta). Huy! Barrientos fell in love with Yola. Seriously! Barrientos fell in love with her. I knew Barrientos well at the time. He was a good-looking young man. He was in the military and he was still a bachelor. He was not yet president. Pedro knew him because he may have driven him to the palace or maybe not even that. But the president, at the time, was Paz Estenssoro. Barrientos came towards Pedro, talked to him and my brother seemed delighted. Barrientos must have told him to present Yola to him. Yola introduced herself and she and Barrientos danced in the palace! It was a splendid dance. I never would have dreamed that I would enter the palace and be with the government. It was a beautiful fiesta! There were waiters who went around with all sorts of delicious dishes. We ate whatever we wanted. Yola was the only one who was *de pollera*, all the others were *de vestido*. So it [must have been] something exotic for Barrientos. I was *de vestido* and my sister-in-law too. We all were dressed in our finest clothes. There were some ladies wearing furs that seem to have cats' heads. The people were mixed. There were people of the high society and others, like we, were *clase media*. The orchestra had some enormous guitars. They began to play the national anthem for the president announcing that he was about to come down. How handsome he looked coming down those luxurious steps while we waited excitedly.

I always tell Yola that maybe she should have married Barrientos. She is a beautiful young woman. I seem old compared to her. She still looks young. Yola preferred to wear *polleras* because she looks prettier that way. She is well-shaped, not like some other *cholas*. Her husband liked her[3] that way and she stopped wearing [Western-style] skirts.

When Yola's husband received his law degree in 1971, he threw a very beautiful fiesta. [I was invited to the fiesta too]. He did it very well. His wife was very happy and proud. She said that it was she, a woman, who had enabled her husband to become a lawyer. Then, in 1972 to 1974, they sent him to work in Copacabana. It is customary for lawyers to first practice in rural areas. He is no longer Señor Isidro but Abogado Isidro. [Yola] went too and so did the children. She cooked and washed and the children went to school there. She didn't work [outside of the home] there. She entrusted her sales site to her mother who sold for her. Now he works as a lawyer and has his office facing the courthouse and she started to sell again. She sells to this day.

Yola is thinking of changing back to *de vestido*. She says, "Now that my husband is a lawyer, I can no longer be a *chola*. I shall have to put a dress on." I am [reconsidering my plans about wearing *polleras*] too because the *pollera* is expensive. More than anything, Yola is thinking of changing to *de vestido* because of her children. She has two sons. The older one is twelve and the younger one seven. She thinks that her sons may criticize her. Her husband wants her to continue [to be] *de pollera*. She is the one who wants to change. Sometimes she is embarrassed. She says that she doesn't want to be seen with her husband when the wives of his clients come to visit. She says that his clients are *de vestido*, they are *gente buena* (higher class). Also, her husband is invited to attend fiestas among lawyers. And she would like to be dressed as well as possible. She says that she would like to talk to the ladies and it's difficult. It seems to me that they don't want to talk to her and so she remains silent. That's why she wants to change [to *de vestido*].

I guess [people] think that a woman who is *de pollera* is inferior and that a woman who is *de vestido* knows better. For example, when Yola tries to talk to them, they may think that she is an illiterate person who hasn't attended school. Of course they would be mistaken. Yola has studied and knows how to express herself, but they must think of themselves as very superior persons. So Yola doesn't want to talk any more either; she goes to one side. Yola laughs [about it]. She says, "I don't like it. Sometimes I am ashamed of the *pollera*. But when I am drunk, then I am no longer afraid and I start to discuss things with them." So they talk about Bolivian history and all sorts of topics and Yola bests the ladies. She says that she tells them that she is proud of wearing a *pollera* and that she is the most enlightened *chola* there is.

Like Yola, Sofía had second thoughts about switching to chola clothing, but for different reasons. In 1980, after Sofía had been wearing polleras for several years, she said:

[For the past two and half years or three years I've worn chola clothing], but sometimes people tell me that because I have a daughter now I will have to change back again. The *pollera* is very expensive. Now that prices have risen I have told my mother that I won't [buy] any more. [Now they cost] two thousand (US$80) or three thousand (US$120) and the mantas fifteen hundred (US$75) or so. It is difficult to earn money now.[4]

An interview with Sofía in 1976 about consumer credit provides some idea why cholas continue to lay such a heavy emphasis on clothing and jewelry as a means of displaying their wealth, rather than engaging in conspicuous consumption by buying consumer goods on credit. As independent entrepreneurs, which many of them are, their monthly incomes are subject to strong fluctuations, making it risky for them to buy things on monthly installments, even if they are able to come up with an item acceptable as a pawn, which stores insist on in the absence of the guarantee of a steady job or a guarantor with a steady job. Consumer goods lose their value rapidly, making them unsuitable as pawns when capital should suddenly be required for their ventures.[5]

Last year (1975), Elvira and I went together [to shop]. She wanted to buy a television set and I a gas kitchen range. We went to the Crédito Popo in the Yanacocha and when we asked about the television set for Elvira, they asked for eighty-four hundred pesos (US$420) or something like that in cash. So I asked whether they would sell it to us on credit [for one year]. They said: "Of course, but what can you leave as a pawn?" The sales girl said that [she] should bring the title to the house and a responsible person, such as the owner of a factory or another person with capital or with a store or other business. Then [she] would have to pay two thousand pesos (US$100) [as a down payment] and she would give [her] the television. After that, [she] would have to pay 550 pesos (US$27.50) each month for eight months [*sic*]. "If you want to pay it in six months then you will have to pay seven hundred (US$35) and something pesos." Anyway, she sold it to us and it came to ten thousand pesos (US$500). Then we asked about the kitchen range that cost some three thousand pesos (US$150) and she said that I could pay one thousand pesos (US$50) down and again she asked whether I wanted to pay in six or in eight months and I had to pay three hundred (US$15) pesos each time and I think that it came to five thousand (US$250). She gave me a little paper and things like that. But then we went to another store in the Calle Comercio and there they charged less. So it would have come to 250 pesos (US$12.50) per month and would have cost me four thousand pesos (US$200) or something like that. They make a profit of almost thirteen hundred (US$65) over and above the thirty-five hundred (US$175) [*sic*]; something like that [for eight months].

[I am not thinking of buying a range on credit]. It doesn't make sense for me. But my nephew [and his wife] are more eager because Máxima works in the Said factory and they have discussed it with her. She went down [with them]. I don't know why those who work in factories are regarded as safer bets. They give them whatever they want in those stores with more confidence. This woman went down and they handed her the television set without any down payment whatsoever. My nephew took it out without paying a cent. He is paying five hundred pesos (US$25) every month, but he didn't pay one thousand in the beginning. He was able to get it just like that. He told me that he has almost finished paying for it. I think that he has two months or so to go. But it makes sense for him to do it because he didn't have to pay anything down.

For me it's different. It doesn't make sense for me to be paying off five hundred (US$25) each month: what if I don't earn five hundred (US$25) during a particular month? I again had the urge to buy one when I went to another store where they told me, "You are going to pay two hundred

(US$10) each month for a year." But they told me that I would have to leave one thousand pesos (US$50). I told them that I would take it, because I can earn fifty pesos (US$2.50) each Saturday which would make two hundred (US$10) a month. But then I told myself that it was better to pay cash.

In that case they will surely give me a discount. They won't charge me the full 350 pesos (US$17.50). They give a discount when it's a cash sale. That's how it is, Señor Hans. That's why I want to pay cash, and some day I will buy it, Señor Hans.

In the mid-seventies Sofía made the decision, which she is unlikely to reverse, to relinquish earlier plans for a more middle class (by North American and some Latin American standards) career as a deacon or as a rural school teacher, deciding, instead, that commerce was both more lucrative and, at least in comparison to teaching in rural schools, less compromising in terms of her personal ethics. As we saw in chapter 1, the family's move to Llamacachi and Sofía's negative experiences when she attempted to go back to school as an adult had already inclined her to abandon these alternative plans, but it was not until 1976 that she made up her mind completely.

The decision to remain in commerce entailed a rethinking of the manner in which she presented herself to others. As we have discussed in the introduction, Bolivians do not apply a unitary classificatory scheme to differences in social standing. Alternative schemes stress length of urban residence, occupation, descent, education, or economic success. Some schemes are meant to apply to everyone, others to a narrow segment of the population. Different schemes apply to men and women. Some schemes resemble modern North American ones, others are more reminiscent of medieval feudalism. Finally, the criteria for upward mobility from the perspective of one scheme may conflict with those of another scheme.

Yet the schemes are not entirely independent of each other. Individuals may measure their standing according to more than one scheme at a time or even amalgamate conflicting schemes, sometimes resolving contradictions and sometimes exacerbating them. Upward mobility by one spouse measured according to one scheme may conflict with that of the other spouse measured according to another scheme, requiring accommodation, or, alternatively, a decision to maintain separate social networks.

Aymara Indians migrated to colonial cities since the sixteenth century where some became highly successful merchants. The latter and the descendants of the inhabitants of the rural communities surrounding the city which were eventually engulfed by the city often displayed and underlined their success by assuming expensive sponsorships both in the city itself and in the nearby village of Laja, where La Paz was originally founded. In addition, the women assumed the expensive dress style described by Sofía. In contrast, the men did not wear distinctive clothing. The archetype of the successful chola *is variously the meat (particularly beef and pork) vendor, the market woman in the major closed central markets (Camacho, Lanza, and Sopocachi, and, before its closure, the flower market), the costume manufacturer from the town of Achacachi, or the milk vendor who traditionally sold milk produced by her family on small plots around the city. Although* cholas *shared a general dress code, they did not necessarily regard themselves as a homogeneous group. Rather, each occupation had, and, to an extent, continues to maintain, its own customs. These groups were highly visible in neighborhood fiestas where they organized their own dance groups (see Buechler 1980: 161 and Albó and Preiswerk 1986). At least into the 1970s, the descendants of the agricultural communities in the La Paz basin continued to be the first to be asked to act as sponsors for neighborhood fiestas (Buechler 1980: 291). To this day, the milk vendors, of whom there are actually only a few left, are celebrated in a dance representing their trade. Sofía herself has danced as a* lechera *in Compi. Finally, the butchers practice distinctive customs at weddings, as Sofía and her family found out to their dismay when one of Moises's sons got married to a beef butcher.*[6]

In some instances, subgroups maintained a ritual ranking. Thus, in the fiesta of Concepción, the term cholada *was reserved for the sponsors and their followers from the lower part of the neighborhood and the designation* indiada *(used pejoratively in other contexts and officially banned by the government since 1952, but used in a more neutral sense in this case) was employed for the inhabitants of the upper part of the neighborhood with a more recent agricultural past (in fact one of the sponsors still had a few dairy cows which his family fed with residues from the beer brewery) (see Buechler 1980: 174–5, 182–7).*

Although cheaper variants of the chola dress style are worn by rural women, it is not primarily associated with ethnic distinctions. Crandon-Malamud (1991) concludes that, contrary to the claims of the protagonists, ethnic dichotomies are problematic. She found that in a Lake Titicaca town she studied, townsmen of peasant and landowner origin shared most of their beliefs and customs. At least into the 1960s, some women who wore chola *clothing regarded themselves as* criollos *(i.e. of Spanish descent) rather than of Aymara origin. Such women, including small-scale landowners living in provincial towns and urban* cholas *with a similar background wore polleras and* mantas *(shawls) but no hats. They were known as* cholas sin sombrero *(*cholas *without a hat). In the sixties and early seventies, Sofía classified herself as a* chota chola, *which might best be described as an intermediate category between a* de vestido *and a* chola decente *(i.e., a person who fits the archetype of the successful* chola*). She wore a loose skirt almost invariably covered by an apron, a sweater (but no* manta*), and a squared rather than rounded hat. And, instead of wearing her hair open and in curls as* de vestido *women do, or in two braids, as* cholas *(and peasant women) do, she wore it in a single braid. This attire did not, as far as we could determine, have a festive version.* Cholas *who were long-term urban residents looked down upon recent immigrants and rural women in their Sunday best who emulated the style of the* chola decente *but could not match the quality of the jewelry and the cloth out of which the latter's clothing were made and could not appreciate the nuances in hat styles nor the manner in which the hat should be placed at an angle on top of the head (see also Gill 1993: 79). Nevertheless, contrary to Gill's negative characterization of the designation* cholas refinadas *(refined* cholas*) as a pejorative employed by poorer urban Aymara women to denigrate the aspirations of some of their peers (1993: 85 n.10), Sofía saw them positively as being on the path towards a more urbane refinement.*

These are the dilemmas and considerations Sofía faced in constructing her social persona. Her friend Yola made similar decisions at about the same time but her marriage to a man with more education created additional problems of identification. Sofía decided to switch from de vestido *clothing appropriate to the more universalistic, Hispanic oriented identification, to the more narrowly focussed, trade related identity as a* chola. *Sofía and Yola's switch from* de vestido *to* chola *clothing does not appear to be an isolated incident. Gill (1993: 79) observes that: "[A] woman may alternate styles over the course of her lifetime, and women in the same family may adopt different forms at the same time." She gives the example of Nora, who, like her four sisters was raised* de vestido. *"Nora did not attend high school, and she married at age seventeen. Because she lacked the education and social connections necessary to land a more prestigious secretarial position, Nora followed the path of other urban Aymara women into a career as a market woman. At the same time, she started to wear her late mother's* polleras, *which the family still possessed, even though her older and better-educated sister, who worked in a record store, remained* de vestido. *Today Nora is a prosperous merchant and the only female member of her family to be* de pollera" *(pg. 83). Gill explains Nora's switch to* polleras *as predicated by limited choices because of her lack of education. Marketing was one of the few career opportunities open to her. Sofía and Yola's example indicate that identifying as a* chola *is an attractive option even for individuals who may have had the option of becoming white-collar workers. Such positions are not always more lucrative than careers in marketing. Thus school teachers have highly uncertain economic prospects in Bolivia.*

While most middle- and upper-class residents in La Paz think that women change their clothing styles only in the opposite direction, Sofía clearly did not regard her decision to wear chola *clothing as indicating downward mobility, provided that she joined the ranks of the* cholas *at the very top. In an absolute sense, she saw her decision not as a lateral move, but as one displaying her upward mobility. The fact that she made the decision in connection with her participation in a dance group in her mother's natal community is significant. Participating in that community's patron saint day festivities announced her identification with the community. Since the dance group was organized in La Paz and its participants included mainly rural-urban migrants and other individuals with strong urban connections, it also denoted a position of high prestige within the stratification system in the community. Full participation in the fiesta entailed a choice. Participants dance in special costumes (most of the components of which are rented rather than purchased) during the main part of the celebrations, but during others, they wear the same type of clothing—for this occasion in coordinated colors—that* cholas *wear on Sundays or for other special occasions.* De vestido *(i.e. European style) dresses have no place in such fiestas. Although Sofía need not have adopted* polleras *outside of fiestas, her participation in fiestas both facilitated the transition, since joining a dance group usually entails a commitment to dance for several years in a row with a new set of clothing each time (and a set of appropriate jewelry) and increased her investment in the* chola *prestige hierarchy. This substantial investment would have gone unnoticed among her rivals in the marketing system, few of whom would have had the occasion to observe her at the Compi fiesta.*[7] *On the other hand, especially during the economic crisis of the 1980s, Sofía sometimes regretted her decision to compete in the* chola *prestige hierarchy with its high costs. Financially, she would have been better off wearing European-style clothing and remaining outside the system of competitive display. Since her contacts with factory and white-collar workers were limited, she would not have felt the need to compete in quite different ways (e.g. by investing more heavily in home furnishings) in the* de vestido/*urban middle class and elite hierarchy.*[8]

Sofía's decision to wear chola *clothing also had other costs. Individuals, particularly outside of the marketing network, who are* de vestido, *hold ambiguous opinions of* cholas. *Sometimes they regard them as belonging to a different prestige system altogether. They may admire and even envy the most successful* cholas *to whom they often ascribe fabulous wealth. One* clase media *woman, who often sews* chola *clothing described them as* costumbristas, *persons who follow traditional customs. She described this clientele has follows:*

> The richer people are now buying ready-made clothing sold in the fashionable boutiques in the new shopping galleries, while those who keep me busy are the people from the Calle Buenos Aires who have their dry-goods stores, micro-buses and large buses. They are not de vestido; they are *costumbristas* [people who follow the traditional customs]. They go from fiesta to fiesta. They celebrate weddings, baptisms and sponsor saints' fiestas. And so, since they have money and compete [for prestige], they would be criticized if they bought their clothing ready-made in the markets; so they have their clothing made. They don't have time to come here because they have to tend to their stores or travel, and so I go to their homes. Buechler and Buechler 1992: 276

The de vestido/*middle class judgement of* cholas *can also be highly discriminatory. According to one of their conceptual schemes,* cholas, *no matter how wealthy, are merely "Indians," a term which almost invariably carries a negative connotation and, as we have seen earlier, whose official use has been banned since the M.N.R. party first came to power in 1952. President Hugo Banzer's characterization of* cholas *as wealthy exploiters of the general population combines elements of both of these middle-class perspectives.*

It is in the light of these contradictory schemes that we must see Sofía's ambiguous feelings regarding her decision to become a chola. *While she is proud of her expensive outfits, she also fears discrimination. As we shall see later, she, like her friend, fears that her children will be subjected to discrimination if she appears in school or at other public events in* chola *dress.*

The case of Sofía's friend, Yola, as presented by Sofía, provides additional dimensions to the chola/de vestido *dichotomy. Yola's mother considered herself as belonging to a higher social class than Sofía's mother. Sofía does not mention whether she wore European-style clothing, but she was more educated and, at least for a time, engaged in more* clase media *economic pursuits such as embroidering petticoats. Nevertheless, as a child, Yola wore her hair in the peasant and* chola *style in braids until she copied Sofía's loose* de vestido *hair style. Yola must have changed back to wearing polleras in the early 1960s. Her husband's preference for Yola's wearing polleras and her own ambivalence about continuing her* chola *identity when her husband had obtained a law degree appears counterintuitive, underlining the manifold considerations that enter into decisions concerning social identities. In some ways, Yola felt out of place as a* chola *among women whose husbands were lawyers and other professionals and who could not imagine that a* chola *could possibly be educated. On the other hand, the* pollera *was becoming and she was unique. She, a* chola, *had financed her husband's education. Had she not stood out from the guests at the presidential palace as the only* chola, *she might not have attracted the attention of General Barrientos, a rising star in the political hierarchy. Barrientos' willingness to be seen in public dancing with a* chola *can also be seen as a political statement emphasizing his image as a populist and reflecting the changing nature of the Bolivian system of social stratification.*

11

ADOPTING *a Child*

Another crucial aspect of Sofía's identity is her role as a good daughter and her search for continuity through children. Unmarried and childless, and responsible for an aging mother who lived alone in Llamacachi for the major part of the week, Sofía attempted to enter into a number of arrangements to have young girls live with her mother and to adopt a child herself, who would take care of her *in her own old age and who would inherit her place should she not have children of her own.*

[Flora was the girl who was living with us some ten years ago (in 1965).] She wasn't an adopted child. She was more like a little servant. We took care of her instead of paying her a salary. We had to clothe her and send her to school. In addition, her mother lived in our house here in La Paz rent-free. We took Flora to Llamacachi so that she would help my mother and father.

My mother's younger sister and Flora's mother lived on the same street. She had always been poor. I had met her before but hadn't talked to her. My brother, who was a police commissioner, knew this woman, and she must have told him that she would be willing [to make such a deal]. So Pedro came and told my mother that this woman wanted to give her her daughter. My father didn't want to hear about it. He said, "I don't know those *cochalas* (persons from Cochabamba), I can't speak to them." My mother didn't want it either and neither did I. But then, when I went to La Paz, I noticed that it was the same woman that I had seen before. So I told my mother that it was all right; that the woman was good. We went there in person and brought her to our house. At that time, Flora was in Chile. When she came back, two weeks later, I picked her up and brought her here. From then on (Sofía says with a smile) I no longer helped [my mother]. They made a formal agreement.

She was ten when we got her and she stayed with us for two and a half years[1] and then she came back here to live with her mother. She might have stayed with us to this day and perhaps we might have married her off; for she is married now and has two babies. But, as I always say, having a family to contend with is something dreadful. When my two sisters-in-law saw that Flora was with my mother and father and that her mother wasn't paying any rent, they decided to make life impossible for the girl's mother in La Paz. They must have thought that she would remain with us forever [and might inherit from my mother]. Finally, she came to see me and told me that she couldn't stand it any longer and she took the child back and moved away. My two sisters-in-law are really mean.

Sofía recalled that another girl had joined her mother under similar circumstances:

Oh [there is another thing I must tell you]. A cousin (*sic*) of mine, whom I hadn't known before, appeared. Remember that I told you that my father had a brother whom we hadn't seen for a long time and didn't even know whether he was still alive? Well that man came to our house. According to what he said, he had learned through the radio that my father had died. He cried and asked me if I was still living alone and when I answered yes, he told me that I had a sister. When I said that my father had never told me that he had [another] daughter, [my uncle] told me that [my father must] never [have] let us know about it because he was afraid, for he had been seeing a woman and that woman had given birth to his daughter. I asked [my uncle] how old she was, and he answered that she was sixteen or seventeen. He added, "She is there now, but I will bring her to you." "All right," I said. "Since she is my sister, bring her here and she can live with me until she marries." But most of all I wanted her to keep my mother company.

I found out that her name was Elena, Elena Velasquez Agramonte. We dressed her [in new clothing]. But I saw her a few days ago and I realized that she could not live in Llamacachi. I noticed that she didn't like the place. I thought to myself that I would take her back and forth. I wanted her mainly to look after my mother and to accompany me on my trips. She was very happy with the arrangement. Then, one day, I left her there under the pretext that I was not travelling with a lot of merchandise and told her to stay behind in Llamacachi because it was not worth paying for two trips and food on the way. I told her that we would travel together again the next time. My sister-in-law Elena told her the same thing. So she stayed. My mother, who is elderly and has had a lot of experience, noticed that she was a bit lazy and willful. She didn't like that, and so when I arrived from La Paz she told me that she didn't want her. "Take her away," she said, "she is willful. When I talk to her she acts as though she hasn't heard me. When I tell her to hand me something, she refuses. She does whatever she pleases."

"O.K., mother," I answered. But I thought to myself that I would let my mother complain but that the girl would eventually get used to the situation. So [on the next trip] I took her to La Paz. But [on the following trip] I brought her back and left her there again under the same pretext I had used before. My mother quarreled with her again. She began to cry and told me that the girl was so badly behaved that she had been ready to hit her. I told my mother that she had every right to hit her because she was her aunt. Then I scolded the girl for answering back to my mother. She bowed her head and didn't say a word. She is already quite grown up, and is crafty and clever. What was I to do?

As we saw in chapter 4, Elena became mixed up in an incident involving the theft of a substantial sum of money that ultimately led to the rupture of Elena's relationship with the family. Upset with the lengthy and costly court proceedings which Sofía felt could have been avoided if Elena had been more watchful, she asked her uncle to take her back.

Since first Flora and then Elena didn't work out, Sofía continued her search for a companion for her mother and, potentially, a child she could adopt herself.

Ever since you left, I wanted to have a child. It was because of my mother. She is old now and needs someone to be with her. I wanted to find a girl who was seven years old, or a five-year-old boy whom I could leave with my mother. So when you left and I had more time, I went to Caranavi, telling my mother that I was working for your father when, in fact, I went to look for a little black boy or girl. I told your mother that I was going to do a market census for the Señora. I took my nephew Teodoro along, and when we arrived in Caranavi we stayed at a very good hostel. We remained there for five days looking for a black child. I have a friend in Caranavi, a woman from Potosí who sells in the cafeteria of the market, the section where they sell cooked food. She is a fat *de vestido* woman whom I had met there a long time ago. [When I looked her up], she asked me why I had come; whether I had brought something to sell such as vegetables. I answered that I was only on vacation. She didn't believe me. She said that I must have some specific purpose. First we talked about my cousin Concha, whose husband—a very nice man—works as a tailor in Caranavi. She thought that perhaps I had come to see him. Then I finally told her that I had come to look for a black boy or girl. She said that she did know some. In particular, there was a woman who had five children whose father was a driver who didn't support the family and so she wanted to give her children away. I begged her [to help me]. I would pay [the mother] whatever she wanted. So the woman told me to come back at a particular time on Sunday. I had come on a Friday and since I had to wait until Sunday, I decided to visit my cousin Concha. She too asked me why I had come and when I told her that I had come in search of a baby, she laughed. Her husband told me that there were blacks who gave their children away and if I couldn't find any [in Caranavi] I should go to Mururata, a community farther up in the valley, where there were many blacks. If I still didn't succeed, then I should go to the fiesta in Coroico on October 20th, which many blacks attend. Sunday came, and I went back to the woman in the food section of the market. She told me that she had talked to the black woman and that she would be coming soon. I had lunch while I waited. After a while, an older black woman came. She was humble and wore tattered clothing. She seemed very poor. She turned out to be very nice. Her name was Blanca. I asked her about her children and she said that she had five children, two of whom were older and were working and three who were still small. She asked me which one of the small ones—all boys—I wanted. She took me to the place where she lived which was near the river. There I saw the three little boys. The youngest was two years old, the next one was three and a half and the third, five. They were appealing (*simpático*). I wanted the youngest one and my nephew also liked him best. The black woman told me to talk to the child's father who drove a truck travelling the route to Puerto Linares and Teoponte. I should wait for him and would find him easily because everyone knew him. I asked about him at the market and I was told that he was a simple man who wore simple trousers and sandals. While we waited, we looked for a parrot and a monkey. There were no monkeys [in the market] but we did see a parrot. They wanted two hundred pesos (U.S.$10) for it. Teodoro didn't want it because he wanted one that could talk, no matter what the price. While we were looking around, we found the father of the child. We talked to him about the child and he was willing to give him to us. He wanted one thousand pesos (US$50). We agreed to sign the necessary papers in front of a notary public on Monday afternoon. However, the next day, the man did not arrive from Teoponte. By evening, he had still not arrived. We returned to the mother, but by then she seemed to have changed her mind. She no longer wanted to give up one of her children, saying instead that she herself would be willing to come with me. She told me that her husband was a womanizer who went off with other women and forgot about her and about her children. She was tired of living like that and promised that if I took her to La Paz with me she would help my mother. I didn't want that. I wanted her to give me her child. But she told me that this stupid ugly man was just fooling me and would never give me a child of his. So we gave up and angrily returned to La Paz. We came back empty-handed—without a parrot, without a monkey, and without a black child.

Three weeks ago, I told a girl from Compi called Seferina, who travels to Caranavi, that I wanted to go there on the sixteenth of July. She told me that she met a black woman who was giving away two daughters. She gave one to a woman who paid her two hundred pesos (US$10) and she had wanted to give Seferina the other one; but she refused to take it. So I asked her to look for one for me so that I wouldn't make the trip in vain again.

[I still want to go and look for one], because [Sulma], the small child [I have adopted now] isn't too sure a bet. [I want a black child to accompany my mother]. Blacks are very faithful. People always say that one should raise a black child. That they are very loyal to their masters. So the black child will take good care of my mother. It should be a black boy or girl who is four or five years old. When they are older, they are crafty, while when they are very small they won't remember their mother and even if they do they [can't do anything about it].

My neighbor in the Incachaca has a black girl who is thirteen living with her. She took the child in when she was seven years old. The child is very faithful, talks a lot and is very cheerful. [Even though she has children of her own, she is raising her like her own child.] The girl has both sons and daughters but the daughters are already older. They are already married and so she wanted a smaller child to be with her and help her. She always carries the water, goes to shop in the market and things like that. [She goes to school.] I would have her do that too. The child would help my mother and would also go to school.

I talked to her just recently during the Fiesta of Gran Poder. There were some *cullawa* dancers there and I went out to watch and so did the black girl. We greeted one another. She speaks well. I asked her about her mother, Pancha, and she said that she was at home. Then I asked her whether she had sisters, and she said that she had two. One of them had come here. She said that her father had given her away because her mother had died. Then I asked her how she had come to live with Señora Pancha. She said that they had requested a child and so her father had sent her. She has been living with Señora Pancha for at least six years. I asked her whether she wanted to return to her father, and she said that her father was not a good man, while Doña Pancha was a good person and she wanted to stay with her.

I asked her about her sisters and she said that she never sees them. At that moment, my niece came along and she asked the girl, "*Che negra*, don't you have a small brother? Give him to me." She answered that she didn't and that she had a sister who had been given away already too. Well, in time I will have a black girl too. I don't care if they want money for her. I am going to buy one. They say that some black women sell [their children] and others give them away. That's why I took money along that day [when I went to Caranavi]. But I couldn't find one and so I returned with rice instead. Yes I am going to get a black girl. They are good and well behaved. Of course it depends on how one educates them too. Some blacks are also lazy.

I would prefer a black girl while my nephew would like a black boy. He would like to have him as a companion. That little boy in Caranavi was really cute. He was fat and this big. He didn't speak, and when I held his head to stroke him he began to cry. I bought him ice cream and then he let me stroke him. My nephew and I quarreled about who would get him. He wanted him and I did too. He said, "Money will decide." So I told him, "Let me see [what you have]." He answered, "What do you know?" "I will win over his father with beer," I continued. And I should have done it, but he told me that he had to leave and would return. So I was only able to talk to him for a little while. If I had caught him and had served him beer I would have been able to take the little black boy along. Even his wife had told me to invite him to some beer. But he escaped promising that he would come back on Monday and he didn't. I had to return because I had told your mother that I would return on Monday afternoon. I only went down on Tuesday and your mother was upset with me [because I was supposed to do research for you, Señora]. I had wanted to give my mother a surprise. I wanted to dress [the child] in red. I like blacks. I like their eyes. So that's the story.

[Let me tell you how we adopted Sulma.] Her real name was Nelly, but we named her Sulma after the artist from Cochabamba Sulma Yurgar, who sings Bolivian songs, because it's a pretty name. I hadn't planned to take in that little girl. Neither did Teodoro. He had just married, and his tailoring business has not been going well and so he asked me to take him to the magician. We came back from Caranavi on Monday, and on

Friday we went to the magician. It turned out that he was in mourning. He greeted us in tears. His wife had died in childbirth. We felt sorry for him. He read our luck, telling my nephew that he had been bewitched and that he should buy offerings so that his business would improve. I asked him what had happened to the child, and he said that he had given the baby, who was only two weeks old, to an unmarried girl from Llamacachi called Rosa but that she came all the time to tell him that the baby didn't sleep and cried all night, so she wanted to give the child back to him. Although she had baptized her, she no longer wanted the child. So I told him that if it was a girl he could give her to me and I would raise her. He agreed. But I was angry that he had let Rosa baptize the child. I told him that if he gave her to me I would baptize her once more [choosing other godparents]. So we arranged that he would give her to me with all the papers and for me to pick the child up on Tuesday. He promised to visit his mother on Sunday to pick up the diapers and a carrying cloth. That Tuesday, I was away, and so I told my nephew that I would tell my mother and that he should pick the baby up. I would come and get her on Friday after buying some clothes for her. Then I would bring the child to my mother in Llamacachi. When I told my mother that I wanted to adopt a child, she was happy about it. But when I told her that the baby was only two weeks old, her face fell. She said, "If the child is only two weeks old, people will think that it is your own child. These days you have always been working with el Señor Hans and they will think that you have conceived a child in La Paz. But you must decide for yourself." I answered that my comings and goings should be clear to everybody and that they could talk if they wanted to. I would take the child in anyway. So she told me to bring her but that I should make sure that all the papers were in order. That Friday, I already knew that the child was at Teodoro's place, and sure enough, when I arrived she was in his bed. She was pretty. I liked her. It turned out that Teodoro had come back with the child at one in the morning. They had been drinking there. The father was crying and told stories. Then only had they gone to pick up the child, I don't know where. The child was in a sad state. Her clothes were dirty. She wore a shirt made out of a sugar bag and her body was covered with boils. So my nephew had bought some clothing for her. He liked the baby so much that he said that he wanted to be her father. I agreed. He could be the child's father and I would be the mother. We would take turns: he would buy milk for one week, and I would buy it for the next. When I wanted to take the child to Llamacachi with me, my niece Elvira, who was expecting a child, told me, "Aunt, I will miss the child. Let me keep it here." So we agreed that she could have her until her own child was born. Elvira cleaned her and I bought the diapers, talcum powder, and milk. Then, when Elvira had her baby, I wanted to take the child with me. Elvira's baby was born while I was away, and so she had given Sulma to my sister-in-law. When I wanted to take her, Elena told me to leave her with her. "You travel a lot," she said, "and mother is too old to raise her." So now Elena is raising her until she is a little older. But Teodoro and I always buy her clothing and milk while Elena takes care of her. Whenever we forget, she comes and requests things. She tells us angrily that she is raising the child and that we can't even remember to bring money for milk. We do give her money. But sometimes she says that we should also pay her for taking care of the child. Now Moises is thinking of recognizing the child too. He wants to give Sulma the surname Velasquez and he wants to register her at the social security office in order to obtain a subsidy. That's why I left her with my sister-in-law Elena, and she has become fond of the child.

We made sure that Sulma's father doesn't have any rights any more. He gave us the child's birth and baptismal certificates and we are asking him to sign a paper that he would never tell the child when she is older that he is her father, and he has agreed to sign it. He says that he is happy that we have her and that he will pray to the spirits to bring us good fortune. He hasn't seen the child since then, and we don't want him to. Once, he did come to the house drunk and said that he wanted to see his daughter, but the renters told him that they hadn't seen her and that we didn't want him to see her. So that's how we got Sulma.

When she is older and ready to go to school, both Teodoro and I will have to pay for her education. Sometimes Elena tells me to take the child and I say, "All right, I will take her." Or sometimes when we get mad at each other I ask her to bring the child to me. I hope that [everything will work out]. But she is not too well behaved. I am afraid that she might be a witch. Also, unfortunately, there is something wrong with her. Her feet are not the same. One foot is large and the other is small. I told Teodoro to take her to a doctor and the doctor told him that the feet would even out and that we wouldn't notice it when she is bigger. But we say that she is *pan coliza* (bread, croissant) because when she walks her feet will sound "pan . . . coliza . . . pan . . . coliza." She has had this since she was born. Now we want to baptize her once more because [both Teodoro and] I want her godmother to be someone else. Perhaps God will smile on her and when she grows up she might be ashamed of her godmother who is from a rural community. Teodoro wants to have his own child and Sulma baptized at the same time. So I told him, "Fine, let's baptize them together." His son is four months old, and Sulma is eight months old now. But she is very sickly. Elena and I have to have a lot of patience. Sometimes her stomach is bloated like a frog's, so we have to give her a suppository. Maybe it's from the milk. Before that she was only drinking Lacta milk and now that we are giving her Nido milk (a whole milk) she is getting a bit fatter. She is only eating [solid foods] now.

[If I die,] she would get my things. That's why my niece Marcela, Teodoro's older sister, tells me to marry. I answer that I will never marry and so if I should die all my things, all my rags, will belong to Sulma. I have a little niece (actually grandniece), Marcela's daughter who looks just like me. So Marcela tells me, "Sulma isn't your daughter, your daughter is the baby I am carrying [in my *awayo*]. You have to will *her* everything." But I answer, "No, I have to give everything to Sulma, when I die, all I have will belong to her."

[If I adopted a black girl] I would give her her share as well, which might consist of giving her an education. If she wanted to, she could become *de vestido* and, in time, she could have something of her own. I would give both something. My inheritance would go to both of them.

If the black child stayed with my mother, she wouldn't give the child anything. All my mother's possessions will belong to me [or rather us]. We are three siblings and we will divide the inheritance among the three of us and the black child would [later] inherit from me. I will look for a black child in order not to give my brothers the satisfaction [of inheriting from me]. Now if Sulma survives she will inherit too. But it isn't certain. Sometimes illness takes children away. The other day Sulma almost died. She is so thin and dark because my sister-in-law Elena used to take her to Río Seco. This woman climbed into a private pickup truck with the baby on her back and in the curve near the Said factory she fell out the door. It was a miracle that she wasn't run over. But the truck dragged her with the baby hanging down and that's why the baby became sick.[2]

Sofía and her family's history of attempting to adopt or obtain the services of a child through some financial arrangement with the parents is rooted in the Aymara tradition of utawawas. Utawawa *is the term used for an adopted child who was usually a close relative, but it can also refer to landless families (not necessarily related) living with those with land who received plots in return for labor. The arrangement whereby the poor mother of Flora received housing in the city in return for "lending" her daughter is based on the same principle. The ambiguous role of these children is seen not only in their treatment, but also in their rights to inheritance which, like those of illegitimate children, are often poorly defined and subject to contestation.[3] Higher-class families also made financial deals with lower-class parents of older children to obtain the latter's services. In those instances, as in the case of Flora, the relationship does not involve any rights to inheritance, although close—albeit asymmetrical—ties might continue over the child's entire life time, even after the child has gained financial independence. The relationship may include providing the child with some education.*

Sofía's description of her attempt at adopting a black child is indicative of the blatant racism and stereotyping with which the small Aymara and Spanish speaking Black minority that lives in the Yungas valleys is treated by other Bolivians. She is fascinated by the Black Yungüeños to whom she ascribes both positive and negative characteristics. She objectifies them as a group that can be used to one's ends because of the supposed ease with which they part with their children. This objectification is underlined when she names monkeys, parrots, and black children in the same breath as objects of her quest. She often refers to persons by skin color and weight and regrets her own dark complexion and heavy weight. Heavy weight used to be a sign of prosperity, but the younger generation seems to prefer being slender. Stereotyping and racism but also the fascination with difference is manifested in the symbolic representation of Blacks in Aymara and Latin folklore. At the Alasitas fair, where miniature objects representing desired goods are sold, black dolls are purchased for luck. The morenada *dance, which represents black wine traders, is one of the favorite costumed dances among peasants, miners, and lower-class urbanites alike. A second dance uses only musical instruments of African origin. Such dances stem from the Aymara tradition of representing the exotic in their festivals. Thus, several dances represent various lowland Indian tribes, herbal doctors from a highland community, and Spanish lawyers.*

The Velasquez's efforts to adopt children are also symptomatic of the way in which childcare and care for the elderly has become complicated through the professional duties of daughters who need to travel and through rural-urban migration. The extended family took care of Sulma jointly and sequentially with tragic results: eventually the child died. Sofía blamed her sister-in-law of child abuse. The care of Sofía's elderly mother remained her charge because she could not arrange for a satisfactory companion in Llamacachi. Fostering or adoption becomes a preferred practice for elderly women whose children have grown and have moved out and for single women without children.

12

RENÉ *and Rocío*

Eventually, Sofía gave birth to a child of her own, which has validated her status as a complete person and, most importantly, will mean that she has a successor.

How Sofía Got to Know René Paucara

I got to know Rocío's father when I sold onions in the Avenida Montes. He was working in the navy then and he still does so now. I met him there one afternoon. He was thin then, he wasn't fat [as he is now]. I am older than he is. Seven years older. I met him when he was twenty-two years old, or maybe only twenty. I was almost twenty-eight (i.e., in 1973). I was already a woman. When I saw him I didn't recognize him. We were just talking about it yesterday. He knew my mother. He came from right next door in Chua Visalaya. He grew up very poor. He was an orphan. His was a sad plight. He would always sell empty beer bottles to my mother. My mother would scold him. She would say, "I am sure that you are stealing the bottles that you are bringing here." But he told me that his mother would give him the bottles instead of pocket money to buy sweets during school recess.

I don't remember it well, but I first met René, when I didn't know you yet, through Madre Chantal. Mother Chantal came to Llamacachi on a mission, with the Augustinian priests. I was the only *de vestido* woman who could speak [Spanish]. Also I had been educated at the school run by the nuns. Anyway, she appointed me as a catechist. I think I told you about that. I taught eighty persons who wanted to take the first communion in Chua Visalaya. I taught them to recite the Lord's Prayer, the Ten Commandments, and the Seven Sacraments. I met with the group every afternoon in the school in Chua. There, we held the first communion. Mother Chantal would bring Induvar shoes as presents, new underwear, sweaters, things like that. The peasants were happy with the presents. They, in turn, gave her gifts of eggs or two pesos. We held a very nice mass. A doctor came along too. Later, they left a first aid kit with me, so that I could treat the people there. Men would come with swollen faces and I would cure them. At the end, they even came to have me treat their delicate parts when they had been hurt playing soccer. I didn't like to do that. My father would get angry and say that that was asking too much.

I knew about René's mother Justita. She was still young. I myself was only eighteen then. One day, his mother came crying, "My son is not well. His foot is in bad shape. Since you deal with the nuns and they have a doctor, please help me. I am a widow and am poor." I told her, "Don't cry. On Sunday, the padres will come and you can come here. Bring some eggs for the doctor and he will look at your son. We will cure him." They came that Sunday, and we held mass and, as usual, there were weddings and baptisms. I would write all that down, so the padres would know how many would be coming for weddings and baptisms. When we had finished in the afternoon, René's mother came to the corner of that hill. René turned out to be quite grown up already. He was twelve or thirteen, but he was already quite a man. Pus was coming out of his leg. He couldn't walk. He was dragging himself along on the ground. We raised the bottom of his trousers to look and asked him what he had done to himself. The doctors and the nuns felt sorry for him. They told his mother that they would have to take him to La Paz, to the hospital in Miraflores. The mother began to cry. She didn't want them to take him to La Paz. But I told her that if she didn't have the leg treated it would have to be amputated. The leg would become gangrenous. Then I told her, "Leave him with me. I will be responsible for the costs." So, we sent René here to La Paz and his leg healed in the hospital. At the hospital, he got to know a nun and he then went to work with the Augustinian priests in La Paz as a sacristan. They were supposed to take him to Oruro to work in that capacity. But when he went to tell his mother about it, she refused to let him go. The peasants always say that one shouldn't let one's children go because they will be sold or cut into pieces. Anyway, thanks to me, he became well again. Later, he entered military service in Tiquina and he became a musician, and he continues to be a musician.

That day, when he came to the Avenida Montes, I didn't recognize him. When he called out to me, I wondered who this little soldier was. I looked at him and he said, "You are my aunt." This man called me "aunt"! Imagine, the aunt had an affair with her nephew! I answered, "Hello, who are you?" He replied, "Don't you know? I am the son of Justita. You know me. I am René. You brought me to the doctor when I hurt my foot." "That was you?" I exclaimed. And I looked at him. The young boy I remembered had become a man. He told me, "I am looking for a room. I would like to become your renter. Don't you have a house in the Garita? Please, rent me a room." I answered, "Fine. Come on such and such a day. Or you can meet me here." So one day he came and knocked. I let him in and we chatted. I rented him the room across the patio where people store meat now. One year later (1978) Rocío came into being.

How Women and Men Get to Know One Another

Now young people get to know one another when they go out for a promenade. As you know, young people used to be introduced by their parents. First the parents would get together and would discuss the matter and then only would they introduce their children so that they would marry. Now it's no longer like that. Now, they get to know one another on the street, or during a fiesta or a wedding celebration. Sunday is the best day for young people to meet. For example, some persons, both men and women who are migrants from the countryside and work as employees, go out for a promenade in the Calle Bautista. In that street there is an area where there are always small groups of *cholitas* and young men who work as employees. It's an area where they sell chicha and hold dances on Sundays. That's where they get to know one another. Some eventually marry, although they rarely do.

People used to marry. Now they don't. Perhaps women don't like to marry . . . Well, it seems that it's for lack of money. Especially their parents don't want to [hold weddings]. For example, last week Rafael Calleja's son, who must be about twenty-five years old [got together] with a girl called Sofía who lives in the Calle Calatayud. The girl is twenty-two years old. He was working in a pharmacy. They say that they have known each other for two and a half years. So we went for an *irpaka.*[1] Rafael came to look for Pedro last Saturday, at 7:30, but Pedro wasn't there. Only I and Teodoro were at home. So he asked us to accompany him because there was no one who could accompany him to ask for the girl's hand in marriage. They called it "asking for the girl's hand" but in reality they were already living together. Before, it was different. They would ask for a girl's hand before they started to live together. Now, after all sorts of things have happened (i.e. the girl is no longer a virgin), he asks for the girl's hand. The young man eloped with the girl during the feast of San Pedro in Compi and took her to his parents' house there. Rafael, the father, who still believes in the old customs, ordered his son to send the girl back to La Paz. But the girl refused. She said, "Don Rafael, excuse me, but I am expecting a child. I can't leave, because I must be together with your son." So she stayed for two days and then Rafael came to La Paz and looked up the girl's parents. They wanted to have the matter settled that very Saturday. That's why I, Teodoro and his wife, the *chola* Carmen, Rafael, his son, and the girl went together [to the parents' house]. The son of Cosmi Condori, also came along with us. He told us that the girl's mother was bad and strongwilled. But we were lucky. It turned out that I knew the woman. When we entered, both she and I were surprised. The woman buys pork from me. She is a food vendor. I said, "Doña Torribia!" And she was very surprised, for she thought that I was the young man's mother. We began to discuss the matter. The girl's mother asked the young man why he had come and how he had met her daughter. The young man answered that he had danced in a *llamerada* dance group in Tambillo and had gotten to know the girl, Sofía, there. The old man asked him whether he was employed and whether he had absolved his military service. The young man said yes. When he heard that, the old man told Rafael that they couldn't whip them because the young man had a job. He was a man in his own right. Then Rafael said that he didn't have any money for a wedding because of the economic crisis, and so they agreed to a private wedding on September third. They wanted to name me *irpaka* godmother, but I refused because I don't have a husband. So Teodoro went with his wife instead. At five in the morning we took the girl back with us totally drunk.

The kind of wedding with a church and an orchestra no longer exists. Those who have money have pompous weddings, those who don't, hold a small wedding at home among relatives. Others live together for years without marrying.

[For a civil wedding, someone from] the civil registry comes to the house. There has to be a witness and that's all. Some live together for two or three years and then they marry. It's because of lack of resources.

[Women now] know everything about sex: how not to have children, how to protect themselves. They teach them about sex in school both here and in rural areas. They teach how a baby is formed and how one can avoid having a child. All the girls in the countryside already know those things. Before, they didn't know. They used to say that one had to take herbs in order not to have children (i.e. to abort). Now they do know. I would like you to ask a girl in the country. She would answer correctly. They say that they have special sex education classes. Women rarely use pills. Instead both partners take precautions. [Actually,] it's more the man who takes precautions. A few of my relatives, for example the wife of Toronto, have had a spiral put in. One has to change the spirals (from time to time). She failed to go to the doctor regularly and became infected. She almost died. That's what happened to Ruth's sister-in-law. You better believe me, the new generation knows everything with the new education they are getting.

They also [learn] from the physician. For example, I have a friend, called Julia, who always buys pork together with me. She had her daughter after I did. The child is Rocío's cousin. She lives with René's older brother. Now the daughter must be seven years old and is in second grade. Well, during those seven years, the woman has not had any more children. I asked her, "Why don't you have more children? You have a husband and so you could easily have more?" She answered, "No, Sofía. I went to the physicians. I have done everything possible to have another child with my husband. I even had sex when the moon was full and timed it according to the menstrual cycle: the last day, the second last day . . . and still I can't get pregnant, Sofía. I continue to menstruate." "Then what could it be," I continued. "Then there must be something wrong with (your husband)"—we talk like that [openly] among friends.

Well, I have a niece who is Moises's daughter from his second wife. This niece, Paulina, is twenty-six. She is married and has three older daughters. She comes around here to work. She runs a *pasanacu* (rotating credit union) gathering sums of two thousand, three thousand, five thousand, two hundred, and one hundred (US$847, $1271, $2119, $85, $42) [from the women around here]. I vouched for them. One day, my niece, Julia, and I got to talk about having children. My niece said that she felt sorry for Julia. She told her, "Doña Julia, there is a gynecologist here on the plaza. Go and see him. I know that your pores (*sic*, tubes) have closed. It will cost you some Bs 200 (US$85), but you will have your child. Go and talk to your husband and go together." And Julia did go to that physician with her husband. She said that the physician had made her lie on a bed and had done something to her with some devices until she bled and gave her an injection and she finally became pregnant. Her son now is five months old, he is nice and plump. See, it's all science. If I want to have a child, I go to the doctor and I can have a child.

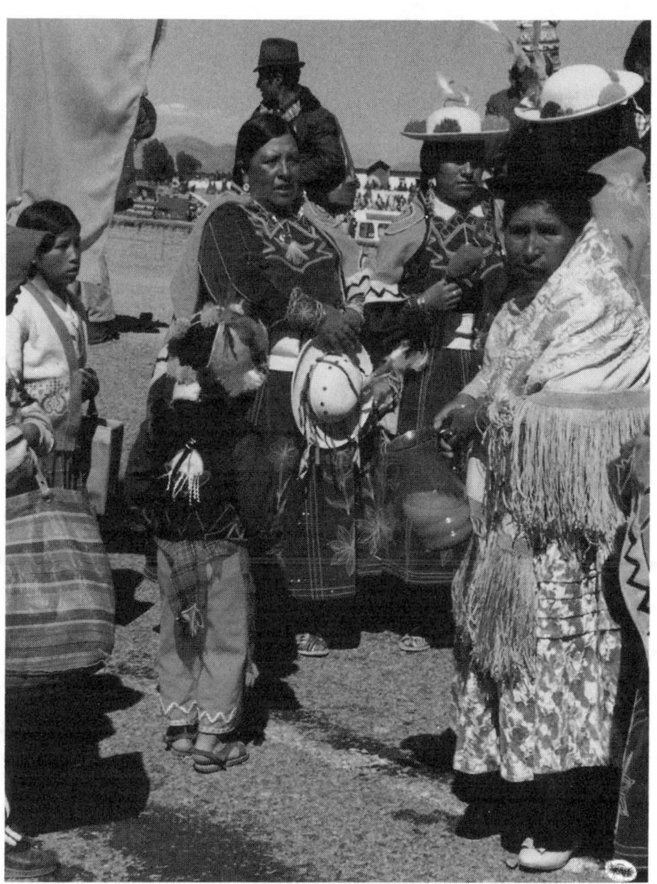

Sofía performing in an Inca dance group in Compi (1981)

Getting René to Return

René disappeared when I was two months pregnant. It [all started] during a wedding. The wedding took place in the dancehall next door. René persisted in calling me "aunt." We even organized an "Inca" dance together in La Paz to take to Compi. At the time when my niece had her wedding, I had a boyfriend called David and this David and I both worked at CIPCA. That is where I got to know him. I was in love with him. But René, who lived in our house, saw me coming and going. Perhaps René already had the intention of being with me.

Now, during that wedding, I drank because I was the godmother or sponsor of the decorations for the dance hall and for the rental of the buses for the guests. So that evening, my friend David brought me home so I could sleep it off. He closed the door and left, but clever René entered into the room to be with Sofía.

The next day I was angry at René. I didn't want to speak to him. I said to myself, "What kind of man is this?" I didn't know that I was pregnant with his child. However, René probably knew already that I was expecting a child and looked for an excuse to give up his room and leave our house. I told him, "Well, go ahead. Go if you want to." He answered, "I am going to leave the room to my brother." "Fine," I replied, "leave the room to him." When I returned to the house a while later, René had taken all his things out of the room and had gone. He had left the room to his brother Mario, who is [now] the husband of my friend Julia.

A month passed and another. I already was suffering from morning sickness. I went to a doctor who told me that I was expecting a child. I didn't know what to do about René. I sent him a letter telling him that I was expecting his child. But René did not come to settle the matter. Since René didn't want to come, I had to tell my brothers and my mother what had happened. My mother came and talked to my brothers. They asked me whether I had had sexual relations with René before that. I said that I hadn't and that it had happened because I was drunk. So they called Mario and told him about it and he was surprised that his brother had caused my pregnancy. Then Mario brought René here.

René and Pedro had a confrontation. Pedro asked him, "What happened with my sister?" René said that it happened while we were drunk; that he had not had sexual relations with me before; that I was older than he; and all sorts of other things. You know how a man tries to escape his responsibilities. Well, that didn't go over well with my brother. He told him, "If you don't like my sister why did you do this to her? Arrange for her to be cured. Have them take the child out of her stomach." René promised to come on a certain Tuesday.

But Tuesday came and went and he did not appear. He didn't come on the following Tuesday either. So my brother told me, "Take a lawyer." And I hired a lawyer and presented the case to his commander-in-chief, Moises Sempertegui. He must have been the commander-in-chief for all of Bolivia. I went all the way to his house in Bologna. I told him what René had done and that he wanted me to have an abortion.

The admiral didn't like the idea that children would be lost [to the nation]. He wanted more children to be born to serve the home country. He said, "How could he do that to you? You have to have the child. I am going to punish him, that Paucara. Where does he work, daughter?" "At the naval barracks near the Guaqui railroad station," I answered. Thereupon, the admiral went up to the barracks and punished (René) in the presence of all the other soldiers. He had him run around the courtyard fifty times because he had wanted to have the child aborted. Later he called him once more and transferred him to Riberalta.

I didn't see him again. He left for Riberalta while I stayed behind, pregnant. I had my child all by myself. [Or rather], his siblings helped me and René's mother came. René only reappeared when my daughter was four months old. But he didn't want to come here to talk. And, since he had had a confrontation with Pedro, he said, "I don't want to talk to Pedro. Pedro isn't her brother [because he was born out of wedlock]. I want to talk to Moises." We went up to El Alto to talk. He said, "I haven't come to patch things up with Sofía. I have come to recognize Rocío. I will make child payments. She will have my surname and I will insure her with COSMIL [the social security fund for the military]." Moises didn't like that. He said, "No, marry my sister first and then you can recognize the child." So René and Moises had a confrontation too. When Moises asked me my opinion, I said, "I am willing for him to recognize her and give her his surname. I don't really want to live with him either. Instead, let him help me." But my brother replied, "This man will just get used to having all sorts of women and then give his name to their children. He has to marry you. If he doesn't want to marry you, let him go away." He told René, "I don't need your surname. My brother and I are here for that. The girl has two fathers. We are going to help her. We will give her money. We are going to provide her with clothing. We will make it possible for her to study. We don't need your surname. You may go."

Once outside, René and his brother had an argument and then René left. He went off to the eastern part of the country. He only returned after ten years [when] they transferred him again. He had himself transferred at the end of 1986. . . . No. Something else happened before that. When my daughter was one year old, René came again. I didn't meet him in person, but he sent me messages. He said that if I refused to let him recognize his daughter, he would find another woman. I replied that he could go ahead. I said, "Let him marry. That's not my problem." Then, when Rocío was three, he came once more. I met him in the street. He told me, "I would like to meet her." I showed him the child. Then he brought her a present and spoke to my mother. He told her that he would recognize the child and make payments. Then he vanished once again.

Finally, René returned permanently in 1986. He was transferred to Chua Kokani. I was told that René was there. But I didn't go to see him.

Señora, René has a family of his own: a wife and two children and so I didn't want to bother him.

In 1987, he continued to work in Chua. My mother died in October, 1986, but I still kept away. I preferred not to go during fiestas, or to the parade in Chua in August. I didn't want to talk to him. However, I did have the intention to have him arrested and imprisoned.

My mother had always bought clothing for my daughter. I finally met [René] in February, 1987, four months after my mother died. He was in a store that sells *salchipapas* (sausage and potatoes). Rocío and I like to eat *salchipapas*, that's why Rocío is fat. We had just come from the fair in Jank'o Amaya. We would always arrive hungry and would go to eat *salchipapas* together in the Max Paredes near the store where they buy gold and where they sell *chola* shoes in the doorway.

That afternoon, I told Rocío to pay. Then I saw René in the doorway. When he saw me, he got a shock. He looked away. That would still have been acceptable. René's wife—actually they are not married, they just live together—was with him, with her baby on her back. She looked at me (in a hostile manner), trying to provoke me. I hadn't done anything to her. She continued to hold her ground and to stare at me. When I get angry, I get really angry. I jumped up from the doorway and went over to René. I told him, "Listen, what has happened to you, you disgraceful man?" "What are you going to do about your daughter?" He answered, "Oh, I don't have time to discuss this matter." I countered, "When are we going get this thing settled? You just wait! I will do whatever has to be done [to get some action]. I want to get this matter settled once and for all." I confronted him in front of his woman because she had bothered me.

After I had done this, I went home laughing. Rocío didn't know who René was. She ran after me asking, "Mother, who is this man?" [I tried to avoid answering her]. But she said, "I know that he is my father, I know that he is my father." Even though she didn't know him, she guessed that he was her father.

Thereupon, I went up the hill to Aida's kiosk in the Garita and told her what had happened. She said, "You are crazy. So, what did the woman say?" I answered, "She remained silent, because she had bothered me."

Later, I made a list of things Rocío needed for school. I myself didn't have money because I had spent a lot on my tooth; I spent some Bs 180 (US$76). And my mother had died [and couldn't help me]. [The school] had asked me to buy seven books: a book for learning English, another for learning French, a dictionary, mathematics. . . . I don't remember them all, there were lots of books. The books were expensive. One could only buy them in the Prado. When I read [the list] I told myself, "Since this woman is bothering me, even though I have allowed her to live with him in peace, I am going to take revenge."

The next day, I really dressed up. I looked really attractive. I left for the bus station all by myself and took the bus to Chua. I asked when René would have his noon break and how long it lasted. They told me that he would come out at noon and return to work at one. Unfortunately I had arrived at 12:30. I was worried that I had missed him. But a girl in Marca Chua told me, "He hasn't come out yet. Oh, there he is, there he is, there he is!" A fat man was bicycling in my direction. I waited for him on the hill slope in Chua. When he saw me, he bowed his head. He didn't know what to do. I stopped him and we had a long argument. I told him, "How is it? Are we going to arrange this matter amicably? I know that you have a family, but I want to get things settled. Are you going to recognize my daughter or are you going to deny her? Tell me one way or another." He began to quarrel with me, "Oh, but your brothers this and your brothers that. . . ." We had a long argument until we were tired and gave up. That is, he gave in. He gave in and promised me that he would come on a certain day. And he came on his own two feet. I was at a meeting in Rocío's school. And so, when I came home, he was already drinking with my brother, Don Pedro. I arrived and he saw Rocío. He began to cry.

He had already spoken with me about Rocío and how grown up she must be. I had answered, "Yes, she is already nine years old." This year Rocío will be ten. At that point, he settled everything making a number of promises. He gave me one hundred pesos (US$42.37). He told me that he would recognize her legally and would pay her school fees, giving me forty dollars for her and clothing too. We worked things out nicely.

But the liar disappeared for almost four months, after making all these promises. That's why I did it. It was a secret, which no one was supposed to know. At the time I used to go to a woman, I think that I told you about her, whose name was Rosita. She died recently. She died on the 23rd of June, before the day of San Juan. She must have been sixty-eight years old. She was a kind of healer, a sort of witch.

I got to know her through a stevedore. There are two stevedores, Mario and Churqui, to whom I entrust meat which they bring into and take it out of the *agencia*. On that day, some meat got lost in the *agencia*. I scolded Mario, but he said that he hadn't stolen the meat. Churqui said the same thing. He added, "We can clear up who did it. There is someone who can catch [thieves]. I said, 'Fine, I will pay for it. Bring that person.' " He answered, "I will do that, but don't tell it to anybody. She is my wife." That's how I got to know the woman.

Soon the woman came. She doesn't like to read coca leaves like Juancito does, nor does she smoke cigarettes [to read the fortune from the ashes]. Instead, she asks for a bottle of white rum, pours some into a little bottle, and reads the fortune from the droplets of alcohol when she sprinkles alcohol on the floor. She told me, "A stevedore came from the street and took it. That man has contacts with an elderly woman." I immediately knew that the woman must be Doña Acencia. "That woman," the witch continued, "did this to you out of vengeance, because you told her to leave. But, in time, she is not going to come anymore. She will no longer sell meat for lack of money." And she was right. That woman no longer comes to sell. That's how I got to know that magician.

I guess the magician must have liked me, because she came to visit me. And she asked, "Where is your husband?" I answered, "I don't have a husband." So I told her my life story. "Just wait," she told me, "Count on me. I will help you. We will make him want to come to you like crazy." So she called his spirit with alcohol and hit it with a crucifix. She said, "He will arrive at the appointed hour."

And René came like crazy. He came crying and drunk asking about his little daughter. Some time later, Rosita returned and asked, "How are things? Well let's do it again." She prepared something, I don't know what—she took it with her again. She didn't leave it here. She told his spirit, "Now you have to recognize your daughter and you must not abandon Sofía again."

One day René returned [from Chua] and told me that he would enter a hospital. He had something wrong with his foot because he drove a motorcycle in Santa Cruz. Apparently he was driving the motorcycle there while drunk. They said that the liquid in his knee had dried out. They operated his knee last year in August (1987). When he left the hospital he recognized the child. It was on September 8th or 11th. He came here on crutches.

René asked Doña Aida to call me. And then he recognized Rocío at the notary public's office. I was happy. We entered a restaurant and Aida, I, he, and my daughter drank together. Then I brought him here with me. The next day, I told Pedro about it, and Pedro was very glad. Since then, René continues to come here. Now, he is working in Següencoma at the naval headquarters. I think that he is acting as a music teacher and he is teaching the beginners. He comes, sees whether Rocío has done her homework, then he goes again. At the beginning of each month he helps with school fees. I pay Bs 55 (US$23) for her school fees and he brings that.[2] Thanks to this woman, who did I don't know what so that he wouldn't leave me again, he continues to come. I can show you the papers. Now she is a legitimate child. He recognized her.

It's important [to be legitimate], especially in school. For example, the school was requesting a certificate from the father, recognizing her. That's another reason why he recognized her. Now Rocío carries the name Rocío Paucara Velasquez. She now has his surname. Here is her certificate.

It appears that René wants to live just like Moises [who has two wives], go up and live there for a few days and then come down here and be with me. But I don't want that. My brother Pedro himself says, "No, we have to arrange this." Right now I have been living with René like this for more than a year. He comes and goes. He comes here twice a week. In the last few weeks he has been here continuously. Then he disappeared for a few weeks. On Saint Peter's Day he disappeared. I have his clothing here and everything. He reappeared here on Monday. He was already here at twelve [that day]. He was wearing his military uniform. I was angry, so I quarreled with him that afternoon. I told him, "You should have phoned me and told me what was happening." He said that his . . . wife became sick. It seemed that she was about to die. She [vomited] bile and he had to ask for permission to leave work to help her. He told me a good tale.

I said, "No more of these things." I told him, "Think about it carefully, either she or I." That afternoon I told him, "You can come and see your daughter whenever you want. Come and see your daughter but don't come and see me any more." What happened after that is that yesterday morning he went into his room and didn't want to come out again. That's why you saw me cry yesterday; I was telling Ruth about it.

Pedro says that one of these days he will put a knife to his throat and tell him, "I don't like these things. Either you arrange things with my sister, or you will have to go." But my brother is waiting for the moment when I am pregnant [again]. But (laughter) I am never going to be pregnant. It depends on what *I* decide. I know how to protect myself. But Pedro wants that [I become pregnant]. He wants to see me in that condition and then confront René. But I told Ruth yesterday to tell Pedro to ask René right away. Either he [stays] or he shouldn't come any more. I don't know when [Pedro] will do it. But René tells me to give him a few months time and he will ask for a hefty loan from COSMIL, and that he will install the other woman in a completely stocked grocery store and [have her] sign a document promising that she will no longer bother him. Then he would come and live with me.

[The woman] is called Celia. He says that he has known her since he has known me. I don't believe that.

Rocío and Sofía's Dreams

As we saw earlier, Sofía claims to have clairvoyant dreams. In one dream, Rocío appears. Sofía's analysis of the dream's meaning is quite unexpected from a Euro-American perspective.

I [continue to have dreams about what is going to happen. I had a clear premonition in my dreams of what happened yesterday at the fiesta [when the band I had hired failed to appear on time]. I told René yesterday: "That's why I had this dream." But the morning after the dream I didn't realize that it was about the fiesta. I dreamt that I was with two small children, two girls that were moving along a steep slope. I looked down into the abyss and my head started rolling down with the two girls, but I held on and shouted "Señor, señora!" and a man came who sent me a woman and she took me away from that place. See?

If I had tumbled down the slope, bad things might have happened. [The two girls that accompanied me] must have meant the [market] union. On the other hand, the night after I talked to Juan about performing a curing ceremony for me, I also dreamt and in the dream all went well. I was walking down Rodriguez street with Rocío, carrying my bundle on my back. When I reached the Rodriguez market a fight broke out among the women and they made me turn back. They turned on a faucet with dirty water at me. The water rose slowly and climbed up the hill. I ran away quickly and called Rocío to follow me. Rocío didn't pay any attention and so I left her in my dream. I told her, "I don't care if the water gets you." When I looked back, I saw Rocío run and fall, run and fall. The dirty water was following her. The fact that I climbed up the hill has a positive meaning. It means that I will continue to advance.

Some time before, I dreamt that I had let my hair hang loosely. That meant that people talked a lot about me. I loosened my hair and couldn't comb and braid it. I was walking down from the Parque Infantil with my hair hanging open. Another time, I dreamt about that the dump trucks of Point Four (American Aid) were spraying me with dirty water as they passed by. Dirty water covered my daughter. Again I was going downhill. But since I talked with Juan I am going uphill again. In that last dream I was able to hold on and didn't slide downhill. And I did have a confrontation. See?

Female/male relations are complex. As we have seen in earlier chapters, Sofía has enjoyed a number of sexual liaisons. Her relationships to these men have been conflicted, at best. The relationships to her brothers and favorite nephew are also problematic. Finally, while her relationship to her father was generally good, he does not seem to have played a central role in her life. She does not talk about him extensively, or mention him frequently. Only one violent episode is mentioned, and this one in connection with his mental illness. She has her male relatives mediate difficult situations—a pregnancy out of wedlock, a lawsuit, an attempted adoption and fostering. Her brothers and nephew stand in for a husband when absolutely necessary, but the narrative makes it clear that Sofía tends to make up her own mind about crucial matters after consulting her mother and/or a magician. Indeed she could not count on her brothers keeping their promise to help her. Neither Moises nor Pedro appears to have contributed financially to Rocío's upbringing. Pedro's initial rejection of René's overtures to recognize Rocío can be regarded as mere machismo. Nonetheless, Rocío does stay with Sofía's kinfolk when Sofía goes on her marketing trips to Jank'o Amaya.

If our memory serves us, Sofía originally ascribed the fact that she did not to marry René to a personal decision. She figured that she would have a claim to a larger share of the inheritance, in particular of property her mother had inherited, if she took care of her mother until her death. Marriage, she argued, might interfere with this obligation. The fact that her marketing activities and the associated network provided her with economic security strengthened her in her resolve to maintain her independence. In this respect, she was characteristic of powerful market women in La Paz whose husbands and lovers remained peripheral to their lives and endeavors. Her decision not to terminate her pregnancy makes sense in the light of her attempts to adopt a child. We do not think that Sofía ever intended to abort Rocío. She had always wanted a child in order to take care of her in her old age and to secure a successor. We often talked about the joys of daughters after our own twin daughters were born. She is very attached to them as well.

Although the decision to have a child and the decision to establish a more permanent union with a man appear to have been independent from one another in Sofía's case, economic necessity induced her to establish the link between such a union and child-rearing. The high expenses she incurred for her mother's treatment and burial, and the high cost of Rocío's education prompted her to bind René to her and to Rocío more tightly. We noticed that other very independent market women also sought partners who would help defray costs during the economic crisis of 1981–86. We must, then, place Sofía's image of herself as a woman and mother into the context of the stage in her life and the economic exigencies of the moment.

Dreams and Power

Although it is clear from Sofía's actions (including the sacrifices that she makes for her daughter's education) that Rocío plays a central role in Sofía's life, her analysis of two dreams in which Rocío appears focuses entirely on other concerns. As we have mentioned before, magic and dreaming also serve to give Sofía some sense of control. While in earlier years her dreams reflected her concern about death, family dynamics, and competition, this time her dream interpretations focused on her position of power in the market. The fact that she is highly selective about the aspects of her dreams, an issue we have commented on at length in chapter 6—is all the more apparent because, from the outsider's perspective, the dream she describes includes disturbing material, which she fails to address. She did not comment on her daughter's fate, which was negative in both dreams. In one dream, she tells her daughter that if she did not hurry and escape from the flood that threatened to envelop them, that was her problem. These aspects of her dreams would clearly fall within her interpretive framework, for, in the dreams we discussed earlier, she does *predict the misfortune of individuals other than herself. In contrast, in 1988, she focused entirely on those aspects of the dreams that concerned her directly. One could speculate that Sofía's selective interpretive framework impinges on the dreams themselves. We could hypothesize that when Sofía is anxious about an impending event, she is more likely to dream and that during such dreams she concentrates on signs directly relevant to her immediate concerns. Her seemingly uncaring attitude towards her daughter's plight could, then, be seen as an indication of this process of focussing which carries over to the act of dreaming itself, rather than indicating a sub-conscious attitude toward her daughter, as a Western interpretation might conclude. In Sofía's focused dreams, Rocío's appearance would become little more than a distraction, to be treated as secondary—not only when she interprets the dream, but also while the dream takes place. The fact that some individuals appear to be able to reorient the unfolding of a dream while they are dreaming gives some credence to this hypothesis.*[3]

Our own interpretation of this dream is that Sofía, at the time, was worried about being able to sponsor the market feast which would affect her future social status and about René's continued support of Rocío which would make her (and her daughter) very vulnerable. She also seems concerned about our two daughters but she holds on to them and a man comes (Hans) who sends a woman (Judith-Maria), and she is thus saved from disaster. In fact, the monetary recompense for the video film which we were in the process of filming has helped her.

Rocío in 1994

By our last visit, in 1994, Rocío had become a lively teenager with ambitious plans for the future. She had also become a major economic asset and her mother's confidante and advisor. In contrast, her relationship to René, who, like many lower-class Bolivians, is suffering from the sluggish recovery from the economic crisis of the 1980s, appeared tenuous at best.

The father of Rocío is just a visitor [in this household]. He only comes once a month. He comes to bring Rocío's school fees. However he does not pay them in full. He only brings Bs 100 (US$42) and they actually come to 160 (US$68). He says that he makes a sacrifice to pay what he does. "I have my own household to take care of," he says. People tell me to welcome him when he comes. They say that other men don't help at all. Now he owes me for two months. He hasn't come for two months. When he came the last time, he said that they were very strict where he works. They have asked all employees to obtain certificates of good conduct, a lung examination, and papers of how long they have worked. He says that they are planning to fire everybody and that the president planned to bring military personnel from the United States to work here. He has been working for three years for the army headquarters (Estado Mayor) and this year they have sent him to Chua Kokani. That's why he hasn't come. He told me, "I owe you school fees, what shall I do?" I answered, "You will have to give me money to pay the fine, because Rocío's school charges interest when payments are late." I think they charge an extra Bs 5 (US$1.05) per month. So, I told him. "You must pay. I don't care where you get it from." So, now he hasn't come. I thought that maybe he would come on July 16th, since it's a holiday.

Rocío is helping me at home for two years now. Before that, she didn't help much, but now she is my right hand, ever since she noticed that I am suffering from high blood pressure and often can't sleep at night because I have a headache. I went to see the doctor who told me that I am at the beginning stage. It must be from menopause. She tells me, "Mother, I am going to help you." I used to make a big sacrifice, getting up at four to cook food [for sale]. So she told me, "No, now its my turn." She gets up at 4:30, dresses warmly and goes out [to the kitchen] to light the kerosene stoves and prepares the food. She cooks better than I do. Her food tastes better than mine. I used to teach her when she was a child and she learned by force. Now, it seems that I have lost my knack. I have lost the magic of preparing tasty dishes. Only Rocío knows how. She has her own recipes. So what I do is cut the meat, grind the *ají* (hot pepper), prepare the bread and things like that, while she does the actual cooking in the morning. I get up at 5:00 just to see what she has done. At 6:30 she packs up the food and has it transported with the stevedore to my sales site on the street in front of the house. At 7:30 she leaves for school.

Rocío also does the washing and ironing. So now I rest. I no longer work hard. I act like a lady (laughter). She also has learned to cook in school. She prepares an *ají* (hot dish) of wheat, bakes cakes with fancy icing and pastries, and makes turnovers. [She doesn't bake at home] because I don't have the necessary molds. She scolds me and tells me to buy molds.

Now I ask her advice as though she were my husband or my mother. When I have some problem I ask her what I should do. She tells me to do this or that. And I follow her counsel. Before, I used to decide everything on my own, but now she directs me. Sometimes, when I do something wrong, she scolds me. She doesn't like bad gossip. She doesn't like lying. She doesn't like it when I owe money to someone. She tells me, "I don't like it when people scold you because you owe them money." Sometimes people from whom I have borrowed money come to my sales site and scold me and she gets upset and tells them not to speak loudly because others might hear. Then, when the woman leaves, she scolds me. So now I am afraid of her.

Sometimes she quarrels with her father. She says, "He comes with his Bs 100 (US$21)." She is going to a private school where high society people go. There are children of congressmen and senators—of wealthy people—and she socializes with them so she knows about a different lifestyle. She says that the young women come with money. They buy things and she can't. I give her only one boliviano for recess. The other girls invite her because she has a pleasant character and so they like her. The other day, one of them had her fifteenth birthday and Rocío was invited too. When Roci had her fifteenth birthday we didn't hold a fiesta for her. She would have liked to have one too, but I just don't have the money. I thought that her father would pay for a fiesta but he didn't. She was very angry. She said that her father had never bought her clothing. "He promises and promises and he never brings anything." She told him, "Father, I am fifteen and you didn't pay for a fiesta so I would like you to give me clothing." He promised but he ever came through. So she said, "I don't have a father." She gets angry. The girl who celebrated her birthday is the daughter of a woman who has a boutique. She had her fiesta in the Prado. It used to be that those fiestas started at 4 p.m. and ended at 9. Now they start at 10 and end at 1 a.m. I couldn't let her go out alone that late, so I had to go with her whether I wanted to or not. We entered the building and there were guards who looked at the ticket she had been given. It turned out that I was the only *de pollera* woman among the guests. I sat in a corner while Rocío went to chat with her friends. It turned out that the young ladies were very nice. She is popular. She is short. The others are tall. She brought her friends over to where I was sitting and they all kissed me. I liked that. They told me, "Señora, your daughter is wonderful." Then she went off to dance. There were police cadets. The dames of honor came in. The girl whose birthday was being celebrated also was with a cadet. The fiesta was really nice. The girl's mother came over and made me sit with the other parents. Rocío told me not to be afraid to eat with the ladies. There was a lot of control so no one would use drugs. I was happy. Later, I told Pedro all about it and told him that I was proud of my daughter because she wasn't afraid to take me along. If only I could have given a fiesta for my daughter. I told her I would do so next year. All this took place in May.

In this house there is a very ugly atmosphere. The children of my brother quarrel with one another and call one another names. So I am not on speaking terms with any of them including my sister-in-law Ruti. The only one I speak to is my brother Pedro and with Moises who doesn't want to come here. We decided to sell the house. People told me to think about the future of my daughter. They told me that if I should die they might harm her. My brother's son-in-law, Felix, wanted to buy it. We had first thought it was worth about US$45,000, but a woman told us that we should ask US$75,000 for it. He finally offered US$55,000 but we want to hold out for US$66,000 which would give each of us US$22,000. With that I could buy myself a house farther up. But Felix refuses to go up with his offer. We are still negotiating. I want to sell and leave. My daughter also wants to have her own bedroom and a living room where she could invite her friends over. She is afraid to bring them here. She and her friends study in small groups of five to ten girls in their homes. She said that if her turn came, how could she bring them here? She wants me to buy a house or to rent one (*en anticrético*).[4] I would prefer to buy a plot of land and build a house.[5]

Rocío has good ideas. She tells me that we should add this or the other thing to what we sell. She wants to study general medicine. She tells her classmates that she will be a physician. She said that she will no longer cook. That she will have a servant to do that. She tells me that she is helping me because I am alone. When she is helping me sell in the street and she sees her friends, she hides from them. They are *señoritas*. When I ask her, "Why are you hiding? Have we have stolen from them?" she says no, but that they might make fun of her.[6] I told her to learn how to play the *charango*.[7] She knows how, but she doesn't like to play. She just wants to study general medicine. One of her teachers asked the class what they wanted to do in the future and everybody said that they wanted to become teachers or secretaries and other things but five of them including her said that they wanted study general medicine.[8]

CONCLUSION

Constructing an Identity

As we indicated in the introduction, our approach to anthropology stresses social networks and—in the case of the life histories we gathered—the contextualization of narratives in concrete events involving other individuals. It is possible that a dialogue between Sofía and researchers with other agenda would have generated a life history with a different emphasis. For example, during the interview with Hans Schlumpf (chapter 9, "The Influence of Women"), Sofía constructed generic women and leaders (while still resorting to concrete cases to exemplify her points). Perhaps, if Hans Schlumpf had recorded Sofía's life story, the stress might have been on the normative. The *fact* that in the narrative Sofía often privileges her relationships to specific others may reflect the nature of our relationship and may have become a mode of communication between us. This manner of narration and interpretation became ingrained in all of us. Few of the interviews were specifically geared to elicit self categorization. That she *portrays* her identity as embedded in relationships to others may, then, be predicated on our relationship and methodology, but *how* she situates herself vis-à-vis others can be teased from the text. In addition, the importance of her social ties is evident from an etic perspective. In what follows, we shall attempt to summarize the most important ties to others in Sofía's narrative; analyze how she constructs her identity over time in the interviews; deconstruct social-scientific categories that appear untenable and/or

Sofía in her bedroom (1988)

biased in the light of the narrative; and, finally, assess how Sofía envisions agency—how she seeks to control the vagaries of life, influence her relations to others, and enhance pleasure and minimize pain in the different stages of her life.

Developing a Social Network

Sofía's life history shows the development of her social network over time in a way that would have been difficult to document through less intensive methods. Sofía sees herself as deeply influenced by her mother and, to a much lesser extent, by the other members of her nuclear family. As a small child, her social universe included mainly close kin and renters who lived in the family compound. In addition, she was already exposed to the frequent guests from Llamacachi who slept in the compound on their visits to the city. Her circle of close friends did not grow substantially during her school years, perhaps because her classmates considered her as socially inferior. Her one new friend, Eva, was herself despised because of her physical handicap. In catechism classes her companions were again kin. She does not mention any friendships that evolved out of her early marketing activities, perhaps because of their short duration. These activities were initiated at the instigation of her friend Yola and facilitated by commercial links established by Yola's mother. However, eventually, Sofía was drawn back into her mother's artisanal and commercial activities.

After the family's move to Llamacachi, Sofía established new friendships. Again the relationship with her closest friend was based on kin ties, further consolidated through ties of ritual kinship. Interestingly, one of her boyfriends was, like herself, an outsider and the other was a *pazeño* from her neighborhood. But the father of her child is a renter and member of the neighboring rural community.

Kin ties facilitated Sofía's entry into the onion trade. Her subsequent progression into selling eggs was made possible by her mother's trade contacts in La Paz. But trading activities may also put ties at risk. The friendships Sofía established with women living in the neighborhood and with fellow market vendors have often been marred by occupational rivalries.

Over time, Sofía's social network also included a few ties outside her social class and beyond the confines of the geographical area in which her life unfolds. It includes nuns who are her teachers and with whom she works for community health care, as well as social scientists and film makers. However, it is interesting to note that, in spite of Sofía's close relation with us and with Jane Benton,[1] her use of those links (or of secondary connections) to expand her network geographically and to other social classes remained limited. For example, she mentions thinking about obtaining scarce sugar through Hans's father, but she did not, to our recollection, ever actually attempt to make use of that tie. We assisted her in obtaining a job working for a team of Bolivian anthropologists, but this did not work out. Neither did she express an interest in accompanying us to the United States, mainly because she did not want to leave her mother alone. To our knowledge, she has not cultivated ties with middle class or elite Bolivians, although her indirect tie with Yola's husband, whom Sofía describes as being a lawyer, might have come in handy in her lawsuit. In this respect, her networking strategies contrast with those of other *cholas* like Doña Flora (H. Buechler 1988, Buechler and Buechler 1992: 109–17) who made extensive use of her ties with foreigners to further her export business and to place her children in jobs abroad and with U.S. institutions in Bolivia.

Sofía's relatively circumscribed social network, then, provides the existential basis for her presentation of self. But the image she constructs of herself is also determined by stereotypic cultural categories she accepts, manipulates, transforms, or resists.

The Constructs of Gender, Class, and Ethnicity

Narratives like Sofía's, recorded over a long period of time lead us to question the utility of attempts to discover a single emic (i.e., informant based) construct of gender, class, and ethnicity, for, as the person reveals himself or herself, we, the consultants and anthropologists deconstruct these categories contextually and historically. In this process, there need be no Cartesian logic or consistency. It seems to us that one of the primary lessons of reflexive anthropology (and perhaps of postmodernism in general) is not the negation of traditional categories and concepts, but the realization that an understanding of the very process of deconstructing and reconstructing categories—*Verstehen* for the anthropologist and the persons studied—is a process of formulation and reformulation of ideas that develop from experiencing and reexperiencing relationships and events during the narration and while writing.

Sofía's depiction of the role of women in their reproductive and productive capacities is often contradictory or at least inconsistent. It is as though each time she focuses on gender she changes or shifts the meaning even if ever so slightly. For example, when she said in 1988 that "in these hard times in Bolivia women go out to work while men take care of things at home," she echoes an observation she made years earlier that the marriage of her nephew to a female butcher obviated the need for his working. She portrayed her nephew as a man whose primary task in a day was to go out, buy a newspaper and return home while his wife was heavily involved in marketing meat. While at *that* time she considered it unusual, in 1988 she identified with this division of labor, regarding it as the norm.[2]

However, her image of women as independent does not mean that she did not seek the economic contribution of men to the household. In 1988, she was in the process of reclaiming a former lover and the father of her child who enjoys a long-term steady job in order to force his economic support of his daughter. To accomplish this, she employed contradictory means to anchor him to her: feminine wiles, attractive dress, threats of legal action and secret coercion by magic. Sofía wanted him to set up his other common-law wife in a store so that she could live independently and he could devote himself exclusively to her (Sofía) and her daughter. But she did not plan to retire. She does not aspire to a traditional middle-class Latin family model. In her actions and musings about René, the image of gender relationships as characterized by complementarity and, in the best case scenario, exclusivity, is—as she probably realizes—highly unlikely in her own case, given the circumstances and the example of at least one of her brothers, who maintains two households.

Should we, the authors, then despair or appreciate that we are privy to the process whereby a person develops meaning in her life based on the manipulation of cultural values and experience? In order not to succumb to the temptation of taking statements at their face value, we need to place them in historical and topical context. Sometimes, the comparison of seemingly inconsistent statements reveals an underlying consistent theme. In the present case, Sofía invariably sees women as autonomous in the sense of responsible for their own and a major portion of their children's subsistence. What on the surface may appear as factually untrue, may actually serve to pinpoint a major insight. Men in Sofía's network are not all staying home (in fact even the lucky husband of the butcher was planning to open a butcher shop with his wife) and many have stable jobs and contribute to households, but women do feel that they can not depend on their support, especially in times of crises. The inconsistency of consultants' concepts is often regarded as resulting from the tension between hegemonic prescriptions and the resistance of the marginalized. Our own view is that while this argument may in fact be valid, it denies the multivocality of those we study. Sofía, in the statement cited above, is not just resisting the dominance of men but is expressing the importance of a long history of female empowerment in the market which is manifested in women's assumption of political leadership and ritual sponsorships. Her statement, then, is not merely an antithesis but a thesis about social patterning.

As we commented earlier, Sofía's narrative provides insight into the diverse roles men play in Bolivia and how context and time influence masculinity: the philanderer becomes a kind father (René), and the practical musician becomes a farsighted magician after series of family misfortunes and psychotic episodes (Juan). Some men are unable to cope with their misfortunes, others adjust. Sofía's father is driven into madness by the lawsuit to reclaim her mother's land, while her brother, Moises, balances the obligations to two unorthodox households in orthodox ways. From Sofía's perspective, all these men can be handled by their women primarily by remaining economically self-sufficient and secondarily by magic.

Sofía is very conscious of social class and ethnic identity. Her varied self-definitions over her lifetime in terms of her position in the urban and national social stratification provide insight into the nuances of class and ethnic consciousness. As we pointed out in the introduction, we find that even the more recent typologies of social class in the Andes are either unitary or dualistic, and thereby underrate the multiplicity of avenues of upward mobility and the complexity of the relationship among persons differently situated within these avenues and the manifold views that they hold of themselves and others. Lagos (1993) and Gill (1993) are to be lauded for recognizing the complexity of socioeconomic roles in post-1952 Bolivia, but, from our point of view, they still oversimplify the ways in which the emic views are interrelated. Dualistic models do not do sufficient justice to the manipulation of social class symbols and stereotypes such as those based on physical type, language and education, profession, place of birth, ritual participation, access to persons in power, and general expenditures for food, fiestas, dress, and home furnishings. Depending on the situation and period, Sofía defines her position as "peasant," "*chola*," "*clase media*," "*chota chola*," "*de vestido*," "*más preparada*" (more educated and prepared for "modern" life), and "*paceña*." These categorizations of herself and of others depend on what she is trying to accomplish at the moment or period in her life, and the stereotypes she assumes others have of individuals like herself. In her role as community liaison person for the nuns in La Paz, she described herself to them as a peasant and farmer, i.e. a person with roots in a rural community. Since, at the time, she had decided against engaging in white-collar work, she may also have tried to convey that she did not aspire to such a position, associated with urbanity and *not* working with one's hands. The use of peasant or farmer in this context, which is rare for Sofía, may thus have connoted subservience, or romanticism of the peasant as producer rather than as merchant. It might have served as a useful technique for avoiding the responsibilities of a catechist, a position which was suggested to her by the nuns. Sofía never employs the term *indio* to refer to herself or to any of her relatives. However, in her narrative, she does employ the word on two occasions to refer to persons who sell pork to her: once in reference to a man from Jank'o Amaya and once with reference to a man who works for a wealthy *Compeño*. In those contexts—while not meant as a direct insult—she uses the terms to designate low status.

Sofía's self presentation as a *chota chola* during the years in Llamacachi could be seen as an attempt to seek refuge in a relatively neutral, or unmarked, category; one that neither emulated the wealthier La Paz *cholas* nor the elite and professionals (see chapter 10). Her choice of changing her hair to a single braid from the open hairstyle she had adopted in La Paz, made her less conspicuously different from the other young women in her rural community, but allowed her to maintain a separate class identity. This symbolic statement made it clear that she had a different background but that she did not want to stand out and appear snobbish.

Sofía ascribes her success as a market leader to being better educated (*más preparada*) than her peers. This is consonant with her self definition as belonging to the *clase media* which, in this context, she extends to all working urbanites with the exception of the elites. White-collar workers and professionals would usually exclude the lower strata: laborers, artisans, market vendors, and servants from this class, and she herself often seems to adopt the latter definition as well, when she contrasts *cholas* and members of the *clase media*. However, in those instances, she often views society in terms of parallel stratification systems in which a *chola* may be the equal of or superior to a person from the *clase media*.

Finally, Sofía constructs her *chola* identity in moral terms and rejects one possible identity as a teacher on moral grounds. She considers the latter as morally lax, since they need to ingratiate themselves to males, thereby losing their autonomy. Her characterization of *de vestido* women as having difficulties in the market place may derive from the same idea. Sofía sees *chola* clothing as protective. One could hypothesize that, in this context, the *pollera* symbolizes the power of the network of like minded women with protective clout, and is not a sign of being humble as Gill (1993: 81) seems to imply when she states that some fathers and husbands insist on their daughters and wives wearing *polleras* because "they believe that women wearing *polleras* are more humble and less available sexually to other men."[3] Her hope to sell the house owned jointly with her brothers for a less conveniently located one, but one where she and Rocío could live alone in a more *clase media* style is in keeping with her daughter's professional aspirations rather than her convenience. As these various self definitions show, ethnic/class identification is not just reactive to dominant models but proactive and created to suit varied circumstances: residence, occupational opportunities and friendship circles.

Self-definition is of course partly contingent on how an individual is defined by others. One of the best examples of the ambiguity, complexity, and, also, the "hidden injuries" of class is that of Sofía's travails with the legal system. In this situation (see chapter 4), she is put down as an ignorant peasant by her rivals and mediators alike, even those who, under other circumstances, would think of themselves as belonging to the same social class. In this case, having the right connections in the bureaucracy counts, while peasant background is denigrated.

While in this and many other instances recent rural origin often has negative connotations in cities like La Paz, the advantages are often recognized even by long-term urbanites. As we have argued earlier (see also Buechler and Buechler 1992: chapter 3), rural origin also carries the positive connotation of rootedness, access to land, and a wide network of crucial connections.[4]

Sofía protects her image of herself against negative stereotyping by narrating examples of how she and others bested those who regard themselves as superior, or how she was accepted by those whom she regards as her social superiors. Her friend Yola amazes the wives of her husband's lawyer colleagues by her knowledge about a variety of topics, while Sofía herself, although initially frightened, finds herself accepted as an "honorary member" of the upper echelon of the *clase media* when she attends the elegant coming-out party of one of her daughter's classmates (chapter 12).[5]

Associated but only partially congruent with social class is the important role of legitimacy. Illegitimate birth (when the genitor and the mother's husband/companion—i.e. the child's sociological father—are not the same) stigmatizes the child even when the child is legally adopted by the sociological father. When Sofía talks about adoption (see chapter 11), she also voices concern about the rights an adopted child might enjoy, as against those of a child reared as a servant. Clearly, René's recognition of Rocío has both economic and social implications, just as, a generation earlier, Sofía's father's recognition of Pedro affected the dynamics of the family.

Life histories, then, highlight the processual nature of gender, class, and birth identification. These are not fixed attributes but are constructed by oneself and others.

Rethinking Conceptualizations of Marketing

Sofía's narrative underlines the class centeredness of such concepts as "the informal sector." As we have argued elsewhere (Buechler and Buechler 1992: 13–16, 278–9; H. Buechler 1992), the "formal"/"informal" dichotomy, which superseded the even more problematic concepts of "dual economy" and "marginality" in the 1970s, is itself based on erroneous assumptions about the differences between large firms and small-scale producers and vendors to which the dichotomy is usually applied;

for these assumptions are based on an idealized construct of "the formal economy" and a class based stereotype of the "informal." Those social scientists who have been most successful in applying the dichotomy have been able to do so only because they, in fact, subvert their own initial definitions by failing to apply them consistently to the cases they examine. Marketers, like Sofía are invariably included into the category of "informal," and yet, by some definitions of "informality" most market vendors would have to be classified as belonging to the "formal sector." For example, in Bolivia, as well as Peru, selling in the market is among the most regulated economic activities and thus the characterization of them as "illegal," a trait frequently ascribed to "informal" activities is, with few exceptions, entirely inappropriate. Furthermore, in Bolivia fresh produce and meat are distributed almost exclusively through women and a few men in street markets, fairs, and covered markets, while many other items, including certain imported foods and even electronic devices, are preponderantly distributed in this manner. These activities are not subsidiary or ancillary as often attributed to activities in the "informal sector."

Some anthropologists, like Babb (1989) prefer to use the term "petty commodity producers" to describe small-scale vendors as well as artisans and peasant farmers in order to circumvent the biases inherent in the formal/informal dichotomy. In order to justify the inclusion of marketers in the category of "producers," Babb argues that among the population of market vendors she studied in Peru, there is no clear separation between producing and selling a product. In addition, she argues that, like peasants and artisans, the majority of the vendors never succeed in accumulating capital, making neoclassical concepts like that of the "entrepreneur" of limited value. However, while such a model might be sufficient to deal with market vendors in a small provincial city, at least in larger cities such as Lima and La Paz, women who engage in marketing activities differ markedly in their success and the degree to which they themselves or their families engage in agricultural or artisanal activities. At the top levels, a *chola* may accumulate substantial amounts of capital. In La Paz, some *cholas* own large compounds of prime real estate, and some are rumored to own entire city blocks, while at the bottom, a vendor may sell a few dozen oranges or peddle a few glasses of fruit drinks. And yet they may share similar values and a similar lifestyle. It therefore makes little sense to attempt to separate wealthier and poorer vendors into different categories and deal with each category within a different theoretical framework. In addition, the Marxist concept of petty commodity production carries with it the burden of its association with unilineal (and unidirectional) evolution. The recent growth of such activities during what Marx would have called "late capitalism" belies the validity of such a model. Rather, we should strive for models that acknowledge both the wide variety of forms that capitalism can take and the debt of these forms to earlier forms of production and distribution which have themselves undergone and continue to undergo manifold adaptive processes. Sofía's marketing activities both harken back to the early colonial role of rural-urban migrants to Andean cities (Burkett 1978, Zulawski 1990) and form an integral part of the modern Bolivian capitalist economy. The responses she develops to cope with the debt crisis of the 1980s provides us with a critical tale of economic restructuring in a nation within the new international division of labor, particularly as it influences capital and commodity flows.

Agency: Joys and Crises

As Sofía sees it, life is full of worries, surprises, dangers, and pleasures. To cope with these in her personal/professional life, she employs mixed strategies. The life history shows her excitement in clinching a good bargain even if it involves deceit on her part; telling a good, rousing tale, even at her own expense; and engagement in the affairs of others. What to our surprise does not come across fully—except indirectly in the last interview in 1994 (chapter 12) and sporadically on other occasions—is her love for good food. This "silence" is due to the fact that our discussions about food invariably took place while buying, cooking, or eating food, i.e., at times when the tape recorder was off. Perhaps the silence is also due to the anthropological neglect of this topic until quite recently (see Johnsson 1986, Weismantel 1988). We do know from a large number (200) of market women interviewed by Judith-Maria and Sofía in the late sixties that one of their favorite pastimes as of a Sunday was cooking for themselves (*sabemos cocinarnos* [*sic*]).[6] Cooking was also one of Sofía's occupations and she and other *cholas*, unlike the middle class, eat out very frequently. Eating well with lots of meat also distinguishes the urban market woman from her rural counterpart. Our eating a quick sandwich for lunch on the run was seen as the height of deprivation by Sofía and our other consultants. The lack of food and food shortages during the economic crisis were the source of greatest concern, taking precedence over other discomforts such as the lack of transportation during the frequent strikes, or even physical danger.[7] Obesity is both the traditional hallmark of the successful *chola* and the result of overindulgence, which in Sofía's case and that of other *cholas* may lead to serious illness (Dr. Ruth Tichauer, personal communication). Preparing and eating good food together was one of the pleasures we shared. Festive meals were a source of high regard for the cook.

For Sofía, drinking has a more ambiguous connotation. She sees no problem with drinking at fiestas in the Aymara pattern where women drink heavily (although less so than men), but she is more ambivalent about the town and urban practice of frequent drinking with peers. She has engaged in this pattern herself, particularly in connection with her activities as a union leader. But she ascribes accidents and corruption to this custom.

Throughout her life, Sofía has encountered a series of major crises: failed or problematic relationships: debt, loss and theft, conflict with city authorities, illness, and death of family members. In her narrative, we see her adept handling of the crises using the social avenues open to her. Some are dealt with by seeking the mediation of individuals with crucial connections such as shopkeepers with access to scarce sugar or individuals savvy in legal affairs. Other crises, such as abuse by the police, demand concerted action by a group such as a market union. The foregoing mechanisms are regarded as appropriate for conditions she shares with others that surround her but insufficient in cases where she appears to be singled out by misfortune. In those cases, she suspects witchcraft that she must divert by magical means. Sofía has admitted to only one instance where she has *initiated* sorcery, namely in order to attract her erstwhile lover. Even though Sofía did not use the term sorcery on this occasion, she classified an analogous example as such in an interview that took place in an earlier year. Sorcery means initiating coercion of others through the use of spirits which is considered dangerous. In contrast, Sofía appears to consider protective sorcery such as preventing others from harming her, but without retaliation, as more justifiable. Finally, general well-being or even an unexpected windfall can be assured through the manipulation of spirits.[8] Although according to Aymara beliefs illness can be caused by sorcery as well, Sofía never directly attributes illness to foul play of this sort. Rather, when she determines that an illness was caused by spirits, the latter are seen to act independently of human agency.

Immersing oneself in this lively narrative of a plucky market trader spanning more than a quarter of a century of turbulence in Bolivia, then, leads us to rethink notions of gender, class, ethnicity, nation, and individual well-being. Sofía is *no* passive Aymara woman in an enduring Andean landscape or nation in inevitable decline.

NOTES

INTRODUCTION

1. The network approach is more evident in the total corpus of taped interviews than is apparent in this book. Interviews with Sofía's kinsfolk and friends had to be left out for reasons of space. We hope to publish them separately at a later date.

2. Another means is to include the voice of the anthropologist in the text. We would have preferred to leave our questions in the book, but in order to comply with editorial space constraints we have deleted them. This also gave us the leeway to maintain Sofía's narrative style and flow as much as possible. Nevertheless, we use square brackets to indicate our insertion of connecting phrases into Sofía's narrative. We use parentheses to indicate our own clarifying statements, i.e., statements where we are not trying to simulate her voice.

3. See, in particular, the section entitled "The Influence of Women" in chapter 18, that records a discussion initiated by a question posed by Hans Schlumpf.

4. Here we use the term *clase media* to correspond roughly to lower middle class persons who wear European-style clothing. Further nuances of the term will be explored later.

5. According to Behar (1993: 11), her Mexican informant employed the narrative mode of victimization to emulate the Christian narrative as a story of suffering and the Catholic confession narrative.

6. The meaning of this social designation for women dressing in a particular dress style will be elucidated presently.

7. Hans's own position within the rural system of social stratification had been of an ambiguous nature. As the only foreigners in a nearby free community—where his father built a weekend house—his family had an unusual position. On the one hand, its position was similar to that of the two or three town families, who considered themselves *vecinos*, i.e. recognized townsmen with its implication of following Latin rather than Aymara traditions: they shared the *vecinos'* urban orientation and

their stake in the local community. In the latter respect, the family's situation was more clearly defined than that of urban absentee owners of a few plots of land near the village. On the other hand, the less hierarchical relationships Hans's family maintained with Aymara peasants differentiated the family from the *vecinos*. On occasion, his father was called upon to assist Aymara community members with procuring scarce commodities, such as cloth for the sailboats with which they plied the straits of Lake Titicaca. While one *vecino* became a friend, relationships with another *vecino* neighbor were complicated by disputes over a right of way, which, in turn, may have originated from the *vecino's* wish to prevent anybody from seeing him personally working his land, a type of work regarded as shameful by traditional *vecinos*. In addition, Hans's father offered to bring a rural-urban migrant baker from a distant community and built a small oven so that the community would have fresh bread. This lead to rivalries between the baker and the *vecino* neighbor. In general, Hans learned to expect condescending behavior towards Aymara speakers from *vecinos* and an ambiguous relationship towards him, at best—often vacillating between embarrassing obsequiousness and aggression when the *vecino* was drunk. Hans's relationship with Sofía's brother's father-in-law, from whom he rented a room (in a separate building) in Llamacachi was of this ambiguous nature.

8. Sofa's "middle class" great grandmother moved from La Paz to Llamacachi as a child and was adopted into a "peasant" family; the family then became impoverished because of the murder of her great-grandfather; subsequently, her mother prospered as a candlemaker; but the family's fortunes declined again due to the obsolescence of her mother's trade and by the father's illness, which resulted in a return to the rural community and in members of the family working for other peasants in Llamacachi and neighboring Compi; finally, with Sofía's slow rise in the world of produce marketing and her brothers' urban industrial and government employment, the family recouped some of its losses.

9. We were sensitized to the issue of narrative style by Behar's discussion of the narrative models followed by Esperanza in telling her story (1993: 11).

10. Even Sofía's own capsule account for the film, which deals with events that occurred over an entire century, while maintaining the correct sequence of the episodes, often does not give a sense of the time frame, much less the various contexts in which they occurred.

CHAPTER 1

1. The Garita de Lima (literally, "Sentry Box of Lima"), located half a block away from Sofía's home, now a small park from which a number of busy market streets radiate, was once the gateway to the city from the direction of Lima, Peru.

2. Sofía must have been around six years old at the time.

3. Presumably Sofía was five or six years old then.

4. We use the term "European" here as shorthand for simple, modern, cosmopolitan fashions. Actually, *chola* fashions are also derived from European fashions, albeit colonial ones.

5. One of the figures in the *tundiqui* dance copied from similar dances performed by descendants of slaves in Yungas valley communities.

6. At the time, Sofía was fifteen years old.
7. Sofía was nineteen then.

CHAPTER 2

1. Alasitas is a fair in the honor of Ekeko, the god of plenty, held annually in La Paz during the week after January 24th. Artisans make miniature replicas of the objects they desire and place them in their homes, often hanging them around the neck of a replica of the god (see Buechler and Buechler 1992: 95—96).
2. In 1988, Sofía revised the age when she began to help her mother to six or seven years.
3. Sofía must have been 12 years old at the time.
4. Ritual cleansing is common among the Aymara. In rural communities it is practiced whenever some calamity has occurred and is designed to ward off further evil. In Compi and Llamacachi, ritual cleansing followed such phenomena as severe hailstorms, the birth of twins, and when a donkey was struck by lightning (see Buechler and Buechler 1971: 98—101). An element of this ritual is the asking of forgiveness of all members of the community by the kinsmen of the afflicted family.
5. However, this does not appear to have led to regular purchases of onions from Llamacacheños. Rather, Sofa continued to buy from strangers.
6. *Cholas* place a strong emphasis on jewelry, which not only constitutes a public display of wealth, but is a major form of investment. Traditional, heavy jewelry with ornate floral designs adorned with pearls are favored. During the economic crisis of the 1980s signs advertising the purchase of gold were ubiquitous in lower-class neighborhoods as *cholas* (and others) were forced to draw on these resources (see our film, *The World of Sofía Velasquez*). At the same time more gilded jewelry was produced, few could afford the genuine article. *De vestido* women place somewhat less emphasis on jewelry, and the designs are simpler.
7. For a detailed analysis of Sofía's father's illness and cure see H. Buechler 1981.
8. "Long live Bolivia" and "Down with Paraguay," a reference to the countries in conflict during the Chaco War (1932–1935).
9. Bolivian currency was known as the *boliviano* until 1956 when it was changed to the *peso* (worth 1000 *bolivianos*). After 1956, however, Bolivians continued to calculate in *bolivianos* rather than in the new *peso boliviano*.
10. The version of this episode Sofía gave in 1988 is somewhat different: "My father opened a store and rented land in Cawaya and Chua and saw that he could produce potatoes and other crops. It was at that point that my mother came to La Paz and sold the land in El Alto. She gave some of the money from the sale of the land to Pedro and to Moises and with the remainder my father bought a plot in Compi. My father cultivated that land and in the process became well again."
11. The government opened certain streets on weekends, so that producers could sell directly to the consumers, thus bypassing intermediaries and mitigating the effects of inflation on purchasing power.
12. In 1988, Sofía elaborated on why she had given up her sales site in the Rodriguez market: "If it hadn't been for the *feria franca* (in the Avenida Montes) I would have continued to sell in the Rodriguez. Because of the *feria franca* I lost my sales site in the Rodriguez. I preferred to sell in the *feria franca* than in the

Rodriguez because one has to sell every day in the Rodriguez. Since I travelled to the countryside, it was better for me to arrive here on Friday in the afternoon and sell on Saturday."

13. In 1988, Sofía stressed the negative aspects of selling onions more strongly. She said, "I sold in the Avenida Montes for almost two and a half years. I sold onions and vegetables. Then my mother urged me to change. She told me, 'You are suffering and you aren't making much money.' . . . She saw that selling onions meant a lot of work. The onions had to be harvested brought to the river and washed—which is difficult during the rainy season—and then carried to the side of the road and bundled. So my mother told me to buy eggs in Jank'o Amaya and, one Thursday, my mother and I went there to buy eggs. That time, I bought almost 500 eggs and later sold them here in La Paz. When I saw that business was good, I went to buy eggs as well as cheese every Thursday. At the same time, I continued buying and selling onions."

14. For a fuller treatment of the Velasquez's divining and curing practices see H. Buechler 1981, from which parts of this discussion are drawn.

15. Tschopik's orthography, derived from the verb *k'atuña*, "to catch," makes more sense than Lucia's own rendition: *k'acjja*.

16. Some informants mention only the *ajayu* and the *animu*.

17. The names for the three souls and their characterization varies. Crandon-Malamud (1991: 133) describes the three souls as the *ajayu* which provides reasoning and consciousness, the *animu* which is strength and courage, and the *alma* which is the spirit that lives on after death. According to her informants both the *ajayu* and the *animu* can be stolen, while the *alma* can only leave the body at death.

18. The invocation of all three spirits at once, as Sofa's mother claims to have done in this case, does not appear to be a common practice.

19. When Hans was a child in La Paz, his Swiss godfather would demonstrate to him by honking the horn (much to the consternation of Hans's godmother), that people who had a scare would invariably and immediately spit on the ground.

20. The ingredients included alcohol and wine, both given as libations to the spirits on all occasions; llama fat, a substance which is an essential ingredient of burnt offerings, as it is considered to be particularly appreciated by the spirits (see Girault 1988: 212); coca leaves, included in all rituals; and wira qua (identified as *Senecio matheswii* by Girault [1988: 168]), an herb similar to thyme, the condiment for the spirits.

CHAPTER 3

1. The *kachua* is a traditional ritual for adolescents performed on specific dates including Saint Andrew's day (November 29th)—the Aymara new year—in the hills surrounding the community, and entails dances associated with the themes of fertility and weddings. Adult men often provide the flute and drum accompaniment to the dances and small children may tag along as well (see Buechler and Buechler 1971: 76—79).

2. August 5th, the eve of Independence Day, is also the day of The Virgin of Snows.

3. Aymara for young man, but here used as an ethnic slur.

4. Guinea pigs are used as a magical cure by transferring the disease to the animal and then sacrificing it, and for divination, by examining their entrails. They are also eaten.

CHAPTER 4

1. A community located some ten miles from Llamacachi in the opposite direction from Jank'o Amaya. The fair is known for its fish, caught by fishermen in the surrounding area and for the goods smuggled by boat across the lake from Peru.

2. A mass and fiesta in the honor of a deceased person held one year after the funeral.

3. Presumably, the authorities wished to keep the supply as high as possible in La Paz, to prevent social unrest in the city.

4. Although that trip did not entail crossing any national boundary, customs officials were aware of the kinds of goods that could only have been obtained from Peru and were on the lookout for them at the roadblocks in major villages and at the entrance to the city where all traffic had to stop and the drivers would have to present papers (*hoja de ruta*) indicating the route they had taken.

5. As we shall see in chapter 11, Elena was also Sofía's half sister.

6. An onomatopoetic expression used in comic books meaning "all of a sudden" or "just like that."

7. Sofia never got her money back, but at least she had the satisfaction that the defendant was forced to pay a hefty sum to be let out of prison.

8. Lambs are sold according to size rather than weight.

9. It is not clear what the figures Sofía gives here represent, since the interview was held in 1988 but she is referring to an earlier period.

10. Interestingly, her sister-in-law, Elena, made a similar switch as a result of a theft that forced her to find an activity which required less capital.

CHAPTER 5

1. Rather than being indicative of a change in his convictions, Pedro's caution about becoming involved in politics again probably reflected the uncertain political climate in 1979–80.

2. Former president Victor Paz Estenssoro was nicknamed *El Mono*, the monkey.

3. Sofía uses the term *agencia* in two ways: to designate a wholesale market and a place where goods sold in the market are stored.

4. Lidia Gueiler was toppled by García Meza, not Natusch Busch. Sofía's uncertainty about which president was involved in that coup gives testimony to the political turmoil in the period between 1979 and 1982.

5. Presumably, Sofía is referring to the nongovernmental development organizations (NGOs) that proliferated in Bolivia in the 1980s and 1990s.

6. Literally, "little boy, little father, little mother," terms used by the peasants during hacienda times to ingratiate themselves with the landowning class, but rarely used in Bolivia today.

7. Hans's assistant.

8. All orientals are called "Chinos." In this case, the persons in question were probably Korean.

9. It would have been worth only US$50 at the official rate and $29.41 at the street rate, while it may have been worth US$4,000 originally.

10. Sofía fails to mention, however, that spare parts must have risen sevenfold in a short period.

11. Dollar equivalencies cannot be given since it is unclear when these transactions took place.

12. Sofía switched from one pig disease to another in this example.

13. This is probably an exaggeration.

14. That is late, but within the culturally defined limits.

15. Although the currency unit (corresponding to one million old pesos) regained the earlier designation "Boliviano" in January 1987, Sofía, who had finally become accustomed to the term "peso," now refused to make the switch back to the term "Boliviano" for the new currency.

16. Since the creation of the new "Boliviano" the exchange rate to the US dollar was allowed to float, thereby minimizing the difference between official and street rates.

17. This doesn't make sense. Sofía must mean that the scale indicates less than the actual weight.

18. In order to obtain a telephone a person must become a share holder of the telephone company at a cost of several thousand dollars. Such shares are transferable and therefore constitute a secure collateral for a loan.

19. In a telephone conversation in October 1995, Sofia again stressed the importance of loans from Banco Sol which she felt were enabling her to cope with a new slowdown in the economy.

CHAPTER 6

1. According to Bastien (1987:40), tarot cards "originated from an ancient cult and continue to be used by gypsies and spiritists throughout Europe . . . The Kallawayas have modified the meanings of tarot cards to fit in with Andean culture."

2. A Manuel Llave is listed on a genealogical chart in Bastien as a "herbalist of Calle Sagarnaga" and brother of Nestor Llave whom Bastien considers as one of the foremost Callawaya practitioners in La Paz (1987: 33). However, some of the details of that family's background do not coincide. For a detailed description of Nestor Llave's medical and magical practices see Bastien 1987:32–66.

3. "Naming," in this case, means designating the pieces of fat for a particular purpose. In other contexts, "naming" may also mean designating a coca leaf or other ritual item to symbolize a particular object or event.

4. Literally, "in this or that place," for the coca leaves fall on and around leaves designated to signify particular individuals and the fortune is read by which side of the leaves is visible, the shape and condition of the leaves, including broken edges, folding, spots and holes, and the direction in which the leaves point as well as their location with reference to the specially designated leaves. Sometimes the specially

designated leaves also signify Jesus Christ (two leaves placed in the shape of a cross) and/or the *achachilas*.

5. Yarn used in magical seances is often spun in reverse (i.e., counterclockwise) to undo misfortune.

6. Possibly, such powers are ascribed to widows because, as spouses of diseased persons, they may be seen as having more direct access to the world of souls and spirits.

7. *Tíos* (literally "uncles") are place (often mountain) spirits.

8. Possibly, Sofía means that the intervention of the spirits she has propitiated has not only averted the neighbors' witchcraft but has turned the witchcraft against them.

9. A spirit resembling a priest who cuts the victim's body to extract the fat surrounding his liver.

10. At another time, Sofía described Manuel Llave's other skulls as well: In addition to Juco, he had a skull called Condori "and the third I don't know, but it is female."

11. The term *Tío* applies to the Christian devil as well as to place spirits with which the devil is sometimes equated.

12. For descriptions of these meanings see Bastien (1987: 44), Carter and Mamani (1982: 318–19), and Paredes (1963: 33–36), among others.

13. We will return to this issue in Chapter 12.

CHAPTER 7

1. Miniature beribboned cards pinned onto the participants in remembrance of an important occasion.

2. The fact that she crossed out the less formal *descripción* and replaced it with the term *redacción* is an indication of the formal and carefully constructed nature of this piece of writing.

3. The essay is not dated, but was almost certainly written in 1967.

4. Or an appointed mayor during military regimes.

5. Market vendors of some urban markets first organized themselves in unions in the 1920s (see Dibbits et al. 1989, Medinaceli 1989: 111–12, and Peredo Beltrán 1993: 103–16) to fight against discrimination against *cholas* and to lobby for the construction of market halls. While all these original unions, which were based on an anarcho-sindicalist model, disappeared by the late fifties, the street markets that flourished in the late fifties and early sixties formed new, more centrally, controlled unions.

6. For a more detailed account and interpretation, see J.-M. Buechler 1972: 131–69).

CHAPTER 8

1. The Dirección de Investigación Criminal (Bureau of Criminal Investigation. The number 110 refers to the telephone number of the police.

2. The upper- and middle-class neighborhoods.

CHAPTER 9

1. That is, for the State of La Paz.

2. The reference to "finding something" is reminiscent of Sofía's magician telling her that she would find an unexpected treasure in the street (see chapter 6).

3. Since in Bolivia all Protestant denominations proscribe the consumption of alcohol, sponsorship of or even participation in fiestas is difficult or impossible for them (see H. Buechler 1980).

4. The reason for the discrepancy between the date Sofía gives for the market's foundation and the time it has been in existence is unclear. No one sold in the Incachaca in the sixties and early seventies, so, perhaps the market was founded in 1959 but did not manage to gain a footing until much later. More likely, the earlier date refers to the establishment of the joint union of the Incachaca, Tumusla, and Garita de Lima. Since we took a photograph of what Sofía described as the inauguration of the Incachaca market in 1981, we are not sure what the thirteen-year figure refers to.

5. All these are towns in the high plateau south of La Paz and the Lake Titicaca area.

6. The sister would, most likely, have been heavily involved in assisting Julia when she sponsored the fiesta.

7. Almost certainly a gross exaggeration.

8. Little printed card pinned on guests of a sponsor by the sponsor himself or by a collaborator.

9. Chicken is more expensive in Bolivia than lamb.

10. A flute of a yard or more in length, associated with the temperate valley of Luribay, located to the south of La Paz.

11. It is not clear whether Sofía means that they had lots of meat to sell or whether, as is customary in community fiestas, the guests were able to take cooked meat home to their families.

12. Sofía is referring to the fact that this woman was angry at our filming marketing scenes.

CHAPTER 10

1. Presumably, Sofía meant a vicuña-colored manta actually made out of fine alpaca wool, or perhaps a mixture with vicuña wool, but by the mid-sixties, it was already illegal to sell vicuña wool.

2. A chola outfit would thus have cost US$750.

3. His mother is also de pollera.

4. Sofía never did make the switch.

5. As we saw earlier, however, in recent years, official credit sources sometimes have insisted on lenders' mustering consumer goods as collateral. And even unofficial lenders take such items as television sets and videocassette recorders as collateral.

6. For a detailed description and analysis of the elopement, betrothal and wedding rituals associated with this wedding see H. Buechler (1980: 199–206, 208–16, 301, 329).

7. As we saw in chapter 4, before she switched to *chola* clothing, Sofía also danced as a *chola* during Carnival in La Paz. In this case, however, the meaning of her choice of dress was not the same. She dressed as a *chola* in order to *disguise* her normal *de vestido* identity.

8. As we shall see in the next chapter, by 1994, Sofía was beginning to experience pressure to conform to *clase media* consumption patterns because of her daughter's aspirations.

CHAPTER 11

1. According to Sofía's mother, Flora was thirteen when she came to live with her.

2. Sulma's life ended tragically when she was still an infant. Sofía, who entrusted her sister-in-law with her care during her frequent trips to Jank'o Amaya and Llamacachi, blames the child's death on Elena's neglect, if not abuse of the child. The death led to a rift with Elena and with her nephew, Teodoro, which lasted for many years.

3. See Buechler and Buechler (1972: 41–42, 112) for a discussion of *utawawas* in Compi/Llamacachi (see also Carter and Mamani 1982: 36, 459).

CHAPTER 12

1. A formal visit with a band to the family of the bride, in order to bring her to the groom's home.

2. The increasingly heavy burden that Sofía had to bear when she had to defray the school fees herself are apparent from a statement she made in 1984: "I am travelling more because my daughter is asking for money now. The school sent me a note that the fees are going to go up to 20,000 pesos (US$10 [official rate], US$5.90 [street]). I will show you the slip. I was speechless (when I heard about it). What am I going to do? I will have to work harder. It's not just the fees. They are asking for other things too. She told me to send fruit: two bananas, two oranges, two tangerines. She said that they will teach them to eat fruit salad. They ask for all sorts of things. Next year it will probably be 30,000 pesos (US$15 [official], US$8.80 [street]). It's expensive."

3. It is interesting to contrast Sofia's use of dreams with that of a more middle-class artisan, whose life history we have summarized elsewhere (Buechler and Buechler 1992: chapter 11), who uses dreams, invariably beautiful ones, as a temporary escape from an unhappy marriage.

4. An arrangement whereby the owner of a property cedes it in return for an interest-free loan. The property reverts back to the owner upon repayment of the original sum, usually at the end of several years.

5. In November 1995, Sofia was still living in the old house.

6. Sofía's heightened sensitivity to slights related to social class is also apparent from a comment she made during out first visit with her in 1994. She complained that her sister-in-law, with whom she is at war, had called her daughter an *imilla*, an Indian girl, denigrating her for the fact that Rocío's father was born in a rural community. She stressed that she herself was a *paceña* (born in La Paz) and that her daughter was a *paceña* too.

7. A mandolin-like instrument, usually made out of the shell of an armadillo.

8. During a telephone conversation in October 1995, as this book went to press, Sofia reiterated Rocío's plan to study medicine or odontology. To help pay for her studies, Rocío planned to work as a hairdresser.

CONCLUSION

1. An English geographer who got to know Sofía through Mauricio Mamani, an anthropologist and former assistant to the American anthropologist William Carter with whom Hans worked for several months.

2. Or, at least she was willing to generalize the example of her nephew and presumably other similar experiences when Hans Schlumpf prodded her to make a categorical statement about "women."

3. We should note that Gill's overall characterization of the social position of *cholas* is that it is ambiguous and contested.

4. Nevertheless, we should not fall into the temptation of assuming a bipolar model of rural connectedness and dense social networks versus loose urban social networks, for the rural-urban ties of migrants may continue over many generations and high-density networks symbolically legitimated in elaborate rituals may evolve in specific occupations such as beef butchers and may persist in urban neighborhoods that engulfed adjacent, once rural, communities (see H. Buechler 1980: 214).

5. It is possible that Sofía might have been inhibited from relating more tales of class and race discrimination in deference to our closeness and the fact that we were middle-class whites, but we also know that when she criticized the Bolivian elite she did not include us in that category. We were seen as outside the system (see Gmelch 1992: 274—6 for a similar observation in his discussion of racism in the narratives of Barbadian return migrants).

6. Sofía's use of the reflexive form is characteristic of Aymaraized Bolivian Spanish and may come from the use of suffixes in Aymara for prepositions.

7. Interestingly, in dream interpretation, gifts of food and their acceptance by the dreamer are seen as a *negative* sign. Their meaning, perdition, may come from the fact that they indicate temptation by evil spirits acting on behalf of a rival or enemy.

8. Counterintuitively, magical intervention did not increase during periods of economic crisis.

GLOSSARY

ACHACHILA Mountain or lake spirit.

AGENCIA Sofía uses this term variously to designate a small wholesale marketplace, usually situated in a patio; a place of business; and a patio where vendors can store their vending tables for a fee.

AJAYU One of a person's three souls that wanders away at night during one's dreams and may be captured by a malevolent spirit, causing illness.

ARROBA 25 Spanish lbs.

AWAYO Carrying cloth.

BRUJO Magician; sorcerer.

CARGA 150 Spanish lbs.

CASERA(O) Regular customer or supplier.

CH'ALLA Ritual libation.

CHICHA A beer usually made out of corn, but on the altiplano sometimes out of quinoa.

CHOLA Urban-born woman who continues to dress in the traditional garb that includes the *pollera* (skirt), *manta* (embroidered shawl), and felt bowler hat. The style is considered the hallmark—but not exclusive province—of market vendors.

CHUÑO Freeze dried potatoes.

COLITA Little printed card pinned on guests of a sponsor by the sponsor himself or by a collaborator.

CORAJE Literally "courage." One of a person's three souls that gives him/her courage to speak up in public.

DE VESTIDO A person who wears modern, European-style clothing. Used both as an adjective and as a noun.

DULCE MESA	Offering to the spirits of sweets, animal fat, and tufts of colored wool.
EMPANADA	Cheese turnover.
ENJALME	A cloth on which money has been sewn which is tied onto the back of a bull at a bullfight. The man who succeeds in ripping it off the enraged bull's back keeps the cash.
HABA	Broad bean. One of the major crops of the Lake Titicaca area.
HUMINTA	A snack made out of ground fresh corn, cheese, and condiments baked in a corn leaf.
IRPAQA	A formal visit to the family of the bride with a music band in order to bring her to the groom's home.
K'AYA	Freeze dried *oca* (*Oxalis tuberosa*), a tuber.
KISPIÑA	Steamed dough made out of ground *quinua* mixed with lime.
LAWA	Barley and milk soup eaten for breakfast.
LLAMPU	Llama fat used as food for the spirits in offerings.
MESA (OR MISA)	Burnt offering to the spirits.
OCA	*Oxalis tuberosa*: a tuber.
ORIGINARIO	A land holder whose family can trace community membership back to at least the last century.
PACEÑO	Person born in the city of La Paz.
PASEO	Sunday promenade. The latin custom for young people (and sometimes adults as well) to go on a promenade (or drive around in an automobile) in a central place in a city on Sundays to meet young people of the opposite sex or just to be seen.
POLLERA	Wide, gathered skirt worn by peasant women (when made from wool or cotton) and by *cholas* (when made from velvet, heavy synthetic cloth, silk).
PRESTE	Section- or community-wide sponsor (rural), neighborhood, market, or factory-wide sponsor (urban), also sponsor of fiestas for private saints.
Q'ATXA	Soul loss caused by the capture of one of a person's souls by a spirit.
QUA	See *wira qua*.
QUINUA	*Chenopodium quinoa*: a high protein grain.
SAYAÑA	A plot of land, usually in the area where the owner's or tenant's house is located.
SUSTO	Literally, Spanish for fright. Illness caused by fright, an etiology common to much of Latin America.
TAMBO	Wholesale marketplace. Traditionally it was also a place where travellers could spend the night.
T"IMPU	A Bolivian dish.
VECINO	Literally "neighbor"; townsman who follows Hispanic traditions and who in prerevolutionary times was regarded as

having the right to be involved in decision-making affecting the town.

WIRA QUA — An herb used to cleanse the body of a patient and as a "condiment for the spirits" in magical offerings.

YAPA — A little extra amount given to a customer.

YATIRI — Magician. Literally, "he who knows."

BIBLIOGRAPHY

Abu-Lughod, L. 1993. *Writing Women's Worlds: Bedouin Stories*. Berkeley: University of California Press.

Albó, X., T. Greaves, and G. Sandoval. 1982. *Chukiyawu: La cara aymara de La Paz, Vol. II. Una Odisea: buscar "pega."* La Paz: Cuadernos de Investigación CIPCA.

——. 1983. *Chuquiyawu: La cara aymara de La Paz, Vol. III. Cabalgando entre dos mundos.* La Paz: Cuadernos de Investigación CIPCA, No. 24.

Albó, X. and M. Preiswerk. 1986. *Los Señores del Gran Poder.* Centro de Teología Popular, Taller de Observaciones Culturales. La Paz: Editorial Alenkar.

Arze, C., H. Dorado, H. Eguino, and S. Escóbar de Pabón. 1994. *Empleo y salarios: el círculo de la pobreza.* Programa de Ajuste Estructural 5. La Paz: CEDLA.

Barth, F. 1967. "On the Study of Social Change." *American Anthropologist* 69:661–669.

Basso, E. 1987. "The Implications of a Progressive Theory of Dreaming." In *Dreaming: Anthropological and Psychological Interpretations.* B. Tedlock, ed., Cambridge: Cambridge University Press.

Bastien, J. 1978. *Mountain of the Condor: Metaphor and Ritual in an Andean Ayllu.* American Ethnological Society. Monograph 64. St. Paul: West Publishing Co. Reissued 1985 by Waveland Press.

——. 1987. *Healers of the Andes: Kallawaya Herbalists and Their Medicinal Plants.* Salt Lake City: University of Utah Press.

Bastien, J. and J. Donahue, eds. 1981. *Health in the Andes.* Monograph 12. Washington D.C.: American Anthropological Association.

Behar, R. 1993. *Translated Woman: Crossing the Border with Esperanza's Story.* Boston: Beacon Press.

Borneman, J. 1992. *Belonging in the Two Berlins: Kin, State, Nation.* Cambridge Studies in Social and Cultural Anthropology. Cambridge: Cambridge University Press.

Buechler, H. 1969a. "The Social Position of an Ethnographer in the Field," In *Stress and Response in Fieldwork.* F. Henry and S. Saberwal, eds. New York: Holt, Rinehart, and Winston.

——. 1969b. "Post-revolutionary Politicking on the Northern Bolivian Altiplano." Paper presented at the 68th Annual Meeting of the American Anthropological Association, New Orleans, Nov.

——. 1980. *The Masked Media: Fiestas and Social Interaction in the Bolivian Highlands.* The Hague: Mouton.

——. 1981. "Aymara Curing Practices in the Context of a Family History." In *Health in the Andes*. J. Bastien and J. Donahue, eds. Special publication of the American Anthropological Association, No. 12. Washington D.C.

——. 1992. "The 'Informal Sector' Revisited: Thoughts on a Misleading Dichotomy." *Anthropology Newsletter* of the American Anthropological Association. December. 1992.

Buechler, H. and J.-M. 1971. *The Bolivian Aymara*. New York: Holt, Rinehart and Winston.

——. 1971/72. "El Aymara boliviano y el cambio social: reevaluación del concepto de 'intermediario cultural.' " *Estudios Andinos* 2(3): 137–49.

——. 1981. *Carmen: The Autobiography of a Spanish Galician Woman*. Cambridge: Schenkman.

——. 1992. *Manufacturing Against the Odds: Small Scale Producers in an Andean City.* Boulder: Westview Press.

Buechler, H., J.-M. Buechler, and H. Schlumpf. 1988. *The World of Sofía Velasquez.* Version in English of video film, *Die Welt der Sofía Velasquez: La Paz, Bolivien.* Distributor: H. Schlumpf, Postfach 835 CH-8025, Zürich, Switzerland.

Buechler, J.-M. 1972. "Peasant Marketing and Social Revolution in the Province of La Paz, Bolivia." McGill University, Montreal. Ph.D. Thesis.

——. 1976. "Something Funny Happened on the Way to the Agora: A Comparison of Bolivian and Spanish-Galician Migrants." In *Women and Migration*. (Special Issue), J.-M. Hess Buechler, ed., *Anthropological Quarterly* 49(1): 62–69.

——. 1978. "The Dynamics of the Market in La Paz, Bolivia." *Urban Anthropology* 7(4): 343–59.

——. in press. "The Visible and Vocal Politics of Female Traders and Small Scale Producers in La Paz, Bolivia." In *Women and Economic Change: Andean Perspectives*. A. Miles and H. Buechler, eds. Vol. 13 in the Society for Latin American Anthropology publication series.

Buechler, S. 1993. *Credit Approaches and Women Microentrepreneurs*. Unpublished report, United Nations Development Fund for Women.

Burkett, E. 1978. "Indian Women and White Society: The Case of Sixteenth-Century Peru." In *Latin American Women: Historical Perspectives*. A. Lavrin, ed., Westport: Greenwood Press.

Caplan, P. 1992. "Spirits and Sex: A Swahili Informant and His Diary." In *Anthropology and Autobiography*. J. Okely and H. Callaway, eds. ASA Monographs 29. London: Routledge.

Carter, W. 1964. *Aymara Communities and the Bolivian Agrarian Reform.* University of Florida Monographs: Social Sciences, No. 24. Gainesville: University of Florida Press.

Carter, W. and M. Mamani. 1982. *Irpa Chico: individuo y comunidad en la cultura aymara.* La Paz: Editorial Juventud.

Chávez Alvarez, G. and C. Toranzo Roca. 1993. *Claves y problemas de la economía boliviana.* La Paz: ILDIS.

Clifford, J. 1988. "Identity in Mashpee" Chapter 12. In *The Predicament of Culture.* pp. 277–346. Cambridge: Harvard University Press.

Crandon-Malamud, L. 1991. *From the Fat of Our Souls: Social Change, Political Process, and Medical Pluralism in Bolivia.* Berkeley: University of California Press.

Crapanzano, V. 1980. *Tuhami. Portrait of a Moroccan.* Chicago: Chicago University Press.

——. 1984. "Life-Histories" (review article). *American Anthropologist* 86:953–960.

Dibbits, I., E. Peredo, R. Volgger, and A. Wadsworth. 1989. *Polleras libertarias: Federación Obrera Femenina. 1927–1965.* La Paz: Hisbol.

Dunkerley, J. 1984. *Rebellion in the Veins: Political Struggle in Bolivia: 1952—1982.* London: Verso Editions.

Geertz, C. 1960. "The Changing Role of the Cultural Broker: The Javanese Kijaji." *Comparative Studies in Society and History* 2:228–249.

Gill, L. 1990. "Painted Faces: Conflict and Ambiguity in Domestic Servant-Employer Relations in La Paz 1930—1988." *Latin American Research Review* 19 (1):119–205.

——. 1993. " 'Proper Women' and City Pleasures: Gender, Class, and Contested Meanings in La Paz." *American Ethnologist* 20: 72–88.

Gmelch, G. 1992. *Double Passage: The Lives of Caribbean Migrants Abroad and Back Home.* Ann Arbor: University of Michigan Press.

Johnsson, M. 1986. *Food and Culture Among Bolivian Aymara: Symbolic Expressions of Social Relations.* Acta Universitatis Upsalensis, Uppsala Studies in Cultural Anthropology 7. Distributed by Alquist and Wiksell International, Stockholm.

Klein, H. 1992. *Bolivia: The Evolution of a Multi-Ethnic Society.* 2d edition. New York and Oxford: Oxford University Press.

Kumar, N. 1992. *Friends, Brothers, and Informants: Fieldwork Memoirs of Banaras.* Berkeley: University of California Press.

La Barre, W. 1948. *The Aymara Indians of the Lake Titicaca Plateau, Bolivia.* Memoirs of the American Anthropological Association, No. 68. Washington, D.C.

Lagos, M. 1993. " 'We Have to Learn to Ask': Hegemony, Diverse Experiences, and Antagonistic Meanings in Bolivia." *American Ethnologist* 20: 52–71.

Malinowski, B. 1922. 1961. *Argonauts of the Western Pacific.* New York: Collier Books.

Malloy, J. 1970. *Bolivia: The Uncompleted Revolution.* Pittsburgh: University of Pittsburgh Press.

Mandelbaum, D. 1973. "The Study of Life History." *Current Anthropology* 14(17): 196.

Mannheim, B. 1987. "A Semiotic of Andean Dreams." In *Dreaming: Anthropological and Psychological Interpretations.* B. Tedlock, ed., Cambridge: Cambridge University Press.

Medinaceli, X. 1989. *Alterando la rutina: mujeres en las ciudades de Bolivia: 1920—1930.* La Paz: CIDEM.

Morsy, S. 1978. "Sex Roles, Power, and Illness in an Egyptian Village." *American Ethnologist* 5: 137–150.

Nash, J. 1992. *I Spent My Life in the Mines: The Story of Juan Rojas, Bolivian Tin Miner.* New York: Columbia University Press.

Nash, J. with Juan Rojas. 1976. *He agotado mi vida en la mina*. Buenos Aires: Nueva Edición.

Oblitas Poblete, E. 1963. *Cultura Callawaya*. La Paz. 1971. *Magia, hechicería y medicina popular boliviana*. La Paz: Ediciones Isla.

Okely, J. 1992. "Anthropology and Autobiography: Participatory Experience and Embodied Knowledge." In J. Okely and H. Callaway, eds. *Anthropology and Autobiography*. ASA Monograph 29. London: Routledge.

Orlove, B. 1977. "Inequality Among Peasants: The Forms and Uses of Reciprocal Exchange in Andean Peru." In *Peasant Livelihood: Studies in Economic Anthropology and Cultural Ecology*. R. Halperin and J. Dow, eds., pp. 201–214. New York: St. Martin's Press.

Paredes, R. 1963. *Mitos, supersticiones, y supervivencias populares de Bolivia*. La Paz: Ediciones Isla.

Peredo Beltrán, E. 1993. *Recoveras de los Andes; la identidad de la chola del mercado: una aproximación psicosocial*. La Paz: ILDIS.

Perez Velasco, A., R. Casanovas Sainz, S. Escóbar de Pabón, and H. Larrazábal Córdova. 1989. *Informalidad e ilegalidad: una falsa identidad*. La Paz: CEDLA.

Rabinow, P. 1977. *Reflections on Fieldwork in Morocco*. Berkeley: University of California Press.

Ramos, P. 1980. *Siete años de economía boliviana*. La Paz: Puerta del Sol.

Said, E. 1978. *Orientalism*. New York: Pantheon Books.

Silverman, S. 1967. "Community-Nation Mediator in Traditional Central Italy." In *Peasant Society* J. Potter et al. eds., pp. 279–93. Boston: Little, Brown.

Smith, S. 1993. "Who's Talking/Who's Talking Back? The Subject of Personal Narrative." *Signs* 18: 392–407.

Stivers, C. 1993. "Reflections on the Role of Personal Narrative in Social Science." *Signs* 18: 408–425.

Tedlock, B. 1993. "Postcoloniality and Feminist Ethnography." Talk given in the Department of Anthropology, Syracuse University, April 23.

Tschopik, H. 1951. *The Aymara of Chucuito, Peru*. Anthropological Papers of the American Museum of Natural History, Vol. XLIV, part 2. New York.

Turner, V. 1969. *The Ritual Process: Structure and Anti-structure*. Chicago: Aldine.

Useem, J. 1952. "South Sea Island Strike: Labor Management Relations in the Caroline Islands Micronesia." In *Human Problems in Technological Change*. E. Spicer, ed., pp. 261–80. New York: Russel Sage Foundation.

Visweswaran, K. 1994. *Fictions of Feminist Ethnography*. Minneapolis: University of Minnesota Press.

Wagley, C. 1964. "The Peasant." In *The Latin American Tradition* C. Wagley, editor. New York: Columbia University Press.

Weismantel, M.J. 1988. *Food, Gender, and Poverty in the Ecuadorian Andes*. Philadelphia: University of Pennsylvania Press.

Whiteford, S. 1981. *Migrants from the North: Plantations, Bolivian Labor, and the City in Northwest Argentina*. Austin: University of Texas Press.

Wolf, E. 1956. "Aspects of Group Relations in a Complex Society: Mexico." *American Anthropologist* 58: 1065–78.

Women's World Banking. 1994. "Best Practice in Providing Financial Service to Microentrepreneurs." *What Works: A Women's World Banking Newsletter* 4: 2–4.

Young, A. 1976. "Some Implications of Medical Beliefs and Practices for Social Anthropologists." *American Anthropologist* 78: 5–24.

Zulawski, A. 1990. "Social Differentiation, Gender, and Ethnicity: Urban Indian Women in Colonial Bolivia, 1640–1725." *Latin American Research Review* 25: 93–114.

INDEX

Designer: María T. Giuliani
Text: Palatino
Compositor: CUP
Printer: Maple-Vail
Binder: Maple-Vail